Popular Complete Smart Series

Complete ScienceSmart®

Grade 8

William Young

Credits

Photos (Front Cover "satellite dish" David Hughes/123RF.com, "gears" alex_star/123RF.com, "jet plane" Lars Christenen/123RF.com. Back Cover "girl on left"/123RF.com, "boy" Jose Manuel Gelpi Diaz/123RF.com, "girl in middle"/123RF.com, "girl on right" Paul Hakimata/123RF.com, "memo board" Sandra Van Der Steen/123RF.com, "children"/123RF.com.)

Printed in China

ISBN: 978-1-897457-80-1

Table of Contents

Section 1 Understanding Life Systems

Students will explore the components, structures, and functions of cells in plants and animals. They will learn about the postulates of the cell theory and understand the role of microscopes in the study of cells. Students will also examine the roles of diffusion and osmosis and their processes within a cell. Furthermore, students will identify unicellular and multicellular organisms and investigate how they satisfy their basic life needs. They will study the organization of cells in multicellular organisms.

ISBN: 978-1-897457-80-1

Section 2

Understanding Structures and Mechanisms

Students will identify different kinds of systems and recognize smaller systems within large systems. They will discover that all systems have purposes, inputs, and outputs. Moreover, they will learn the scientific definitions of the words: energy, force, work, and efficiency, and learn to calculate how much work some simple machines do and their mechanical advantages. Students will also study the causes of heat and ways to minimize heat in mechanical systems. Furthermore, they will investigate how systems evolved in our society and how systems improved the productivity in industries.

ISBN: 978-1-897457-80-1

Table of
Contents

Section 3

Understanding Matter and Energy

Students will examine the properties of fluids including viscosity, and the relationship between buoyancy and density. They will learn to explain, using the particle theory of matter, how different states of matter vary in density. They will also calculate the density of a fluid with its mass and volume. In addition, students will study the difference between the compressibility of liquids and gases, as well as how their compressibility works in hydraulic and pneumatic systems. They will also explore the use and control of fluids in society.

ISBN: 978-1-897457-80-1

Section 4

Understanding Earth and Space Systems

Students will examine the conditions under which each state of water exists and the relative amount of each state. They will learn about watersheds and water tables, their importance in water management and planning, and the impacts of nature and humans on them. In addition, students will study the characteristics of glaciers and polar ice caps, and the factors that affect their sizes. They will also learn how large bodies of water affect climate and weather patterns. The uses of our water supply and the treatments that it goes through will also be discussed.

ISBN: 978-1-897457-80-1

ISBN: 978-1-897457-80-1

Section 1

Understanding Life Systems

ISBN: 978-1-897457-80-1

1 Postulates of the Cell Theory

Understanding cell theory is understanding what living things are made up of, as well as how they function. In this unit, you will review what all living things have in common, and relate that to the postulates of the cell theory.

After completing this unit, you will

- know the characteristics of all living things.
- understand the postulates of the cell theory.

The larger the organism is, the more cells it has.

Vocabulary

cell: the smallest, almost always microscopic, unit of life

postulate: a suggested truth about something that further discussion is based on

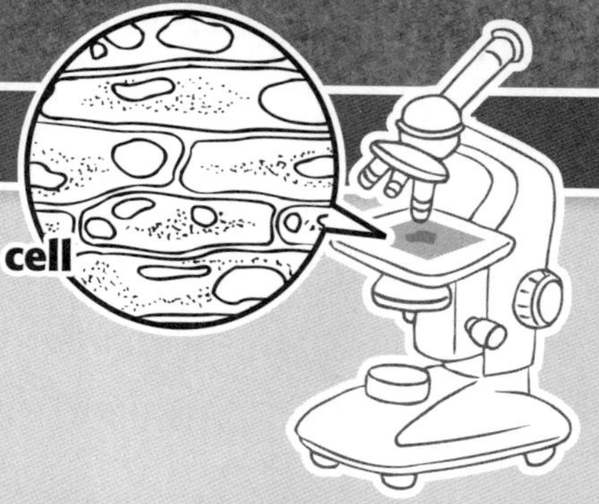

ISBN: 978-1-897457-80-1

Extension

Do you know what your body is made up of? Yes, it is your bones, blood, skin, and other organs. However, what are all of these body parts made up of? They are actually made up of very tiny living things called cells. Each part of your body is made up of millions of cells and different types of cells make up the different body parts. The cells in your body work together to keep you alive. While some of the cells in your body last throughout your life, others only live for a few days, and when they die, they are replaced with new cells.

How long do your brain cells last, about 2 days or 30 years?

Answer: about 30 years

A. Fill in the blanks with the words provided in the picture to complete the descriptions.

Cells make up every part of a living thing which carries out the seven life processes.

Seven Life Processes

1. ______________ : Living things grow.
2. ______________ : Living things respire.
3. ______________ : Living things move.
4. ______________ : Living things reproduce.
5. ______________ : Living things need food.
6. ______________ : Living things produce waste.
7. ______________ : Living things respond to the environment.

ISBN: 978-1-897457-80-1

B. Fill in the blanks to complete the passage. Circle the correct words to complete the three postulates. Then write T for true and F for false.

Postulates of the Cell Theory

living things | functions | microscope | pre-existing | structure | division | cells

In 1665, the British scientist Robert Hooke examined a piece of bark under a 1.____________ and saw that it was made up of tiny 2.____________ . Over the next couple of hundred years, it was observed that all other 3.____________ were composed of cells.

Postulate 1

All living things are made up of one or **more / fewer** cells.

Over time, it was also noted that cells provide more than just a 4.____________ to build life: cells perform all the 5.____________ of living things.

Postulate 2

The cell is the basic **tool / unit** of function in living things.

However, new cells do not arise spontaneously from nothing. They come from 6.____________ cells through a process called cell 7.____________ .

Postulate 3

All cells come from pre-existing **bones / cells** .

T/F

8. Only animals have cells; plants do not have cells. ______
9. A living thing must have at least one cell. ______
10. Two cells make one cell in a cell division. ______

ISBN: 978-1-897457-80-1

C. State the postulate of the cell theory that each picture illustrates.

A
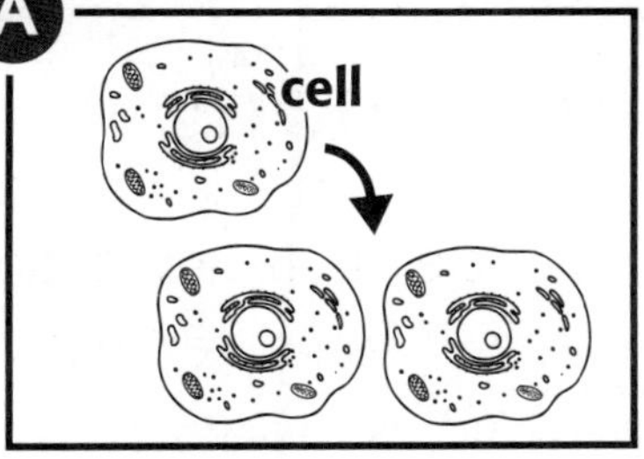

B
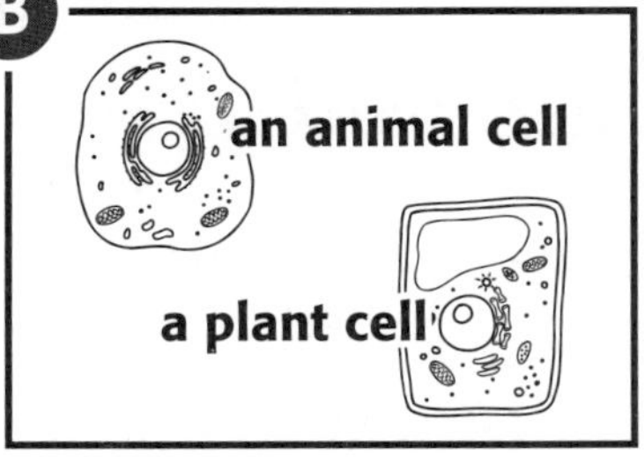

C
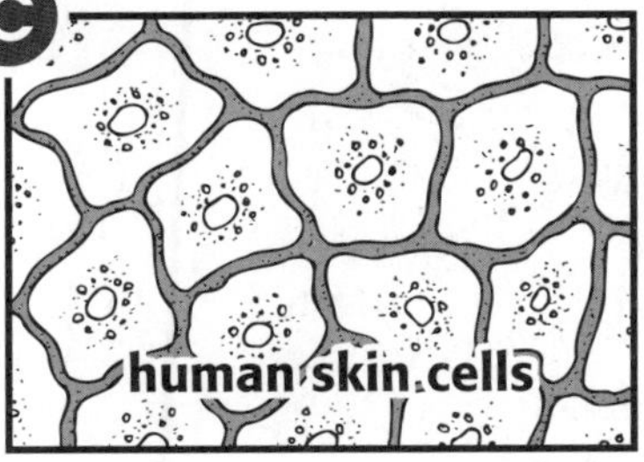

A ______________________________

B ______________________________

C ______________________________

D. Check the correct answers.

1. The average human being is composed of around ________ individual cells.

*__Trillion__ means 1 000 000 000 000.

(A) 10 thousand (B) 1 million (C) 100 trillion*

2. Cells are found in plants, as well as in ________ .

(A) pockets (B) animals (C) the air

3. All cells are produced by the ________ of pre-existing cells.

(A) division (B) multiplication (C) addition

4. ________ working together can form a wide variety of creatures.

(A) Cells (B) People (C) Plants

ISBN: 978-1-897457-80-1

E. Read the passage. Fill in the blanks to complete the timeline.

Cell Theory:
Years and Years in the Making

The cell theory took many years, many scientists, and many advances in microscope technology to form. Some key events and figures in the history of the cell theory are as follows:

In 1595, Zacharias Janssen, with the help of his father Hans, invented the compound light microscope.

In 1663, Robert Hooke saw the dead cell walls of a bark under a light microscope and named each compartment a "cell", a word that comes from the Latin word cellula, which means little room. Hooke discovered the first cell.

In 1674, Anton van Leeuwenhoek was the first person to perceive a live cell under a light microscope.

In 1809, Charles-François Brisseau de Mirbel was the first to recognize that each plant cell is contained in a continuous membrane.

In 1824, Henri Dutrochet concluded that cells of both plants and animals are the basic units of life.

In 1838, Theodor Schwann and Matthias Jakob Schleiden proposed that all living things are composed of cells and cell products.

In 1855, Rudolph Virchow declared that all living cells arise from other living cells.

ISBN: 978-1-897457-80-1

History of the Cell Theory

1500

1595

Scientist: 1. ____________________

Invented item:

2. ____________________

1600

3.

Scientist: 4. ____________________

He saw the dead cell walls of a 5. ____________ under a light microscope and discovered the 6. ____________ cell.

7.

Scientist: 8. ____________________

He was the first person to perceive a live 9. ____________ using a 10. ____________________ .

1800

1809

Scientist:

11. ____________________

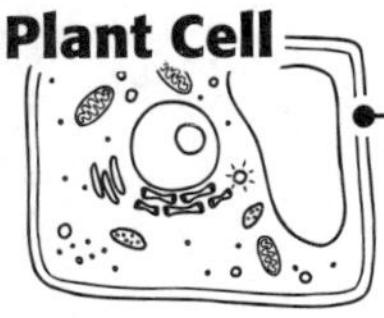

– a 12. ____________ membrane

13.

Scientist: 14. ____________________

He discovered the basic unit of life – 15. ____________ .

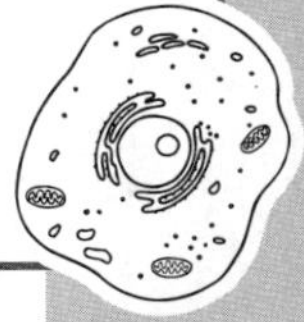

16.

Scientists:

17. ____________________

18. ____________________

cells + 19. ____________ → **Living Things**

1855

Scientist: 20. ____________________

He declared that all living cells arise from 21. ____________________

____________________ .

ISBN: 978-1-897457-80-1

2 Parts of the Cell

A cell, the basic unit of all living things, is a living thing itself. It is complete with little organs (organelles) that allow the cell to function. In this unit, you will examine the parts of a typical animal cell and the functions of a cell's components.

After completing this unit, you will

- know the different components of a cell and their functions.
- understand the role of microscopes in the study of cells.

Vocabulary

organelle: specialized structure within a cell

chromosome: substance that carries genetic information

electron: particle with a negative electrical charge

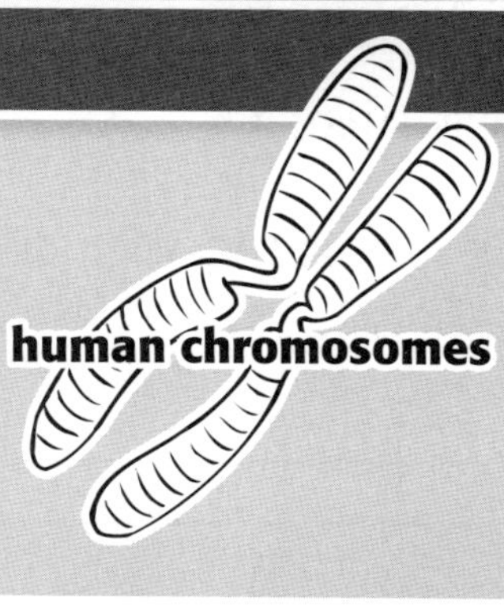

ISBN: 978-1-897457-80-1

Extension

Most cells are extremely tiny and are visible only when they are viewed under a microscope. Some of them are so microscopic that you must magnify them hundreds of times in order to view the cells' parts clearly. For instance, to view the basic parts of an onion cell, you will need to magnify the cell at least 200 times. However, there are a few cells that we can see with the naked eye. The yolk of an egg is a large single cell that we can see without magnification. In fact, the yolk of an ostrich's egg, which has the size of a baseball, is the heaviest single cell.

A. Look at the diagram of a cell. Then label the parts and fill in the blanks.

Basic Parts of a Cell

nucleus cytoplasm cell membrane | controls protects encloses chromosomes membrane

1.

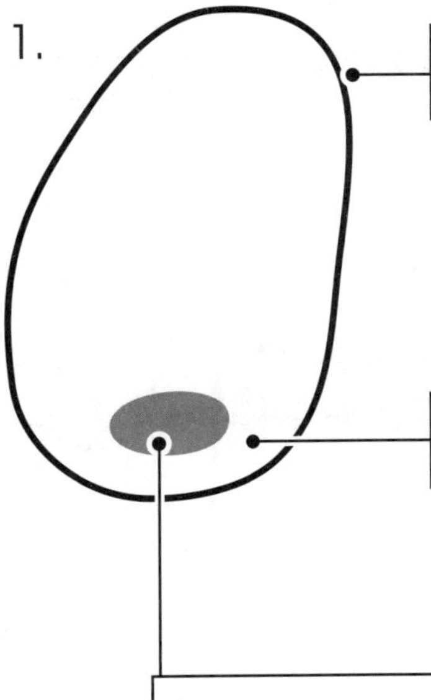

a. ________ : It b. ________ the cell, keeping the cell's parts within, and c. ________ them. It is permeable to some substances and impermeable to others.

d. ________ : This is everything within the e. ________ of the cell, except for the nucleus.

f. ________ : It is the information storehouse of the cell; it contains g. ________ and h. ________ all cell activities.

2. Cells of most animals and plants contain these three basic parts:

____

ISBN: 978-1-897457-80-1

B. Read the paragraph. Name the organelles with the help of the diagram. Then fill in the blanks.

Cell's Organelles

Organelles are tiny structures with varying shapes and functions. They are part of a cell's cytoplasm, suspended in the supportive liquid called cytosol. The nucleus is an organelle with the important job of housing all the cell's information in chromosomes. Each of the other organelles has a specific function.

Structure of a Cell

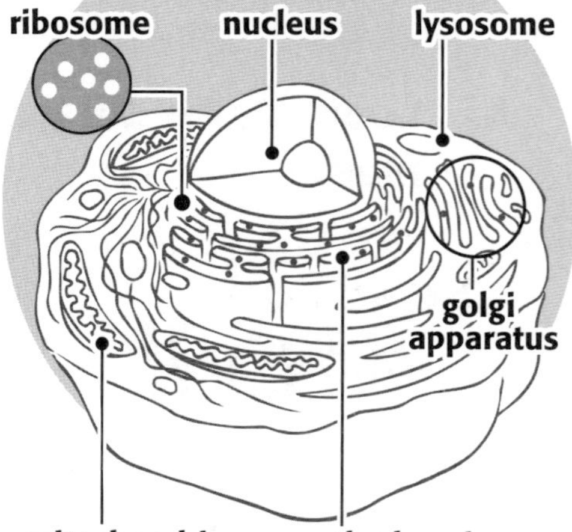

1. n__________ : houses all the cell's information
2. m__________ : controller of energy
3. r__________ : makes protein
4. l__________ : breaks down other cell parts
5. g__________ a__________ : stores and moves protein
6. e__________ r__________ : canal, either rough or smooth, that carries substances through the cytoplasm

Test Yourself!

7. All organelles are part of the cell's __________ .
8. The organelles are suspended in the liquid called __________ .
9. The organelle __________ contains the cell's chromosomes.
10. Mitochondrion controls the cell's __________ .
11. List six organelles: ____________________

____

ISBN: 978-1-897457-80-1

C. Name the microscopes. Circle the correct words to complete the descriptions and match the pictures of cells with the correct microscopes. Then answer the questions.

electron microscope
light microscope

1. [ ]

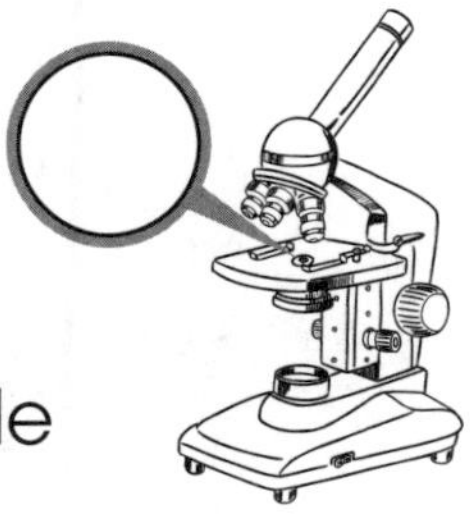

- allows us to **see / taste** live cells
- cells and their basic **parts / functions** are visible

2. [ ]

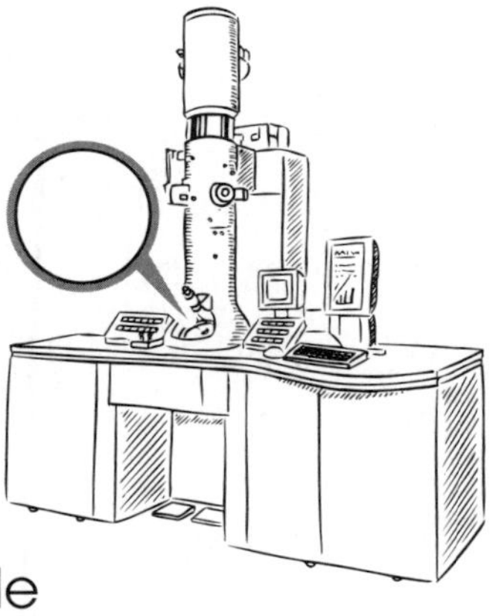

- does not allow us to see live cells because the living tissue is **destroyed / generated** by the intense beam from the microscope
- allows us to see materials that are many times **larger / smaller** than with a light microscope
- cells and their **organelles / movements** are visible

3. *Which microscope should I use if I want to view...*

a. the cells without destroying them?

____

b. the detailed structure of a ribosome?

____

c. the components suspended in the cytoplasm?

____

D. Read the passage. Label the parts of a microscope with the words in bold and circle the correct words. Then answer the questions.

The most common kind of microscope, the one you are likely to use in school, is the compound light microscope. Compound means that it contains more than one lens, and light means it uses light. Different light microscopes have different parts and varying levels of magnification, but all light microscopes share a few basic parts.

The **eyepiece** is where you place your eye, and the ocular lens is the lens closest to your eye. The objective lens is the lens closest to the specimen. There are typically three to four **objective lenses** held together by a **rotating nosepiece**. The largest objective lens, or the high-power objective, is the one with the most powerful magnification; the smallest objective lens, or the low-power objective, is the lens with the weakest magnification. The **arm** is the part that connects the lenses and their protective tube to the microscope's supporting **base**. Both the **coarse focus knob** and the **fine focus knob** are found on the arm. The coarse focus makes big focus adjustments, and is often the larger of the two knobs, while the fine focus makes much smaller adjustments. The microscope's **stage** is the part that holds the slide on which the specimen is placed. A pair of **stage clips** keeps the slide from moving. Below the stage, in the base, is the **light source**, often a light bulb. Directly beneath the stage is the **diaphragm**, which controls how much light reaches the stage.

ISBN: 978-1-897457-80-1

1. A Light **Microscope**

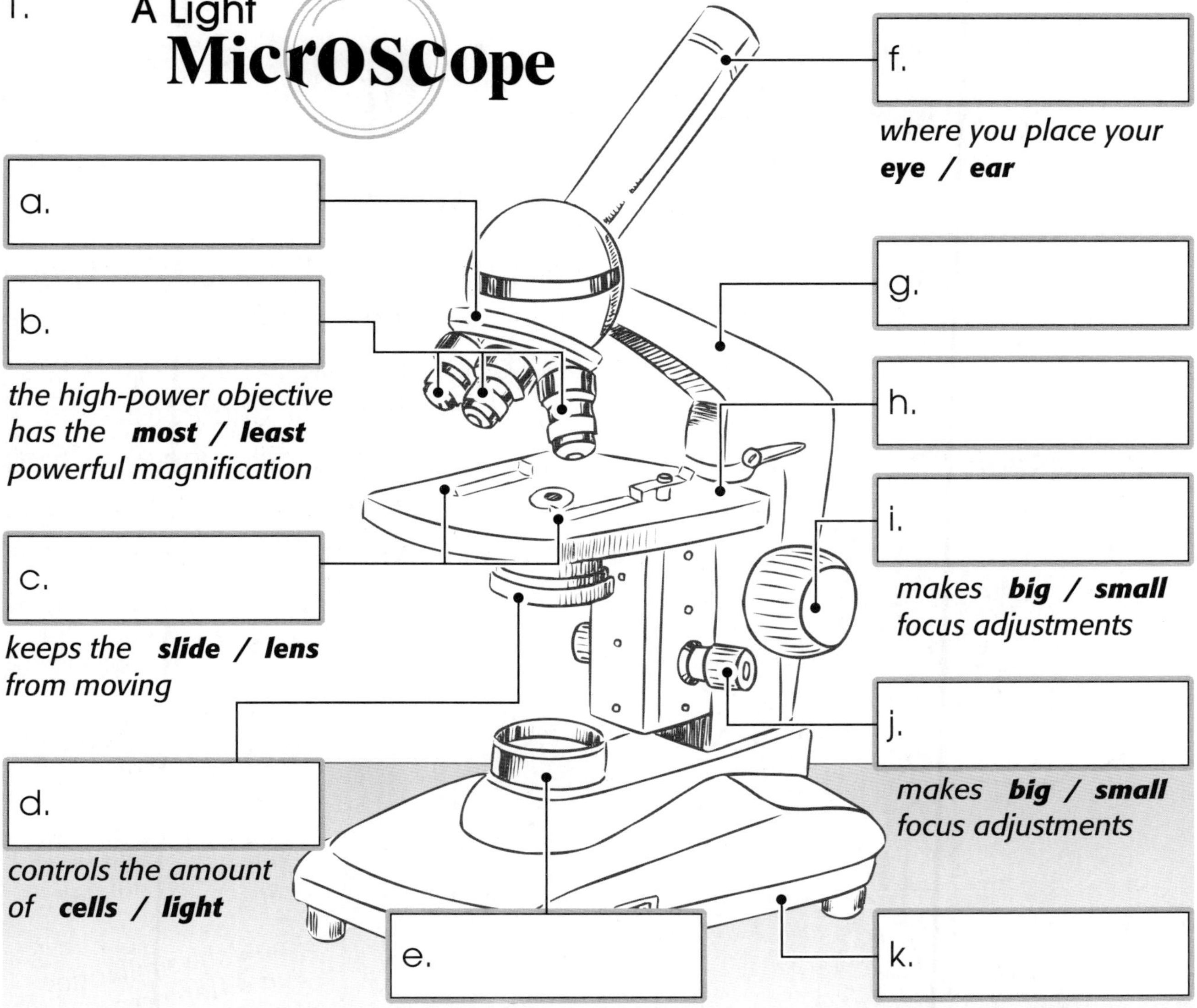

2. Which objective lens should be used to see something very tiny?

(A) 4X

(B) 10X

(C) 100X

"10X" means the lens has an effective magnification of 10 times the life size.

3. What does a compound light microscope use to see cells?

____

____

4. If it is not bright enough to see an image, which part of the microscope should be adjusted?

____

ISBN: 978-1-897457-80-1

3 Animal Cells and Plant Cells

There are similarities and differences between plants and animals, and between their cells. Both plants and animals have similarities in their structures, which give them the characteristics of living things. They also have differences in their structures to protect themselves in different ways. In this unit, you will examine and compare the structures and functions of these two types of cells.

After completing this unit, you will

- be able to identify the parts of a plant cell and an animal cell.
- know the similarities and differences between a plant cell and an animal cell.

Vocabulary

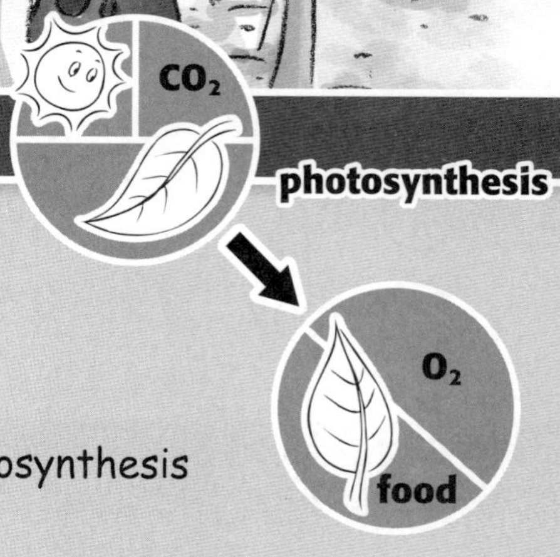

photosynthesis: the process by which green plants make food and release oxygen using the sun's energy

chlorophyll: green pigment in chloroplasts, used for photosynthesis

ISBN: 978-1-897457-80-1

Extension

One of the major differences between animals and plants is that plants have the ability to make their own food but animals do not. To make its own food, a plant needs to go through a process called photosynthesis. Chlorophyll, a chemical that can be found inside the cells of a plant, is needed to make photosynthesis possible. Chlorophyll in green leaves takes in carbon dioxide, soaks up water from the soil with the plant's roots, and receives sunlight from the sun to produce sugar. This sugar is all a plant needs to grow.

A. Fill in the blanks to complete the diagrams of cells.

Animal Plant	Parts of a Cell:	cell membrane	cytoplasm	nucleus

1. A Typical a. ______________ Cell

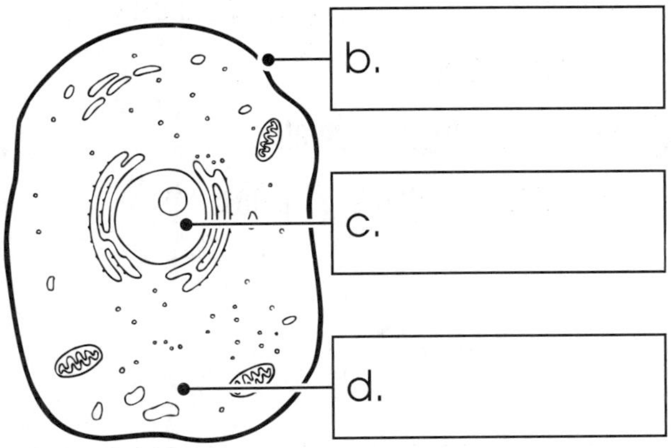

2. A Typical a. ______________ Cell

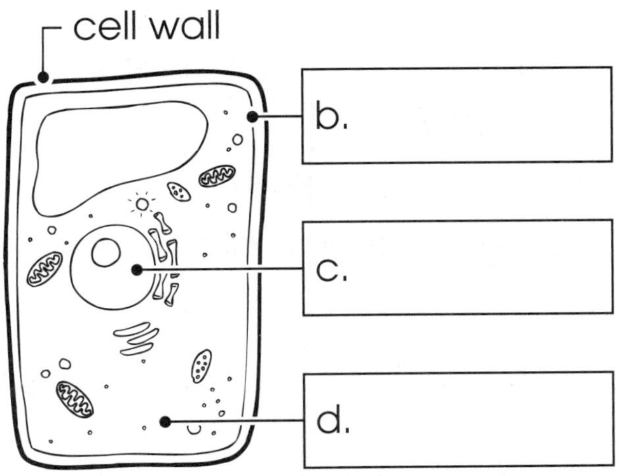

ISBN: 978-1-897457-80-1

B. Read the paragraph. Label the parts of the cells. Then complete the charts and answer the question.

Three important differences between animal and plant cells are highlighted by three structures: a ***cell wall****, an organelle called a* ***plastid****, and another organelle, a* ***vacuole****. Instead of a bony skeleton, a plant's cell wall, which is just outside the cell membrane, supports the plant. Being unable to move around to find food, a plant contains plastid which is responsible for making food. The vacuole, which can also be found in animal cells, plays a bigger and different role in plants. It provides shape and stores food.*

1. **An Animal Cell**

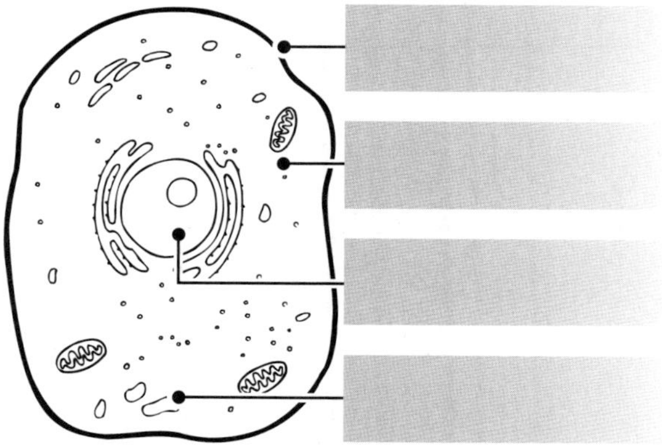

Check the parts that an animal cell has.

- ◯ cell wall
- ◯ nucleus
- ◯ plastid
- ◯ cytoplasm
- ◯ cell membrane
- ◯ vacuoles: large / small
- ◯ chloroplasts: green / yellow

2. **A Plant Cell**

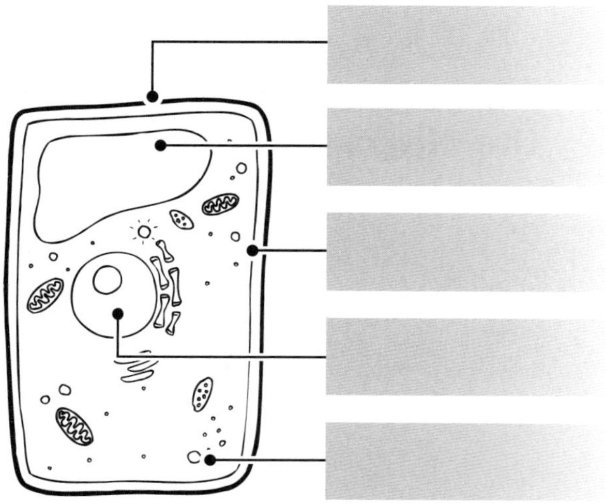

Check the parts that a plant cell has.

- ◯ cell wall
- ◯ nucleus
- ◯ plastid
- ◯ cytoplasm
- ◯ cell membrane
- ◯ vacuoles: large / small
- ◯ chloroplasts: green / yellow

3. Why is it important for a plant to have a cell wall?

____

____

ISBN: 978-1-897457-80-1

C. **Draw an animal cell and a plant cell in the boxes. Then draw lines to match the descriptions with the correct kinds of cells.**

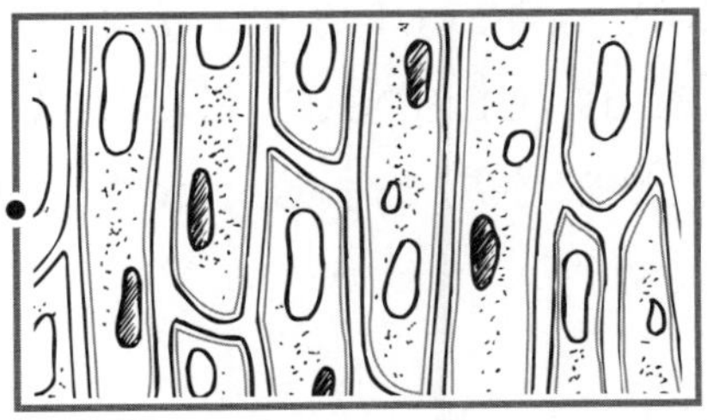

Plant Cell

Animal Cell

- cells can burst if too much water is absorbed
- makes own food
- gets food from outside cell
- no danger of cell bursting with too much water

ISBN: 978-1-897457-80-1

D. Read the passage. Name the cells and label their parts. Then answer the questions.

Many, Many Animal Cells

Animals are made up of many cells and many types of cells. A person is made up of about 100 trillion cells of over 200 types. Here are a few types:

Neurons, or nerve cells, are the cells that carry messages through the body. Like other animal cells, neurons are surrounded by a cell membrane and contain a nucleus and other organelles. Unlike other cells, though, neurons have special extensions that allow them to do their jobs. An axon is a long, arm-like extension that generally carries information away from the neuron body. Dendrites are shorter extensions that generally transmit information to the neuron body.

Muscle cells have one job: to contract, that is, to stretch and snap back into shape after being stimulated by a neuron. Like other animal cells, they contain a nucleus (in some muscle cells, there are more than one) and a cell membrane. Unlike many other cells, they are long and fibre-like; in fact, they are made up of many fibres. These fibres push many of the muscle cell's organelles to the edge of the cell.

Red blood cells deliver oxygen to the body. Like other animal cells, they have a cell membrane, but they do not have a nucleus or most of the organelles found in other cells. They are also much smaller than most other human cells and have a very distinct partially concave disc shape.

ISBN: 978-1-897457-80-1

1

N________ or N________ Cells

Function: ______________________________

(✔ or ✘)

◯ cell membrane

◯ nucleus

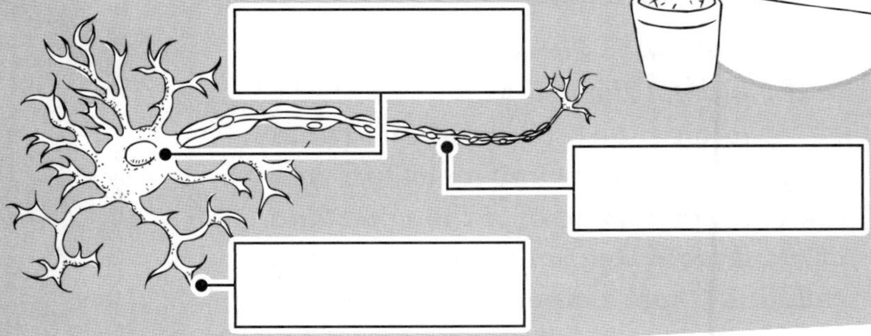

2

M________ Cells

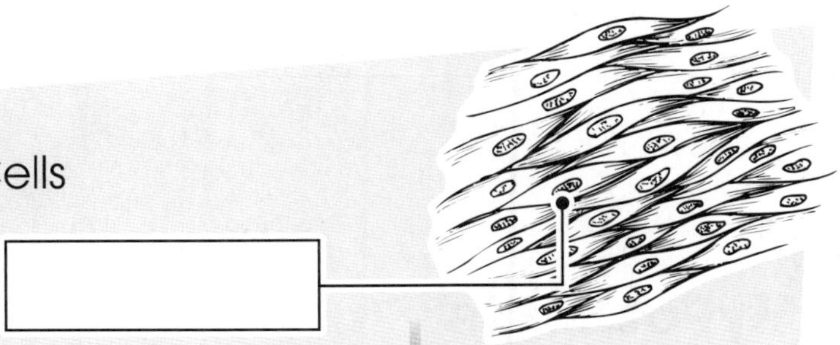

Function: ______________________________

____

Shape: ______________________________

(✔ or ✘)

◯ cell membrane

◯ nucleus

3

R________ B________ Cells

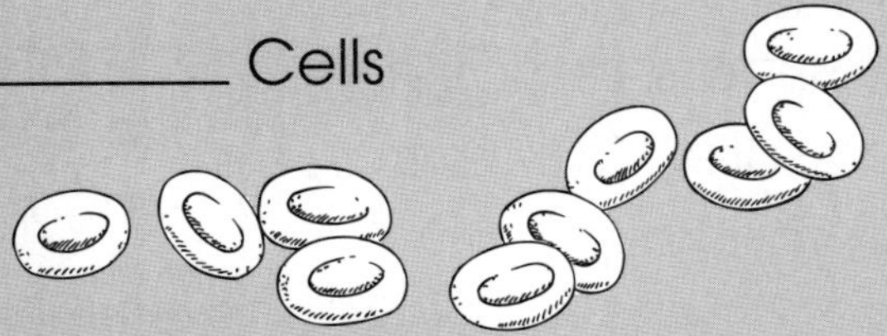

Function: ______________________________

____

Shape: ______________________________

(✔ or ✘)

◯ cell membrane

◯ nucleus

ISBN: 978-1-897457-80-1

Experiment

Introduction

A cell wall adds stiffness and structure to the plant. The cell wall is composed of cellulose, but its amount varies between different kinds of plants and even between varieties of the same kind of plant. Red Delicious apples have less cellulose than Granny Smith apples. Since cellulose is a strengthening fibre, will Red Delicious apples break down quicker than Granny Smith apples?

Hypothesis

A Red Delicious apple breaks down slower than / faster than / at the same rate as **a Granny Smith apple. (assuming the apples are about the same size)**

Steps

1. Preheat the oven to 200°C.
2. With the paring knife, cut the apples into quarters, removing the inedible core. (Be extra cautious with the knife.)

Materials

- ***a Red Delicious apple***
- ***a Granny Smith apple***
- ***a small oven***
- ***a paring knife***
- ***a baking tray***
- ***oven mitts***

Have your parent's approval before using the oven, or you may ask your parent for help to do this experiment.

ISBN: 978-1-897457-80-1

3. Lay the quarters with the skin side down on the baking tray; put the Red Delicious on one side and the Granny Smith on the other.

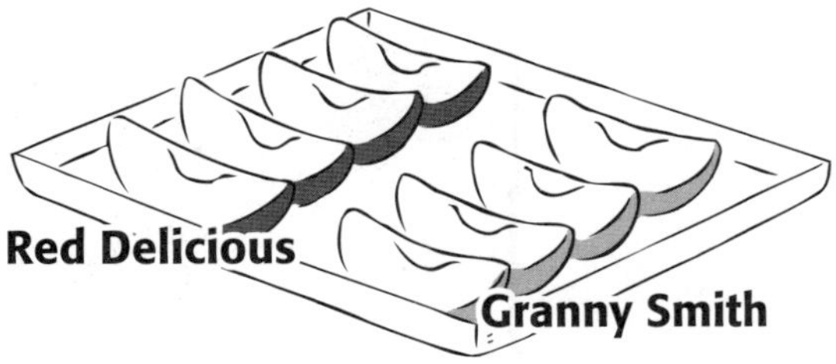

4. Put the tray in the oven and bake.

5. At ten-minute intervals, remove the tray with the oven mitts and check the apples slices. Poke the pieces with a spoon to check softness, and record your findings.

6. Remove the tray from the oven after 40 minutes.

Result

Check the softer apple at each interval.

		10 min	20 min	30 min	40 min
Softer Apple	Red Delicious				
	Granny Smith				

Conclusion

The hypothesis was: ______________________________

____

My experiment ______________________________ the hypothesis.
supported/did not support

*Acidity of an apple also affects how cellulose breaks down.

ISBN: 978-1-897457-80-1

4 Diffusion and Osmosis

For the processes of life to occur, some substances need to move in and out of cells. This is achieved naturally through diffusion and osmosis. In this unit, you will examine diffusion and osmosis as methods of passive transport through cell membranes.

After completing this unit, you will

- understand the process of diffusion and its role within a cell.
- understand the process of osmosis and its role within a cell.

Vocabulary

permeable: allowing to pass through

impermeable: not allowing to pass through

concentration: the relative amount of a substance in a solution

ISBN: 978-1-897457-80-1

Extension

Have you ever noticed that when you eat something salty, you feel thirsty? The salt circulates in your body through your bloodstream and attracts the water within your cells like a magnet. As a result, water begins to leave the cells, and your cells send signals to your brain to tell it that they are "thirsty". Your brain then tells you that you are thirsty.

A. Fill in the blanks with the given words. Then label the diagrams with the words in bold.

The Cell Membrane

permeability contents diffusion water substances osmosis out

A cell membrane keeps a cell's 1. ______________ inside it, allows some things into the cell, and keeps many things 2. ______________ of the cell. In other words, it is **permeable** to some 3. ______________ and **impermeable** to other substances. Its 4. ______________ allows nutrients, waste, gas, and 5. ______________ to enter or leave the cell. A cell membrane moves these substances in and out in a few different ways. Two of these ways are 6. ______________ and 7. ______________ .

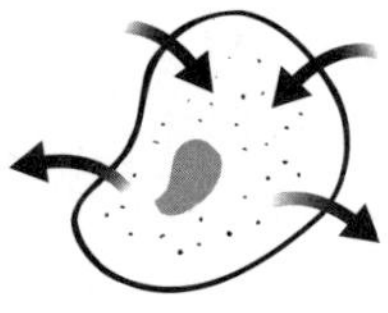

8. ______________ to some substances

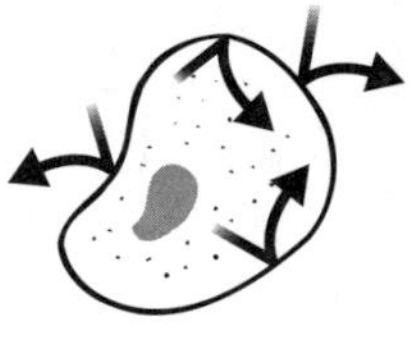

9. ______________ to some substances

B. Circle the correct words and number each set of pictures from 1 to 3 to show the correct sequence of diffusion. Then check the examples of diffusion and give one more example of your own.

1. **Diffusion** is the natural movement of a **substance / solid** from an area of **high / low** concentration to an area of **high / low** concentration.

2. **Examples of Diffusion**

A ✔

B ✔

- [ ] C adding salt to soup
- [ ] D spreading grass seeds in your backyard
- [ ] E a smelly gas spreading in a room
- [ ] F a collection of coins in a piggy bank
- [x] G ____________________

 ISBN: 978-1-897457-80-1

C. Circle the correct words and fill in the blanks. Then describe the concentration of water on both sides. Draw arrows to show the movement of water molecules.

Osmosis is the **concentration / diffusion** of water that occurs on either side of a cell's selectively permeable **membrane / nucleus** .

low sugar water concentration out

The membrane between two substances is permeable to 1. ______________ molecules but impermeable to 2. ______________ molecules. Water molecules are drawn from the side where there is a high concentration of them to the side where there is a 3. ______________ concentration of them. When the 4. ______________ is equal on both sides of the membrane, the water molecules moves in and 5. ______________ of the cell at an equal rate.

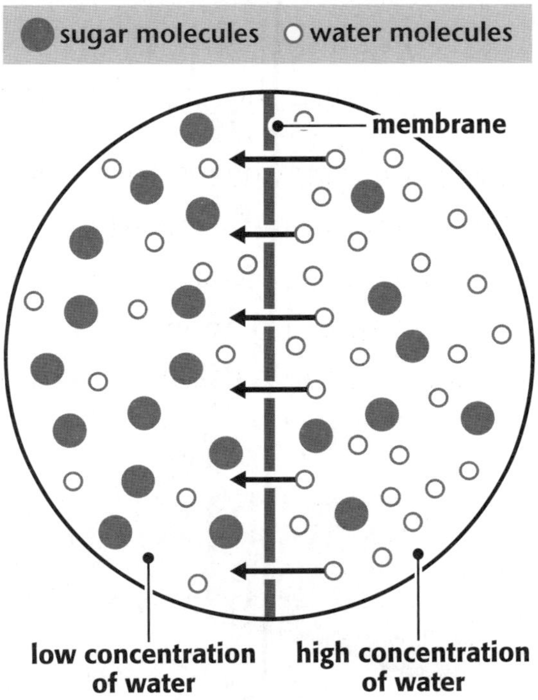

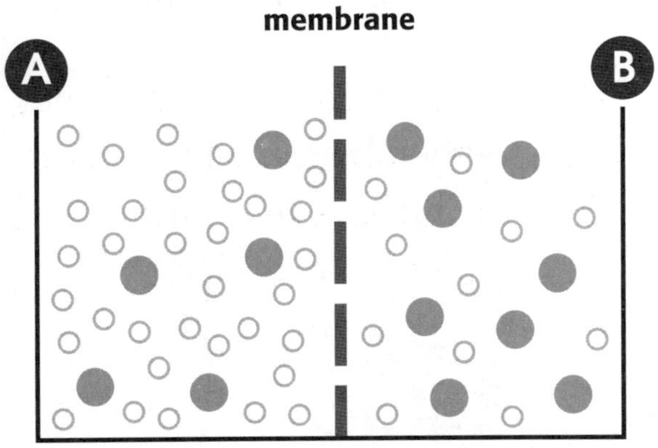

____

____

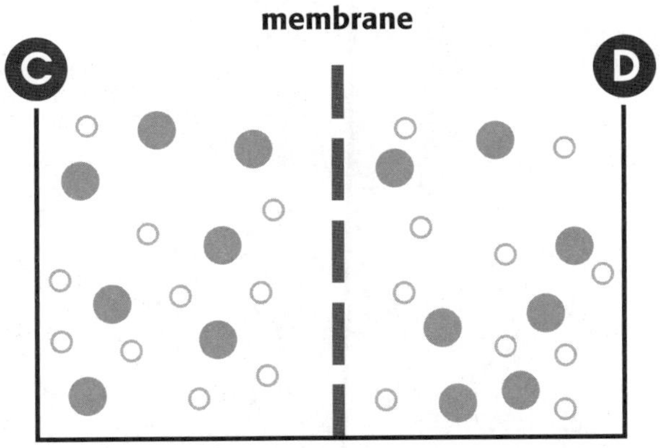

____

____

ISBN: 978-1-897457-80-1

D. Read the passage. Then answer the questions.

Preserved Food:
Sugar, Salt, and Osmosis

The purpose of preserving food is to stop or slow spoilage that would lessen the look, taste, or nutritional value of food. This food spoilage is often caused by micro-organisms, so the aim of many preservatives and preservation methods is to slow or stop the growth of these micro-organisms.

There are many ways to preserve food. Food can be heated, frozen, smoked, chemically treated, mixed with helpful micro-organisms, and even given a mild electric charge. Many foods are preserved by rubbing them with salt or sugar, or by immersing them in a salt or sugar solution. Both methods are used to manipulate the natural process of osmosis.

Salt and sugar preserve food because they kill micro-organisms. Their presence creates a lower concentration of water outside the cells of micro-organisms than inside their cells; osmosis then occurs, drawing water out of the micro-organisms until they are no longer functional.

Salt is used to preserve fish, meat, and vegetables, while sugar is used to preserve fruits and vegetables.

ISBN: 978-1-897457-80-1

1. Name four ways to preserve food and give one example of each.

Ways to Preserve Food		Examples
______________________	:	______________________
______________________	:	______________________
______________________	:	______________________
______________________	:	______________________

2. Why can salt and sugar be used to preserve food? Explain and complete the diagram to illustrate the idea.

____

____

____

____

____

____

____

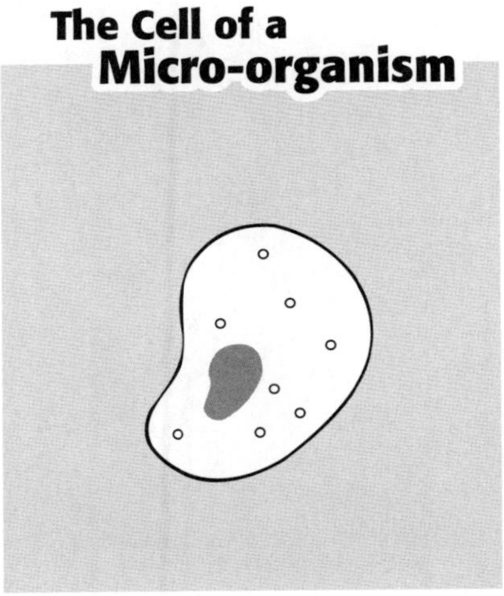

3. Draw lines to show what happens to the peeled and diced potatoes after 30 minutes.

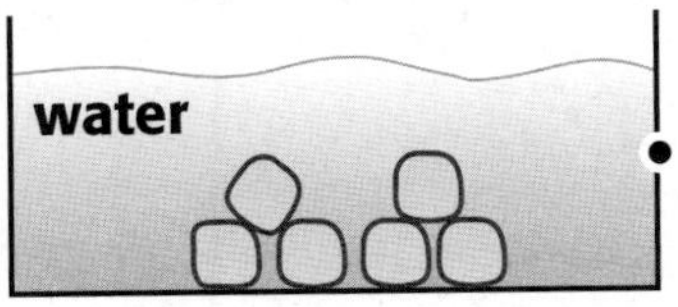

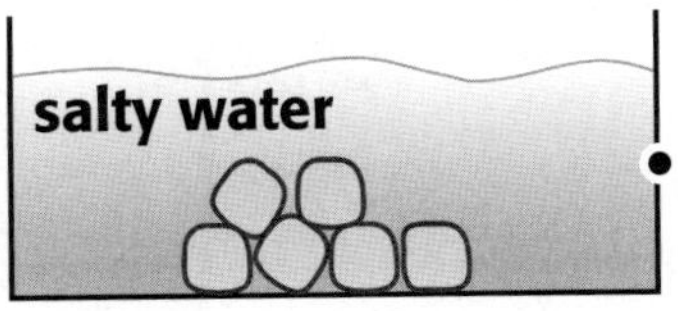

- The potatoes will become softer than before.
- The potatoes will become harder than before.

ISBN: 978-1-897457-80-1

5 Unicellular and Multicellular Organisms

Like us, dragonflies and broccoli have many cells. Other organisms, almost always microscopic, are made up of only one cell. In this unit, you will identify unicellular and multicellular organisms, and examine how unicellular organisms satisfy their basic life needs.

After completing this unit, you will

- understand that there are both unicellular and multicellular organisms.
- understand how unicellular organisms satisfy their basic needs.

Vocabulary

unicellular: made up of one cell

multicellular: made up of many cells

microscopic: only seen with the help of a microscope

ISBN: 978-1-897457-80-1

Extension

While we generally cannot see bacteria, they are everywhere. In fact, they outnumber any other kind of organism by far and have been around for much longer. Scientists believe that bacteria have been on Earth for 4 billion years, making them the oldest form of life. A single human has up to 1000 different species of bacteria living inside him or her, and another 1000 species living in and on his or her skin. Do some research to see just how many species of bacteria live on Earth.

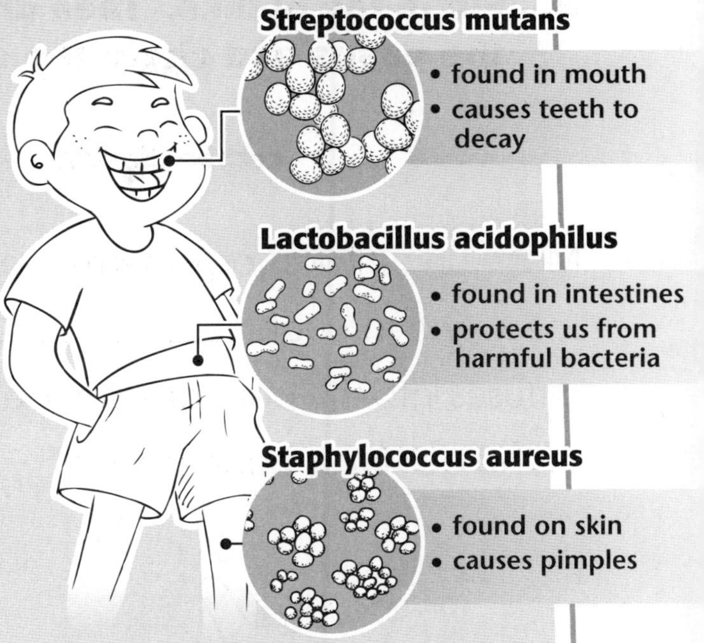

A. Fill in the blanks. Then identify each organism as "multicellular" or "unicellular".

1. A **multicellular** organism is made up of a. ____________ (more/fewer) than one cell.

   A **unicellular** organism is made up of b. ____________ (ten cells/one cell).

2.

a. ____________

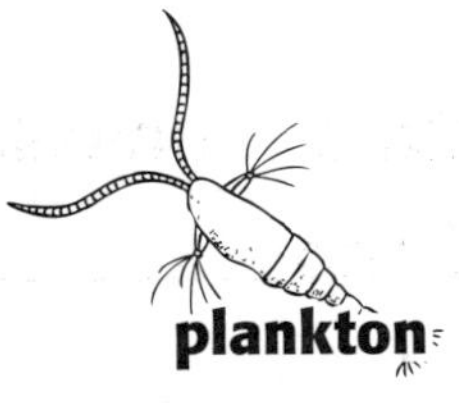

b. ____________

c. ____________

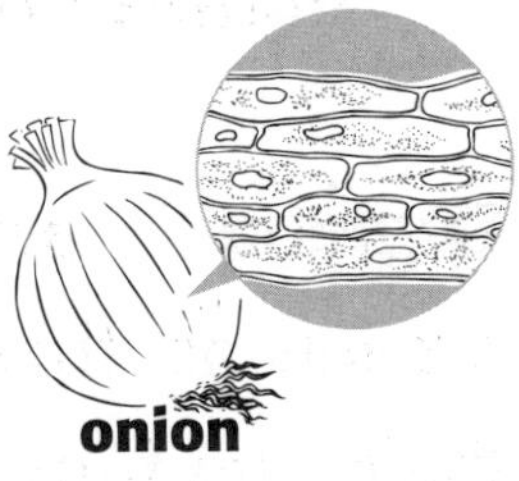

d. ____________

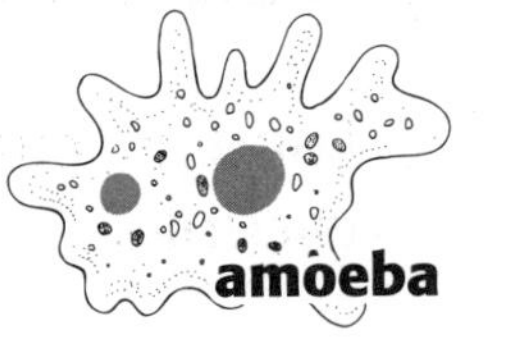

e. ____________

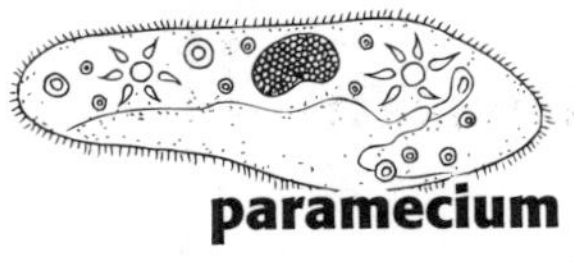

f. ____________

ISBN: 978-1-897457-80-1

B. Fill in the blanks. Then draw arrows to show the movement of the gases and circle the correct words.

carbon dioxide **diffusion** **oxygen**

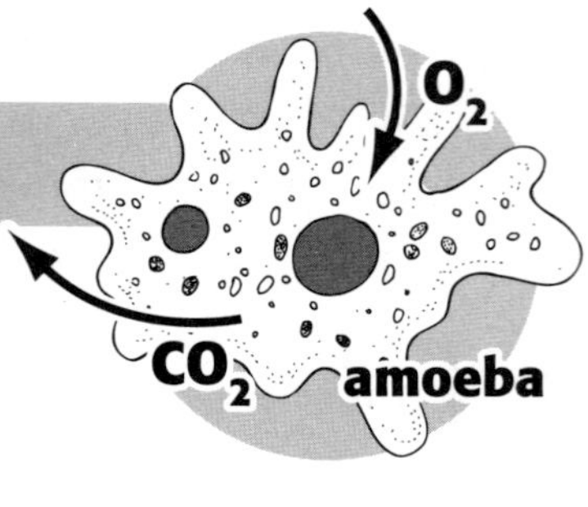

Most unicellular organisms need oxygen, which they get through 1. ______________ . 2. ______________ diffuses into the cell from outside the cell, and 3. ______________ diffuses out of the cell from inside the cell.

4.

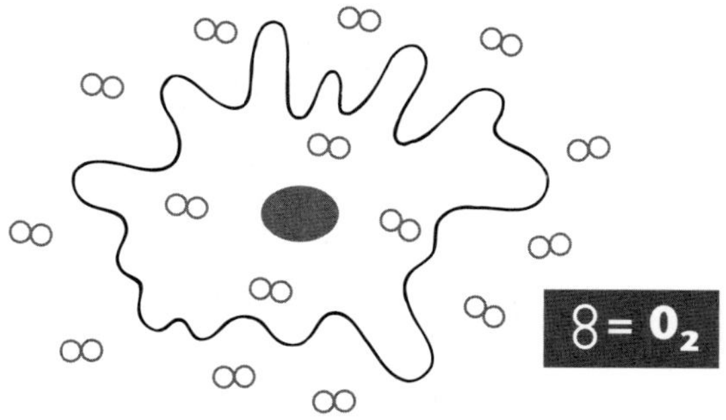

The oxygen will go **out of / into** the cell.

5.

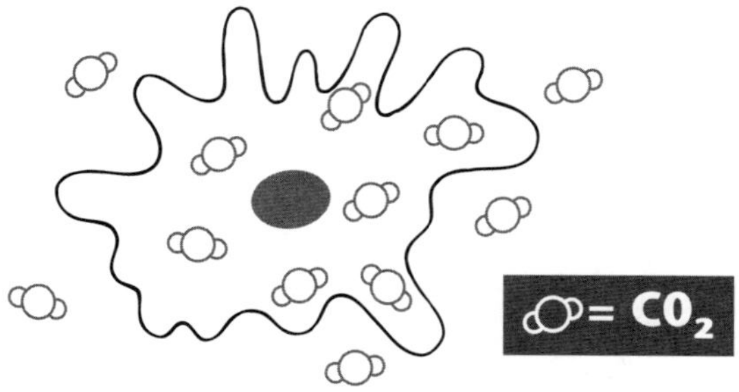

The carbon dioxide will go **out of / into** the cell.

C. See how unicellular organisms make or find food. Fill in the blanks and number the steps.

chloroplasts **make** **eat** **photosynthesis**

Euglena are unicellular organisms that 1. ______________ their own food.

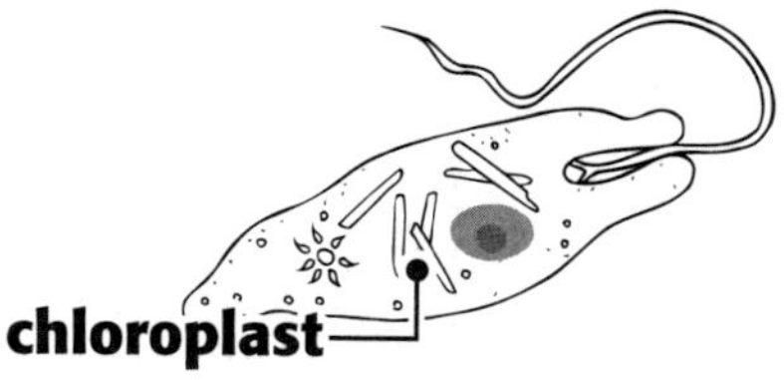

Euglena contain 2. ______________ for 3. ______________ .

Paramecia are unicellular organisms that must find and 4. ______________ their food.

◯ Food goes into the oral groove.

◯ Waste is released.

◯ Food is contained in a vacuole.

◯ Nutrients from food diffuse into the cytoplasm.

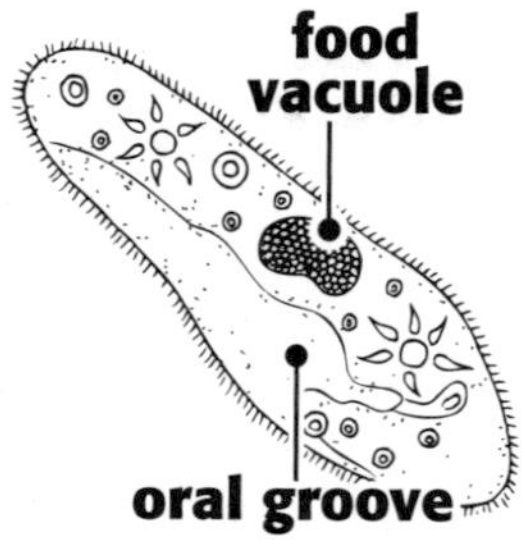

ISBN: 978-1-897457-80-1

D. Fill in the blanks with the given words. Then use the words in bold to describe the pictures.

How Unicellular Organisms Move

food spiral tail locomotion watery shape propel invader

Some unicellular organisms, such as **amoebae**, move by changing their 1.____________ . They stretch out a part of themselves in a process called **cytoplasmic streaming**. In this way, they can gather a 2.____________ particle or swallow up an 3.____________ . Other unicellular organisms use actual 4.____________ to move around in the 5.____________ environment. For example, **paramecia** use tiny, hair-like protrusions called **cilia** to 6.____________ through water. Others, such as **euglena**, have a single, long 7.____________ called a **flagellum** to 8.____________ themselves around.

9.

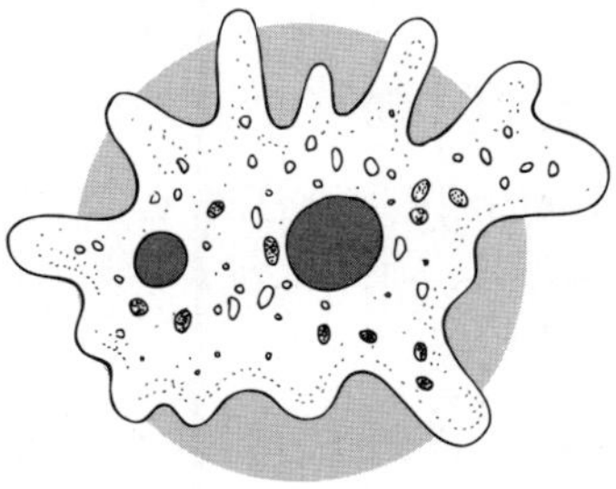

____________ use ____________ to move.

10.

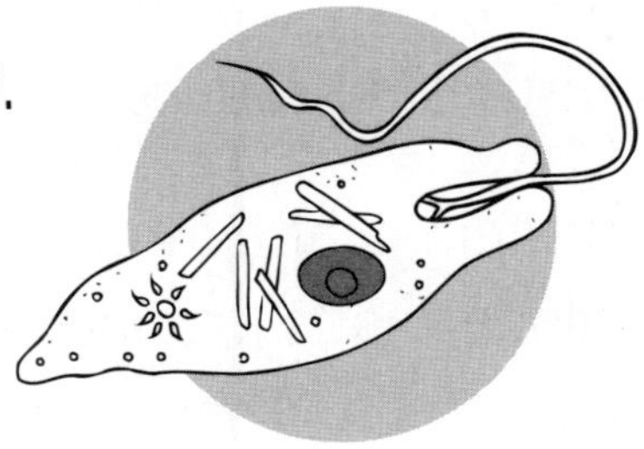

____________ use a ____________ to move.

11.

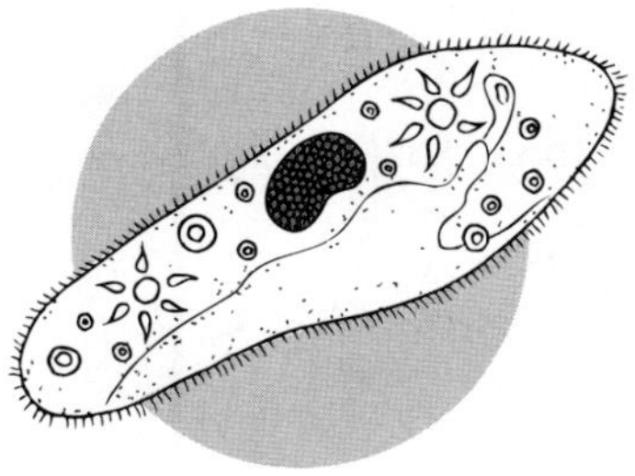

____________ use ____________ to move.

E. Read the passage. Then complete the table and do the quiz.

Are Viruses Living Organism?

Unicellular organisms are everywhere. Bacteria, for example, live all over your body, house, and neighbourhood. However, viruses are even more abundant. Scientists believe that for every organism in existence, there is at least one virus. Then, are viruses living organisms?

Size: An average virus is 20 to 250 nanometres* long. Bacteria are typically 1000 nanometres long.

Life Processes: A virus has almost none of the life processes of a bacterium (or any other living cell). In fact, when outside a living cell, it has no recognizable life processes: it is dormant. However, bacteria need energy, expel waste, and respire, to name just a few of their life processes common to all living cells.

Reproduction: Viruses can reproduce inside a living cell, whereas bacteria can reproduce independent of another organism. Additionally, the way bacteria, and all living cells, reproduce is very different from the way viruses reproduce.

Parts: A virus is made up of two to three parts: genes, a protein coat that protects the genes, and sometimes something called a lipid envelope that surrounds the virus when it is outside a cell. Unlike bacteria, viruses are not cells. They have no cell membrane, no cytoplasm, no nucleus, or any other organelles.

By most definitions, viruses are not organisms, but they are life-like in some ways.

There are one billion nanometres in one metre.

ISBN: 978-1-897457-80-1

1. 

Viruses vs. Bacteria

	Viruses	Bacteria
Size	20 to ______ nm long	about ______ nm long
Life Processes	need to be **inside / outside** a living cell to grow; if they are outside a cell, they are ______	**are / are not** able to live on their own
Reproduction	______	______
Parts	made up of two to ______ parts: • ______ • ______ • ______	common parts found in a cell: • ______ • ______ • ______

2. **Quiz Yourself** T/F

a. Bacteria are one-celled organisms. ______

b. A virus must have a living cell to survive. ______

c. Bacteria do not need energy. ______

d. A virus cannot reproduce outside a living cell. ______

e. Bacteria are usually bigger than viruses. ______

f. Viruses are dormant when they are inside a cell. ______

No. of Questions You Got Right: ______
(5 or more: ***Excellent;*** *3 or 4:* ***Good;*** *2 or fewer:* ***read the passage again)***

6 Cells in Multicellular Organisms

Multicellular organisms are not just a bunch of cells stuck together in any way. They are highly organized. In this unit, you will examine the organization of cells in the human body and other organisms.

After completing this unit, you will

- understand the organization of cells in multicellular organisms.
- understand the functions of the different tissues, organs, and organ systems in multicellular organisms.

Vocabulary

cell: basic unit of life

tissue: group of similar cells

organ: one or more tissues with a specific function

organ system: organs working together to perform a function in an organism

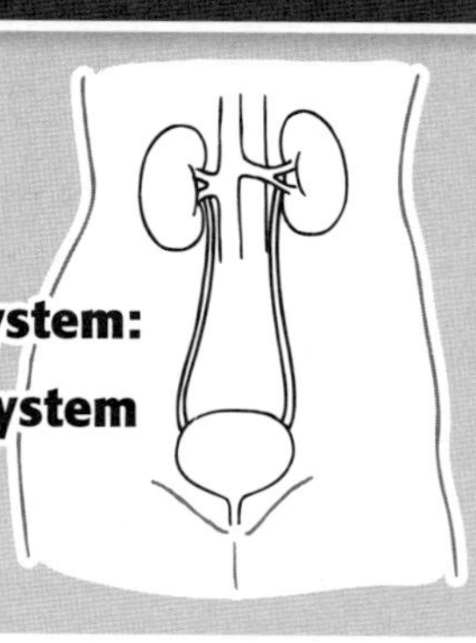

an organ system: excretory system

ISBN: 978-1-897457-80-1

Extension

Humans and other animals have internal organs made up of similar cells like hearts, brains, livers, and skins. Though we do not think of trees or dandelions as having organs like these, they have organs and organ systems, too.

	Main Organs
reproductive system	flowers and fruit
vascular system	stems
photosynthetic system	leaves
absorptive system	roots

Try to identify the organs and organ systems of plants around your house.

A. Read the paragraph. Label the pictures with the words in bold. Then put them in order from the most basic to the most complex using the numbers 1 to 5.

Organization of Cells in Multicellular Organisms

In a multicellular organism, cells are highly organized. Similar ***cells*** *make up tissues.* ***Tissue****, sometimes more than one kind, makes up an* ***organ****, and organs work together to make up an* ***organ system****. All of these make up an* ***organism****.*

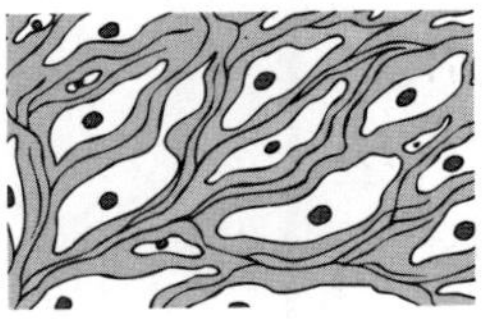

1. ____________ ( )

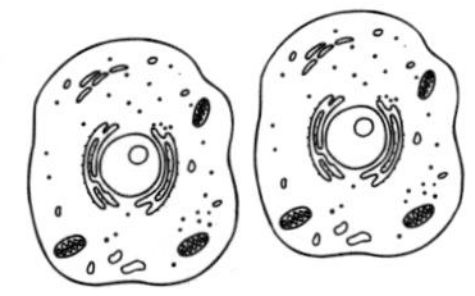

2. ____________ ( )

3. ____________ ( )

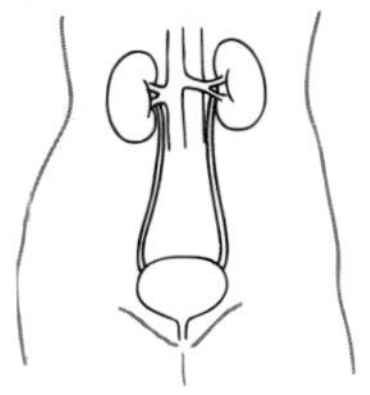

4. ____________ ( )

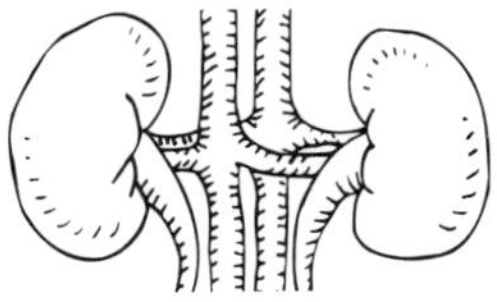

5. ____________ ( )

B. Name each level of organization. Then write the letters to match the characteristics of each level.

Characteristics of Each Level of Organization

tissue cell organism organ organ system

1. 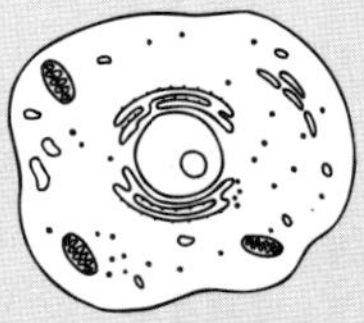

   ____________ ( ) ( )

2. 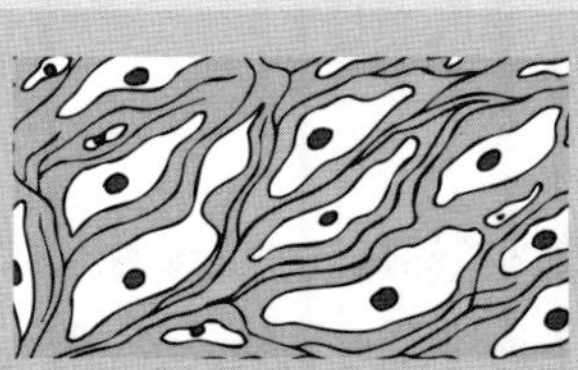

   ____________ ( ) ( )

3. 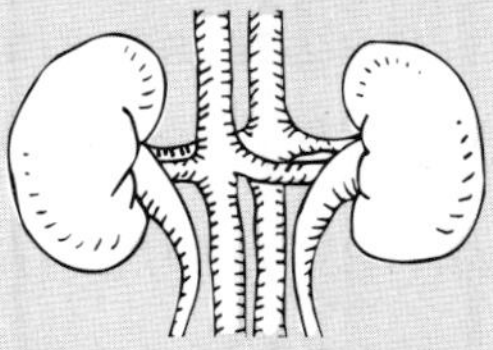

   ____________ ( ) ( )

4. 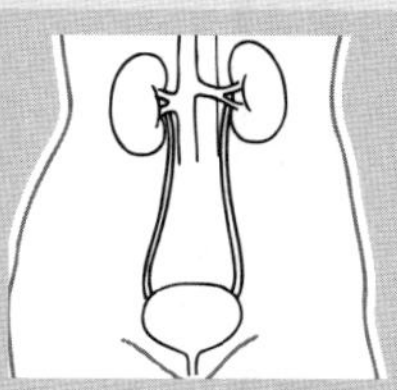

   ____________ ( ) ( )

5. 

   ____________ ( ) ( )

A basic unit of life

B examples are fat, hair, and blood

C examples are skin, kidneys, and heart

D work together to allow a living thing to function

E of the same type; they make up a tissue

F examples are digestive, circulatory, and reproductive systems

G composed of cells similar in form and function

H can be made up of many organ systems or just one cell

I a living thing; carries out all the processes necessary for life

J can be made up of one or more kinds of tissue

ISBN: 978-1-897457-80-1

C. Fill in the blanks with the four types of tissues.

Four Types of Tissues

muscle | epithelial | connective | nervous

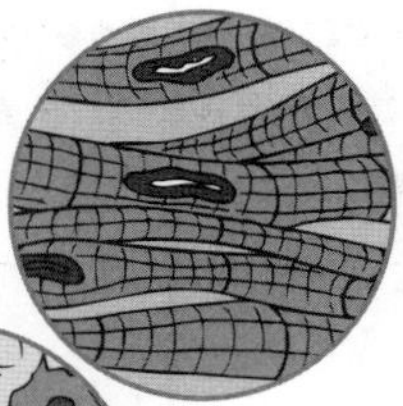

1. ________________ tissue: makes up our muscles

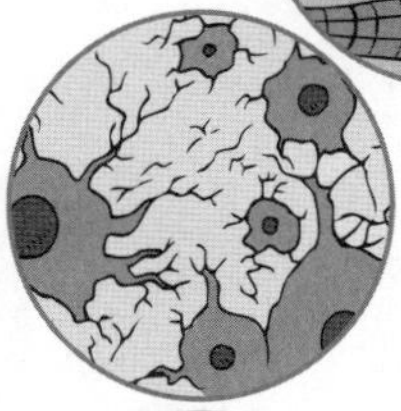

2. ________________ tissue: is made up of message-passing neurons

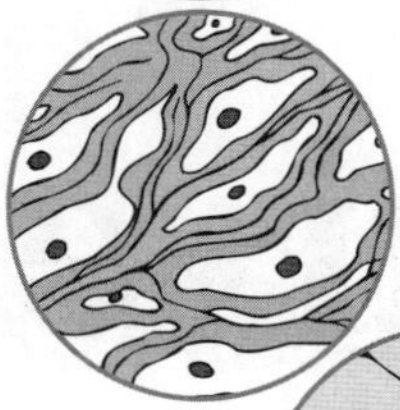

3. ________________ tissue: examples are blood and bones

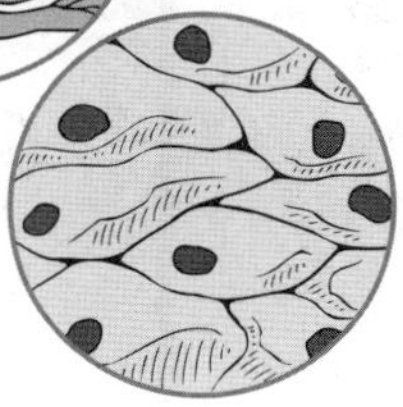

4. ________________ tissue: lines our organs

D. Sort the organs into the correct organ systems. Name the organ systems. Then name one more organ in each system on your own.

bones | brain | stomach | Respiratory | Circulatory | Muscular

Organ System — **Main Organ**

1. Digestive System: ________________ ; ________________
2. Nervous System: ________________ ; ________________
3. Skeletal System: ________________ ; ________________
4. ________________ System: smooth muscles ; ________________
5. ________________ System: trachea ; ________________
6. ________________ System: blood vessels ; ________________

ISBN: 978-1-897457-80-1

E. Read the passage. Then answer the questions.

The Digestive System

The digestive system extracts nutrients from the food we eat. It includes organs such as the mouth, stomach, and small intestine. Let's take a closer look at the function and structure of the small intestine.

The small intestine is the main site of digestion and nutrient absorption. Food makes its way to the small intestine from the stomach, where it has been only partially digested. In order to absorb nutrients from food as it moves through the digestive system, the small intestine must actually be quite large. In humans, the small intestine is anywhere from 3 to 7 metres long and 2.5 to 3 centimetres in diameter.

The small intestine is made up primarily of epithelial tissue, which is a type of tissue with many functions, one of which is absorption. In the small intestine, this tissue is folded and has many projections called villi; the folds and villi increase the small intestine's surface area, which means more nutrients can be absorbed to keep a human body in working order. After absorbing nutrients, the cells of the small intestine deliver the nutrients into the bloodstream. The bloodstream then delivers the nutrients to every cell in the body.

ISBN: 978-1-897457-80-1

1. Name the important organs of the digestive system and write one major function of each.

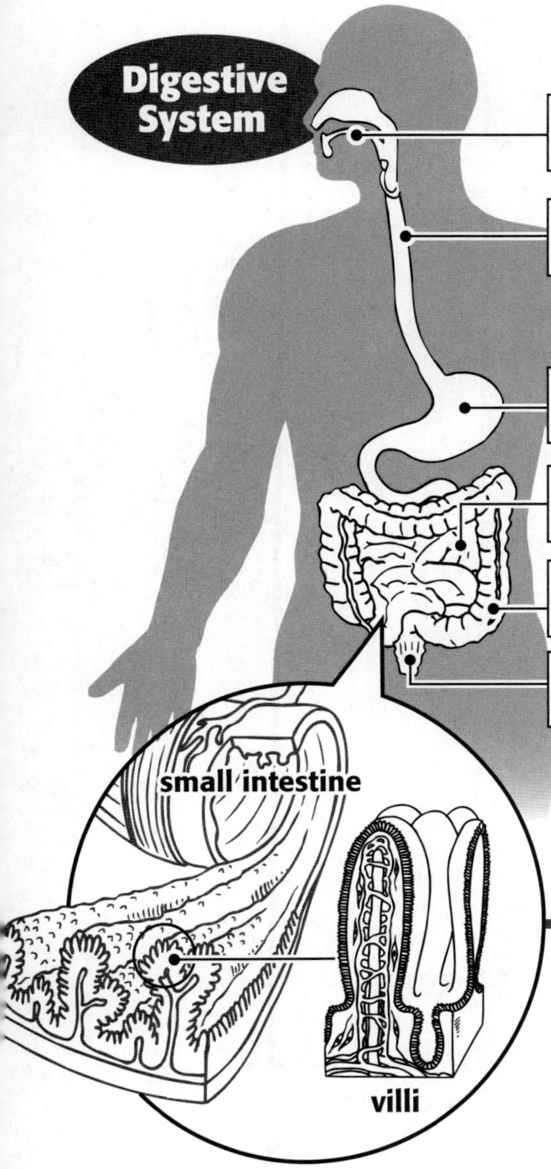

Organ	Major Function
a.	; ______________
b.	; ______________
c.	; ______________
d.	; ______________
e.	; ______________
f.	; ______________

2. Description of the small intestine:

- length: a. ______________
- diameter: b. ______________

- made up primarily of c. ______________ tissue; this d. ______________ (folded/smooth) tissue has many projections called e. ______________
- the folds and villi increase f. ______________ so as to absorb g. ______________ nutrients

ISBN: 978-1-897457-80-1

Experiment

Introduction

Diffusion is the movement of a substance from an area of higher concentration to an area of lower concentration.

If a soft cookie is left out long enough, it will become stale – dried out – as its moisture diffuses into the air, which contains less moisture. If a soft cookie is paired with a slice of apple, will it affect the time it takes for the cookie to go stale? Will it draw moisture from the apple through diffusion?

Hypothesis

If a soft cookie is paired with a slice of apple, it will affect the time for it to go stale.

Steps

1. Cut a small slice of apple.
2. Place a soft cookie in a container with the apple slice.
3. Place the other soft cookie in a container without the apple slice. This is the control*.

Materials

- ***two soft cookies***
- ***an apple***
- ***a paring knife***
- ***two plastic containers with lids***

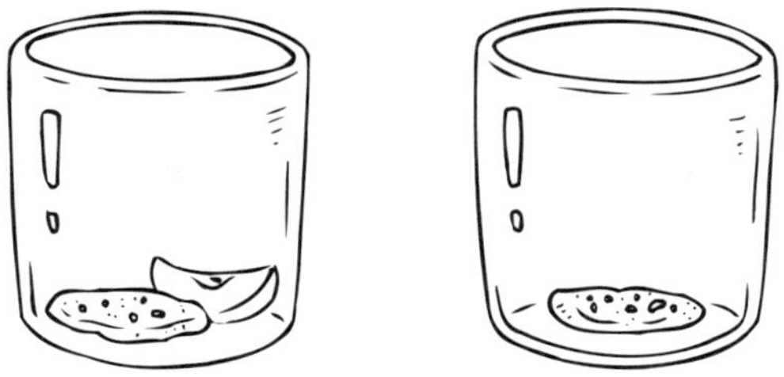

*control: the portion that no experiment is performed on; serves as a state to be compared with

ISBN: 978-1-897457-80-1

4. Put the lids on the containers.

5. Feel the cookies in the containers each day for 5 days. You may take off the lid, but reseal it after each touch.

Result

Put a checkmark under the softer cookie. If they have the same softness, check both.

Do not consume the cookies or the apple slice after the experiment. They can be contaminated.

Day		
1		
2		
3		
4		
5		

Did the cookie draw moisture from the apple slice through diffusion? If yes, describe the diffusion process.

____

____

____

Conclusion

The hypothesis was: ______________________________

____

My experiment ______________________ the hypothesis.
supported/did not support

ISBN: 978-1-897457-80-1

This review consists of five sections, from A to E. The marks for each question are shown in parentheses. The circle at the bottom right corner is for the marks you get in each section. An overall record is on the last page of the review.

A. Write T for true and F for false.

1. Cells make up living things, but they are not living things themselves. **(2)** ______

2. A cell membrane can be found in plants, but not in animals. **(2)** ______

3. Plant cells have much larger vacuoles than animal cells in proportion to their sizes. **(2)** ______

4. The vacuole contains the cell's chromosomes. **(2)** ______

5. 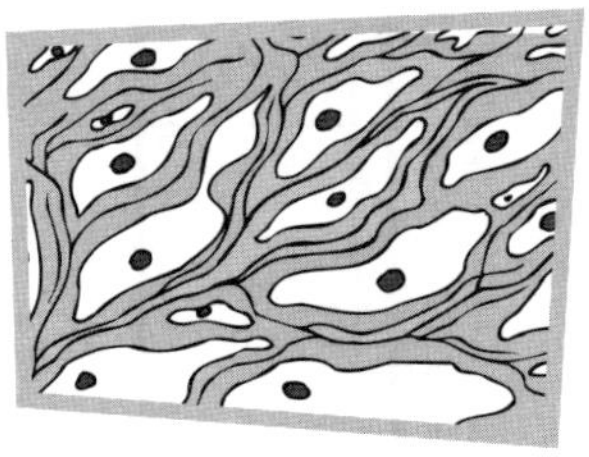

Tissue is made up of cells. **(2)**

______

6. 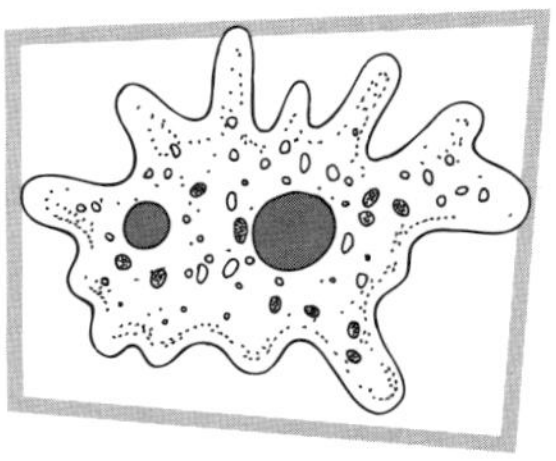

All unicellular organisms use cilia to spiral themselves around. **(2)**

______

12

ISBN: 978-1-897457-80-1

B. Do the matching.

1.

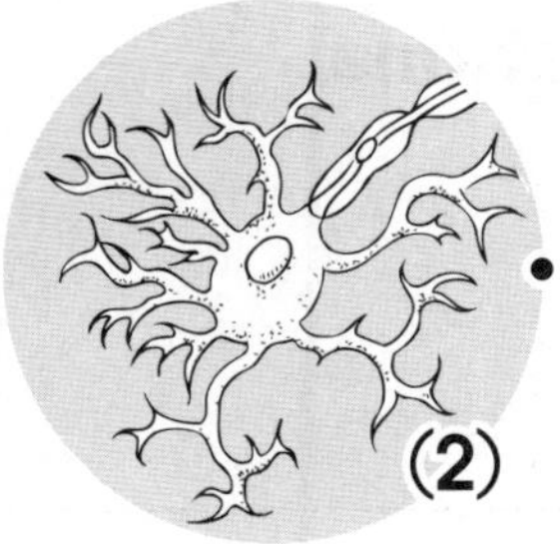

2.

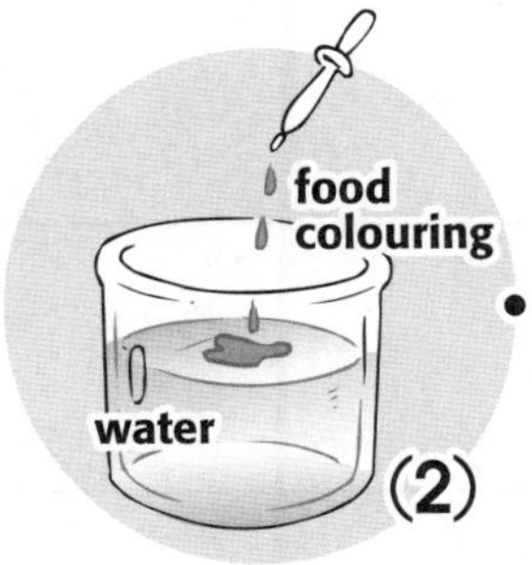

3.

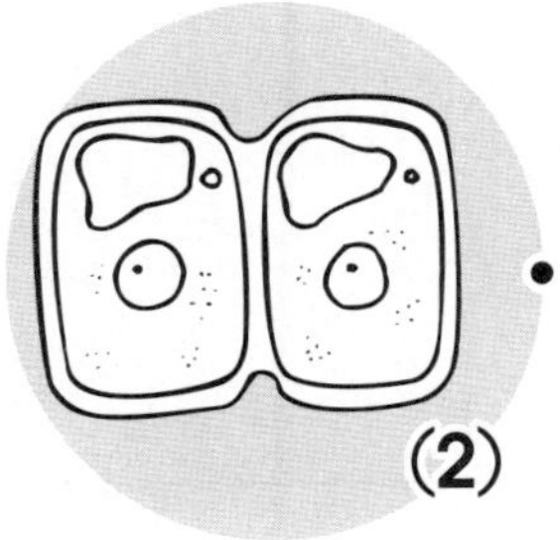

4.

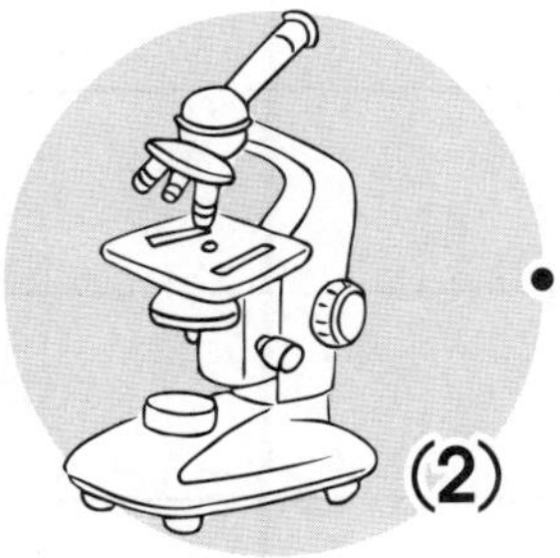

5.

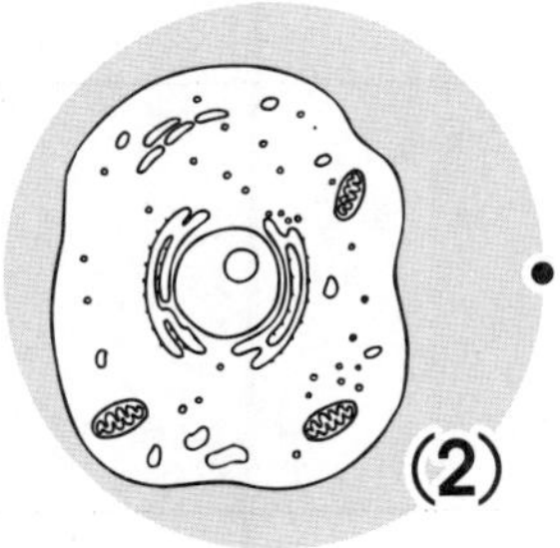

6.

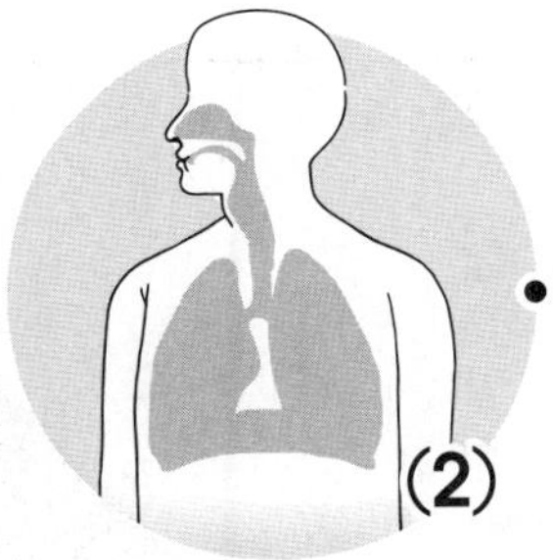

- an organ system
- an example of diffusion
- a nerve cell
- enables us to see live cells
- in the process of cell division
- can burst if too much water is absorbed

12

C. Write the postulates of the cell theory to match the descriptions. Identify the cell, label its parts, and write the functions of the parts. Then answer the questions.

1. **Postulates of the Cell Theory**

1 ______________________________ **(2)**

There are trillions of cells that make up an organism.

2 ______________________________ **(2)**

A cell is a building block.

3 ______________________________ **(2)**

You come from your parents' cells.

2. **A Typical ____________ (2) Cell**

Animal/Plant

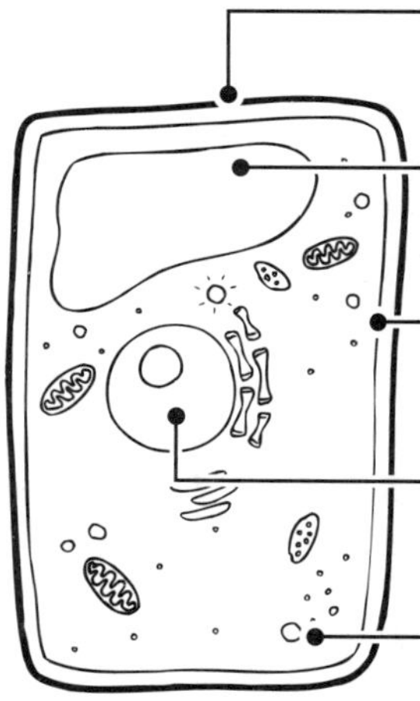

a. : ______________________________ **(3)**

b. : ______________________________ **(3)**

c. : ______________________________ **(3)**

d. : ______________________________ **(3)**

e. : ______________________________ **(3)**

3. Name two special features of this kind of cell. **(4)**

____

____

4. Name the three basic parts that most animal and plant cells contain. **(6)**

____

33

ISBN: 978-1-897457-80-1

D. Fill in the blanks with "high" or "low" to complete the descriptions. Then answer the questions.

1. ***Osmosis Process***

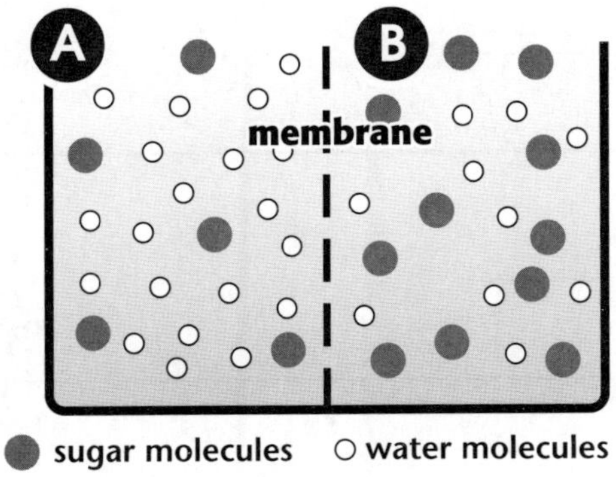

A ________ concentration of water (**2**)

________ concentration of sugar (**2**)

B ________ concentration of water (**2**)

________ concentration of sugar (**2**)

2. Describe the permeability of the membrane in the diagram. (**4**)

____

____

3. Which part of a cell is involved in osmosis? (**2**)

____

____

4. Describe the process of osmosis. (**4**)

____

____

____

5. Most unicellular organisms need oxygen. Describe how an amoeba, a unicellular organism, gets oxygen. You may use the diagram to illustrate your answer. (**4**)

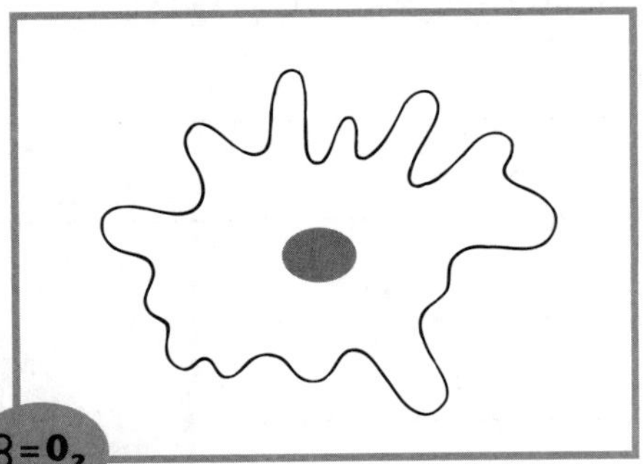

____

____

____

$8 = O_2$

22

ISBN: 978-1-897457-80-1

E. Answer the questions.

1. 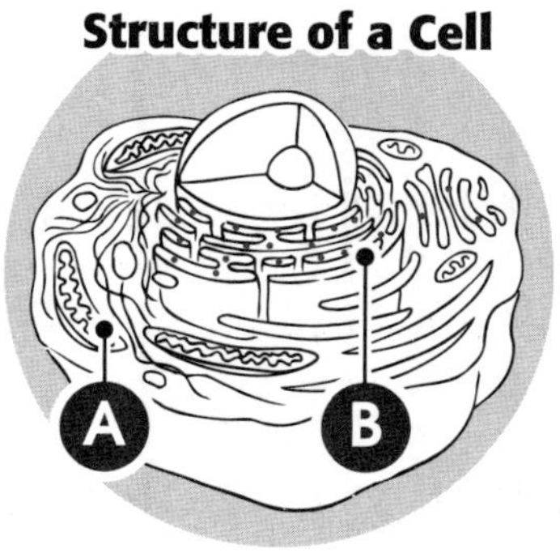

Name the organelles and write their functions.

A ____________________ :

____ (3)

B ____________________ :

____ (3)

2. 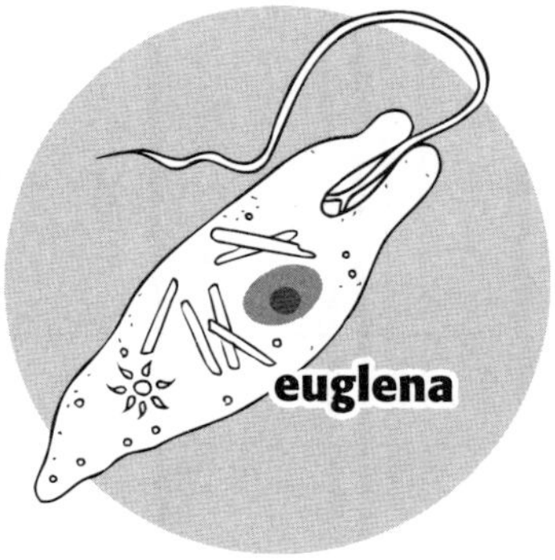

Are euglena unicellular or multicellular organisms? Describe where their food comes from. (**4**)

____

____

3. 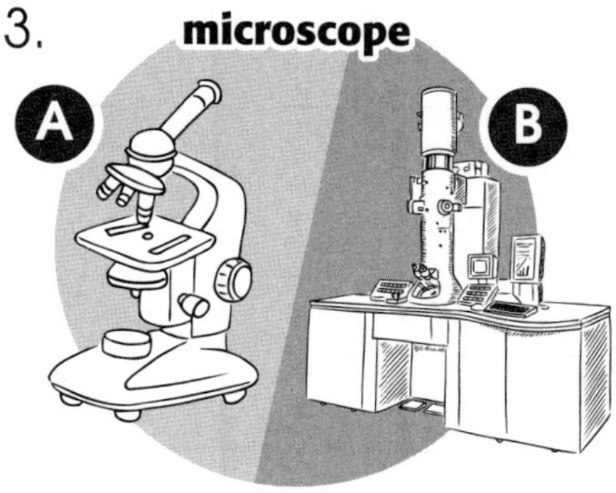

Name the microscopes. Write one feature of each.

A ____________________ :

____ (3)

B ____________________ :

____ (3)

4. 

Write what makes up an organism. (**5**)

____

____

____

____

21

ISBN: 978-1-897457-80-1

My Record

Section A	12
Section B	12
Section C	33
Section D	22
Section E	21

Total

100

80-100

Great work! You really understand your science stuff! Research your favourite science topics at the library or on the Internet to find out more about the topics related to this section. Keep challenging yourself to learn more!

60-79

Good work! You understand some basic concepts, but try reading through the units again to see whether you can master the material! Go over the questions that you had trouble with to make sure you know the correct answers.

below 60

You can do much better! Try reading over the units again. Ask your parents or teachers any questions you might have. Once you feel confident that you know the material, try the review again. Science is exciting, so don't give up!

ISBN: 978-1-897457-80-1

Scientists at Work

The Cell Biologist

The cell is the functional basic unit of life that is classified as a living thing, and is often called the building block of life. The more we understand cells, the more we know ourselves and the living things around us.

There are scientists who specialize in studying cells. They are called cell biologists. A cell biologist studies the properties of cells: the functional structures within them, interaction and communication among cells, and their life cycle, division, and death.

Anthony Pawson

Anthony Pawson is a world-renowned Canadian cell biologist. In 2008 Pawson was awarded the Kyoto Prize, which is Japan's equivalent of the Nobel Prize given annually to those who make significant contributions in advanced technology, basic sciences, arts, and philosophy.

Pawson was given the award for his pioneering work on cancer cell signalling – how cells control one another's behaviour through chemical signals. His research has led to a better understanding and treatment of cancer, diabetes, and disorders of the immune system.

ISBN: 978-1-897457-80-1

Cool Science Facts

ISBN: 978-1-897457-80-1

1. Why do many deep sea fish have large eyes and large mouths?

2. How do you oust mosquitoes from your garden without using any chemical mosquito repellents?

3. Antibiotics are a kind of medicine. What did scientists in the past put in antibiotics?

4. We should thank the bacteria in antibiotics which cure us when we are sick. How do the bacteria work in antibiotics?

Find the answers on the next page.

Cool Science Facts

1 Due to the extremely harsh environment, with high water pressure, low temperatures, and a lack of oxygen, food is scarce in deep seas. Hence, deep sea fish developed large mouths to collect as much food as possible. Moreover, to adapt to the environment that is lack of light, deep sea fish need large eyes to gather every single source of light.

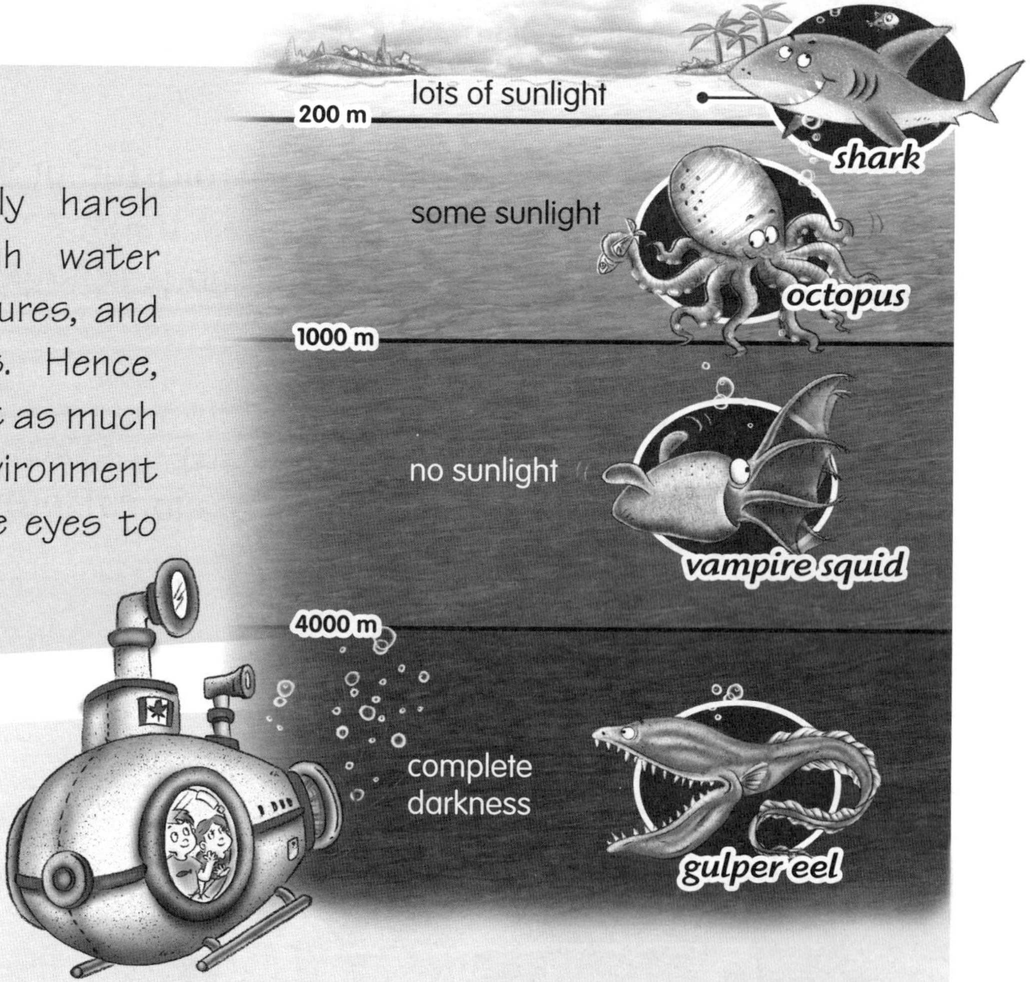

2

You can plant some mosquito repellent plants such as lavender, mint, and rosemary in your garden. It is a natural and an effective way to keep mosquitoes out. When you are working in your garden, simply break off a branch of the mosquito repellent plant and rub it over the exposed areas on your skin. This will ward off mosquitoes.

ISBN: 978-1-897457-80-1

ISBN: 978-1-897457-80-1

3 The early antibiotics were made from bacteria, fungi, or other micro-organism living in soil. Many of these early antibiotics are manufactured chemically nowadays. Newly discovered antibiotics have also been synthetically made, usually by altering the chemical structure of an existing, naturally produced antibiotic.

4 All the different types of antibiotics work in one of the two ways: an antibiotic, which is also a bacterium itself, either kills the harmful bacteria or stops them from multiplying so that we can fight the limited number of harmful bacteria with our immune systems. Remember though, antibiotics are only effective for treating an infection caused by bacteria, but not by viruses.

ISBN: 978-1-897457-80-1

Section 2

Understanding Structures and Mechanisms

ISBN: 978-1-897457-80-1

1 Systems

Systems exist in the natural world and as human-made constructs. What they all have in common is that their component parts work together as a whole. In this unit, you will learn about the characteristics of systems, identify different systems, and look at smaller systems that make up larger systems.

After completing this unit, you will

- understand the purpose and characteristics of systems.
- be able to identify different kinds of systems.
- recognize smaller systems within larger systems.

Vocabulary

system: a group of parts that work together as a whole

subsystem: a system that works with other systems as part of a larger system

component: a part of a whole

ISBN: 978-1-897457-80-1

Extension

Throughout history, we have created systems in order to make our lives easier. Many of the greatest inventions and innovations are systems or parts of systems. Take a look at the timeline to see what systems were invented.

Which innovation or invention has the most impact on you? What would you add to the timeline?

____

____

640 **Windmills in Persia**

1044 Movable type printing in China

1335 Clock in Europe

1698 Steam Engine

1826 Photograph

1846 Sewing Machine

1873 Typewriter

1879 Light Bulb

1895 X-rays

1908 Automobile

⋮

A. Fill in the blanks with the given words. Then label the bicycle with the words "system" and "subsystem".

subsystems   more   together   nature

A system is a group of parts that work 1. ____________ to accomplish a task. It uses resources 2. ____________ efficiently than the parts working alone. Systems occur in 3. ____________ and as human-made constructs. They can be made up of smaller systems or 4. ____________ that work together to make up the whole.

Bicycle

ISBN: 978-1-897457-80-1

B. Name each system and determine whether it is a "natural" or "human-made" system. Then write two component parts of each system and give one more example.

system

solar electrical
digestive ecosystem education

component

trees Earth electricity esophagus
wires school stomach lion
sun student

1. ______________ system
(**natural / human-made** system)
components:
____
____
______________ *(my example)*

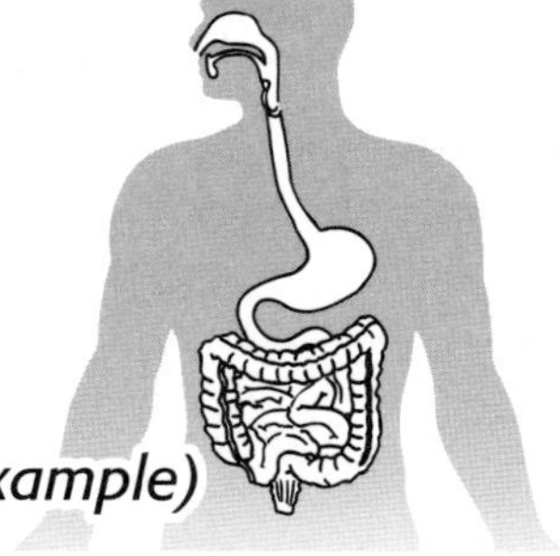

2. ______________
(______________ system)
components:
____
____
______________ *(my example)*

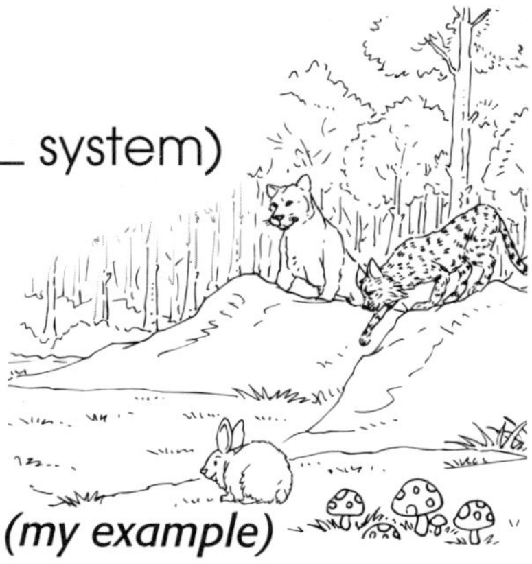

3. ______________ system
(______________ system)
components:
____
____
______________ *(my example)*

4. 

______________ system
(______________ system)
components:
____
____
______________ *(my example)*

5. 

______________ system
(______________ system)
components:
____
____
______________ *(my example)*

ISBN: 978-1-897457-80-1

C. Complete the diagram to show the subsystems of the transportation system. Then answer the questions.

transportation	*component*
land air water	subway horses gliders lighthouses hot-air balloons ships runways canoes cruise ships freighters cars buses locks helicopters barges railways trains bicycles airplanes ferries airports

1.

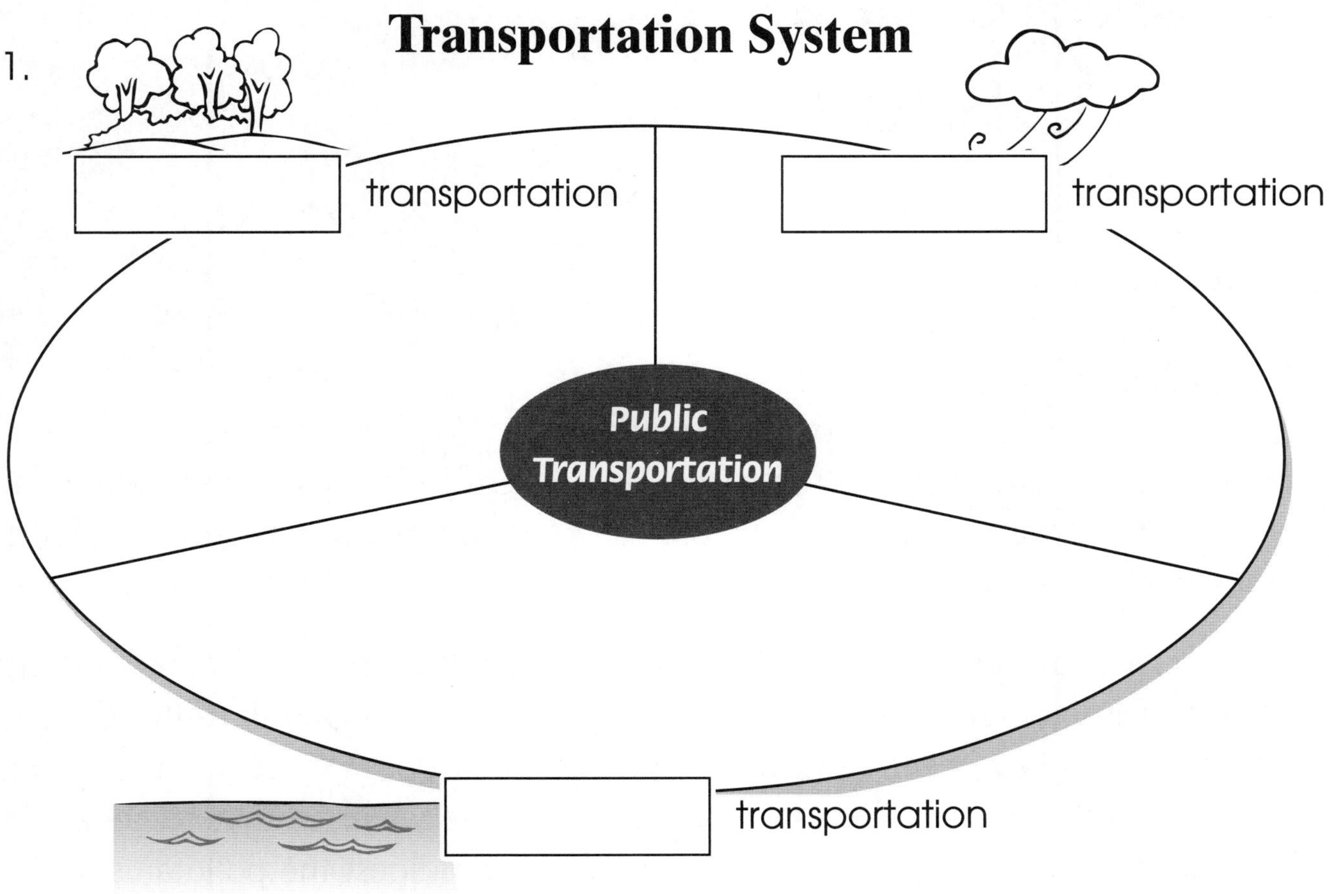

2. What are the subsystems of the transportation system?

____

____

____

3. *Name a subsystem of the land transportation system.*

____

ISBN: 978-1-897457-80-1

D. Read the passage. Name the parts in the subsystems to complete the diagram. Then answer the questions.

Keeping Water Clean

As you know, humans use a lot of water! We use it to flush toilets, clean ourselves, clean other things, play sports, and much more. To keep a steady and clean supply of water, we have to use a complex system called a sewage* treatment system. When water goes down the drains, it travels through pipes that lead to a treatment centre. There, it gets treated by a whole bunch of subsystems.

In the first subsystem, we pass the sewage through a screen to remove large objects. Those objects have to be disposed of and go to a landfill. After sludge, grease, and oil have been removed, the waste water goes into an aeration tank, which is another subsystem. Air is pumped into the water so that bacteria will have just the right environment for them to eat and digest the pollutants in the water. The function of the third subsystem is to filter out the dirt left behind. Then the last subsystem uses chlorine to disinfect the water. Don't worry – the chlorine gets removed before the water goes to the surface water.

Now imagine what would happen if not enough air was pumped into the water in the second subsystem. The bacteria would not be able to feed on the pollutants and we would have bacteria- and pollutant-filled water. As you can see, we need each component in each subsystem to work to keep our water clean.

**sewage:* *the water that we have used, along with whatever else we put down the drains*

 ISBN: 978-1-897457-80-1

Subsystem

1.

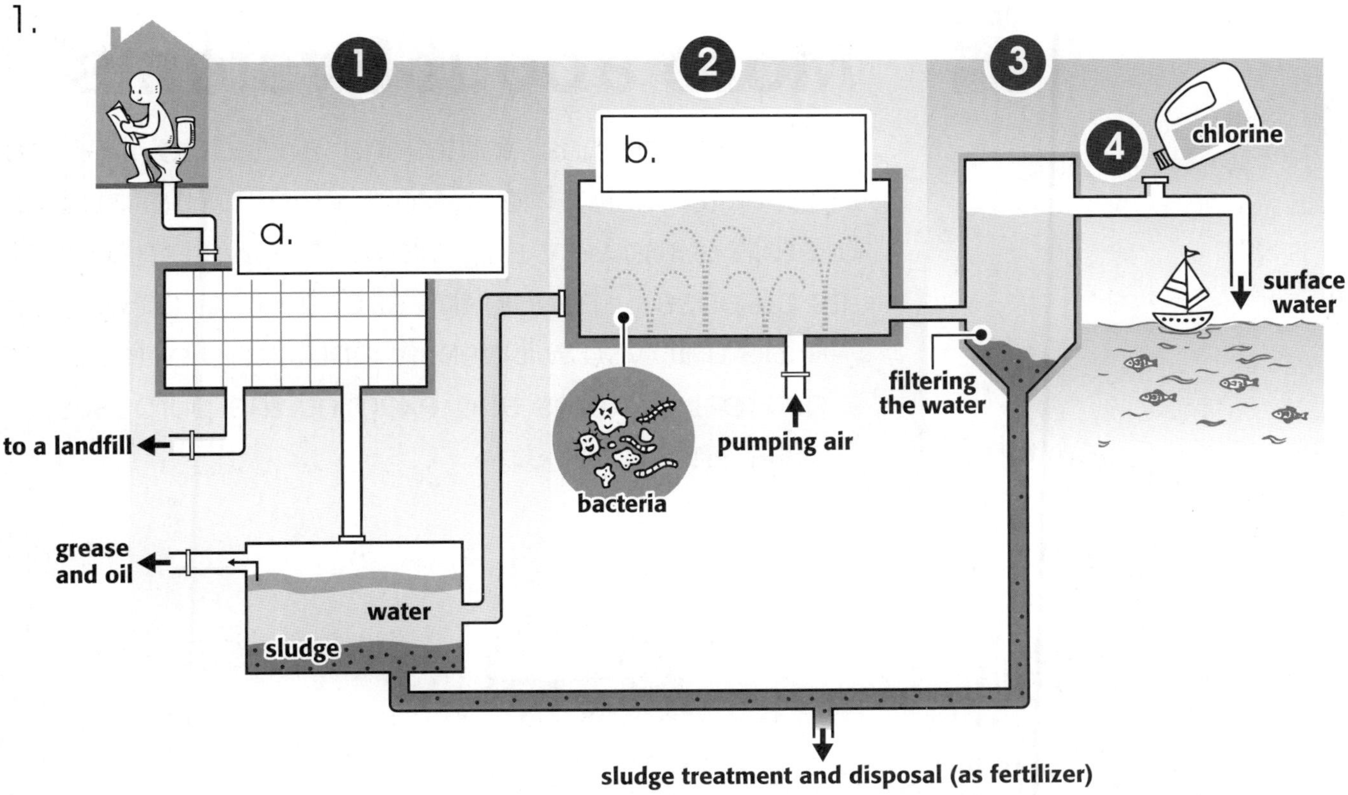

2. Function of Each Subsystem

1 ______________________________

2 ______________________________

3 ______________________________

4 ______________________________

3. Name three components in the second subsystem.

____

4. What would happen if not enough chlorine was added to the water in the last subsystem?

____

____

2 More about Systems

Every system has something added to it – the input – to make the system work. The input is used in some way that allows the system to fulfill its purpose. Then, in the end, there is an output. In this unit, you will identify inputs and outputs for different systems and examine the purposes of different systems.

After completing this unit, you will

- understand that systems have purposes.
- understand that systems have inputs and outputs.
- be able to identify the purposes, inputs, and outputs of different systems.

Vocabulary

purpose: the reason for a system to exist

input: what is put into a system

output: what is produced by a system

ISBN: 978-1-897457-80-1

Extension

We are all a part of many systems, many of which are connected to one another.

Here are some systems you may be a part of:

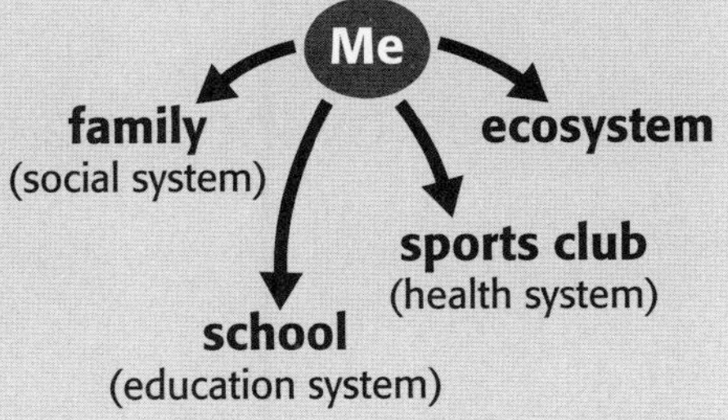

Think about the questions below:

- *What other systems are you a part of?*
- *In what ways are these systems connected?*
- *Do you know why you are a part of these systems?*
- *What are the purposes of these systems?*

A. Circle the correct words. Then fill in the blanks.

A system's purpose is its reason for **reading / existing** . A system's success depends on whether the system **achieves / states** its purpose and does it efficiently.

gear	affairs
factory	goods
health	less
hydraulic	speed
political	illness

System

1. 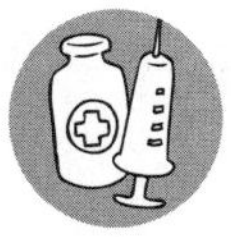 ______________ system: to keep people healthy and to treat ______________
2.  ______________ system: to mass produce ______________
3. 

______________ system: to administrate a country's ______________
4.  ______________ system: to move or lift large loads with ______________ effort
5.  ______________ system: to change the interaction between the speed of a driving mechanism and the ______________ of the driven parts

ISBN: 978-1-897457-80-1

B. Fill in the blanks with the words in the diagram. Then complete the diagrams.

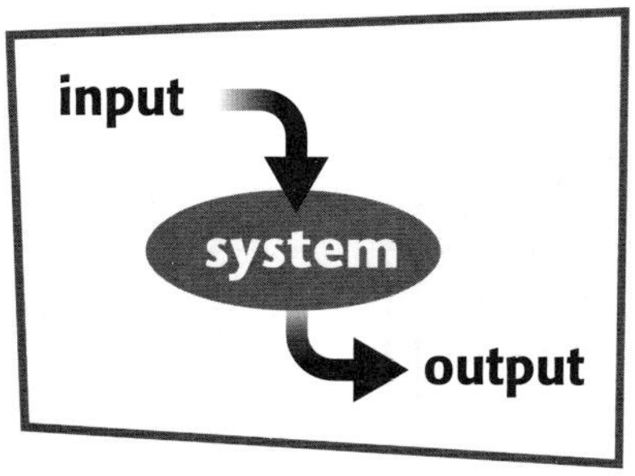

_______________ : what is put into the system

_______________ : what is produced by the system

system

night light respiratory system hydroelectric plant

input/output

electricity oxygen ingredients oxygen plant light cookies

1. [ ] input → system → output → **carbon dioxide**

2. **electricity** → input → system → output → [ ]

3. **moving water** → input → system → output → [ ]

4. [ ] → input → system **Bakery** → output → [ ]

5. [ ] → input → **ecosystem** → output → [ ]

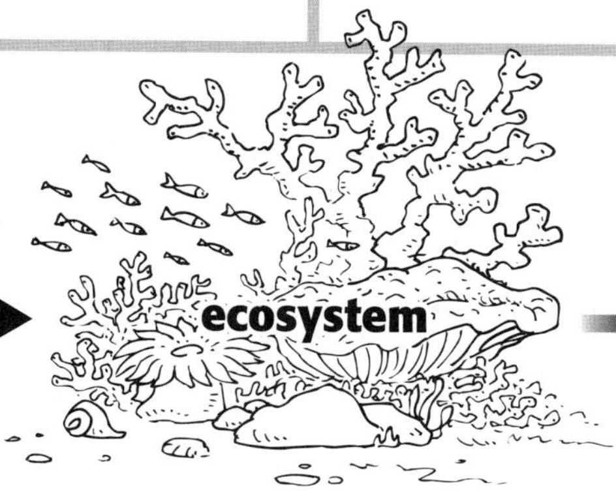

ISBN: 978-1-897457-80-1

C. Read the paragraph. Then write about the septic system and the computer system.

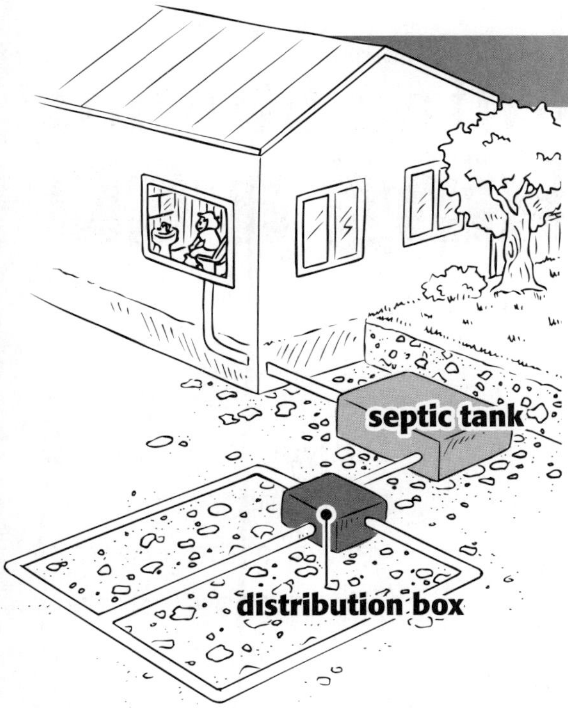

The Septic System

In houses not serviced by a city water system, a septic system is used to treat waste water and sewage. A house's waste water and sewage begin in toilets, sinks, and bathtubs, go down drains into drain pipes, and then into the septic tank, distribution box, and septic field where they are filtered and cleaned. The septic system eliminates pollutants from waste water and sewage, and clean water is what results.

Septic System

purpose: ____________________

components:

____________ ____________

____________ ____________

____________ ____________

____________ ____________

inputs: ____________

____

output: ____________

Computer System

purpose: ____________________

components: ____________________

input: ____________________

output: ____________________

ISBN: 978-1-897457-80-1

D. Read the passage. Then label the arrows as "input" or "output" and name the components in a recording system.

The Recording Studio: Making a CD

Did you know that a recording studio is a very specific system? The purpose of this system is to record what musicians played live in their studio onto a CD so that fans can listen to the music anytime, anywhere. There are many components necessary for this system to work.

When a musician plays an **electric guitar** or **keyboard**, or sings into a **microphone**, the sounds he or she makes are sent as electrical signals through wires. The **mixer** receives these signals. Then the mixer sends the signals to an **amplifier**, which increases the signals' strength, and a **computer**, where a song editor can modify the sounds before he or she puts them onto a **CD**. The CD is the output produced by the input components involved in the recording.

However, in the system that plays the CD, the CD can be considered an input component. Electrical signals are stored on the CD. In order to play the songs, the **CD player** needs an amplifier and a **speaker system**. The speaker system turns the amplifier's electrical energy into sound energy and this is how we hear music. Without the input components above, we could not have the output – the sound energy, or music. What a complicated process in transforming a sound wave produced by a person into one produced by a CD!

ISBN: 978-1-897457-80-1

Recording System

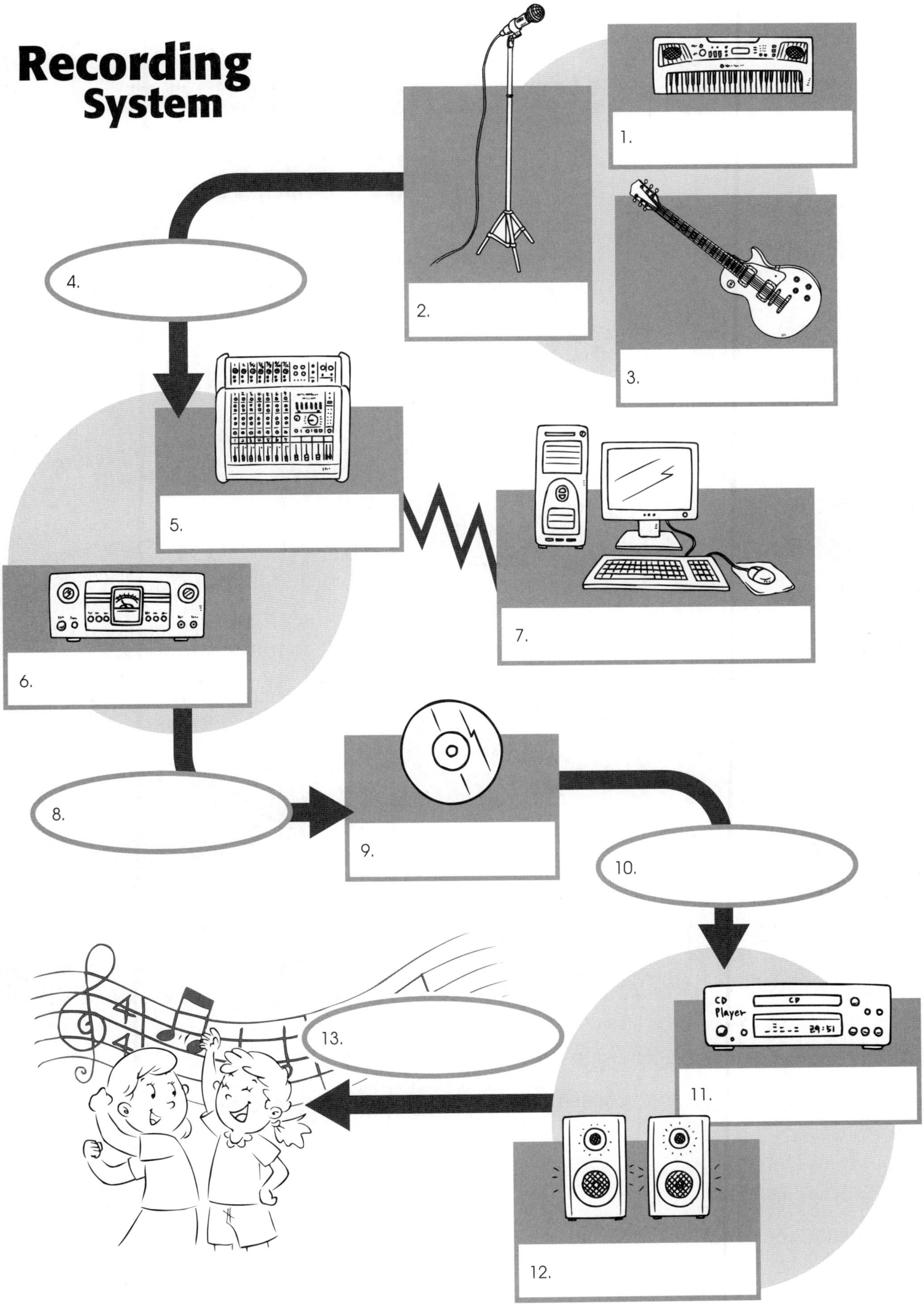

ISBN: 978-1-897457-80-1

3 Systems in Action

The terms energy, force, work, and efficiency have scientific meanings that differ from their meanings in our everyday use of the words. In this unit, you will look at how these terms differ in their meanings, and examine how the quality and working order of system components affect a system's efficiency and safety.

After completing this unit, you will

- know the more precise definitions of the words: energy, force, work, and efficiency.
- understand that systems perform efficiently because of their processes and components.

Vocabulary

energy: the capacity to do work

force: a push or pull that causes movement or stress on an object

work: the effort it takes to cause an object to move or change shape

ergonomic: designed for comfort and safety

ISBN: 978-1-897457-80-1

Extension

Have you used the terms "energy", "force", "work", and "efficiency" in conversations and writings in your everyday life? What do these terms mean to you? Write the definitions, everyday or scientific, of these terms in the space below. When you have finished this unit, go over your definitions and see if your understanding of the terms has changed.

energy: ____________________

force: ____________________

work: ____________________

efficiency: ____________________

A. Draw a line to show the correct scientific meaning of each term.

Energy •

- the capacity to do work
- something that helps you stay awake

Force •

- all of the police officers in the city
- a push or pull that causes movement or stress on an object

Work •

- the effort it takes to cause an object to move or change shape
- what we do to make money

Efficiency •

- being organized
- the ratio of useful work to the amount of energy it takes to do the work

ISBN: 978-1-897457-80-1

B. Read each situation. Answer the questions with the terms in scientific meaning.

A

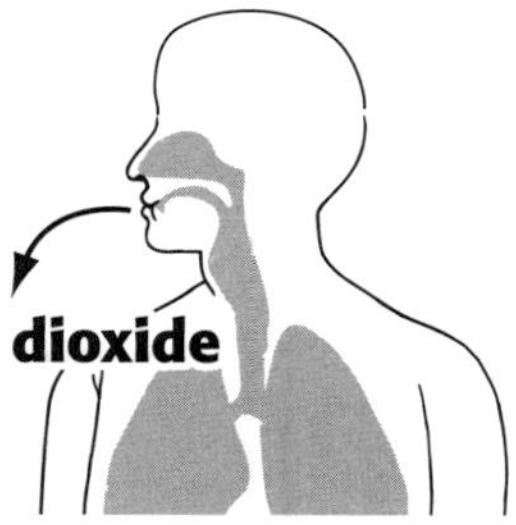

The respiratory system moves carbon dioxide out of the body.

B A boy pushes a wheelbarrow of rocks with all of his force, but it does not move.

C Car A travels 450 km before needing to be refilled with 50 L of gas. Car B travels 1000 km before needing to be refilled with 55 L of gas.

D

Tom and Peter have a tug of war. Peter wins.

E Jeff drives four truckloads of bricks from the store to the job site, and Jim moves four truckloads of bricks from the store to the job site with a trolley.

A Is work being done? Explain.

____

B Is work being done? Explain.

____

C Which car is more efficient? Explain.

____

D Who exerted more force? Explain.

____

E Who needs more energy to do his work? Explain.

____

 ISBN: 978-1-897457-80-1

C. Fill in the blanks with the given words and match each component with what happens if it is inefficient. Write the letters.

Functions of a Computer's Components

safety amount efficiency ergonomic necessary

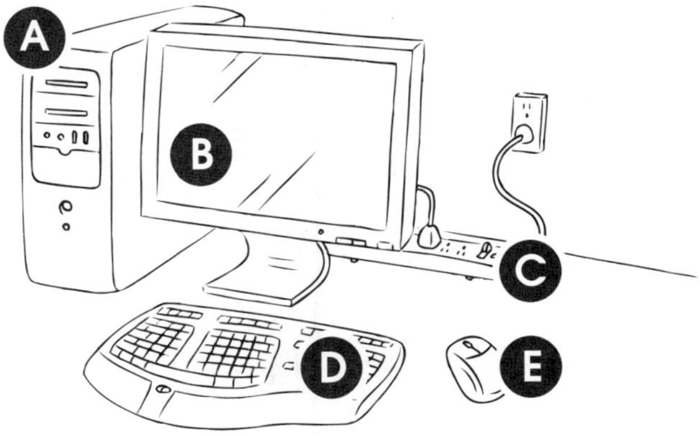

(A) Performing many tasks at the same time on a computer requires a large ____________ of computer memory.

(B) Changing the computer monitor from an old, boxy screen to a cooler-running, modern flat screen improves the computer's ____________ .

(C) Using a surge-protecting power bar to plug in the computer components is an important ____________ measure.

(D) An ____________ keyboard is perfect if you type often.

(E) The mouse and keyboard are ____________ for your interaction with the computer system.

Things That Happen If a Computer's Components Are Inefficient

◯ Your wrists hurt after typing a long essay.

◯ Everything is turned off because of a short circuit.

◯ The mouse is not working, so you cannot surf the Internet.

◯ The flashing light from the monitor hurts the eyes.

◯ You are uploading pictures, typing an assignment, and talking to a friend online, and your computer is working very slowly.

ISBN: 978-1-897457-80-1

D. Read the passage. Then answer the questions.

Old Technology
Makes New Again

You have probably noticed that stores constantly get new models of cellphones, computers, and music players. We often want the newest technology so that we can do things more efficiently, but what should we do with old technology that we do not need anymore?

Electronics and batteries contain harmful chemicals, like mercury or lead. If they are disposed of in a regular landfill, those chemicals can leak into the ground or water, damaging the health of humans, fish, and soil. Therefore, they should go into the recycling drop box in an electronics store, or to a local Household Hazardous Waste Depot. There, the chemicals can be extracted and put into a secure chemical landfill where they will not leak. Sometimes, the chemicals can even be recycled. For example, the lead in used car batteries can be recycled into new batteries.

Non-toxic materials in electronics can be recycled as well. Plastics can be made into CD cases or computer parts, while metals, like copper and gold, can be used in jewellery or industrial products. In addition to properly recycling our old technology, we should think about the new technology we buy. Many TVs and computer monitors are made with fluorescent lights containing mercury, but some are made with LED lights, which do not contain mercury. Choose the most environmentally friendly option whenever you can!

ISBN: 978-1-897457-80-1

1. Identify the cellphones. Write their years of production in the boxes. Then give two reasons why people get new cellphones.

1983	2009	1990	2002

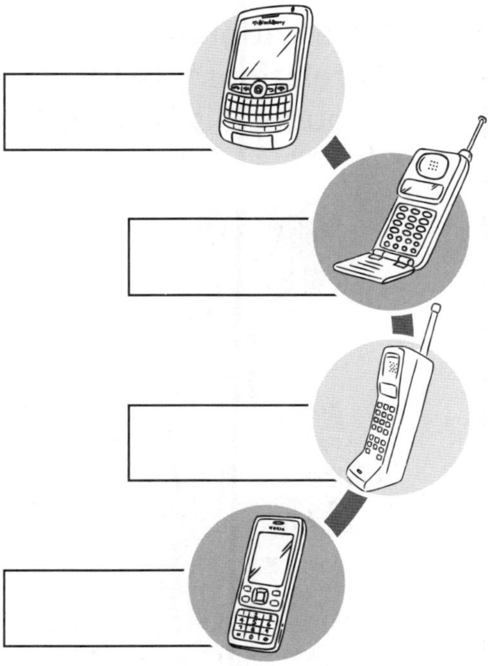

Reasons for Getting a New Cellphone:

a. ______________________________

____

b. ______________________________

____

2. When your parents or friends get new cellphones, how should they dispose of the old ones?

____

____

____

3. Describe two ways to treat or recycle toxic and non-toxic chemicals in electronics.

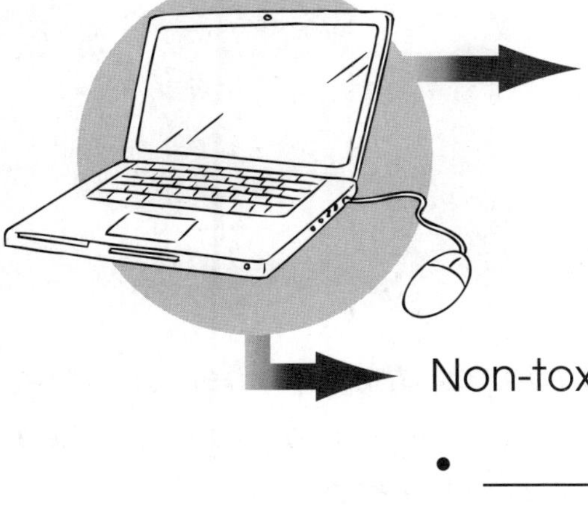

Toxic Chemicals

- ______________________________
- ______________________________

Non-toxic Chemicals

- ______________________________
- ______________________________

Experiment

Introduction

Observational studies look at data to determine relationships, or correlations*, between events. It is not possible to determine causation* through this kind of study, though. However, if a relationship between two events is established, a hypothesis is set to put forward the cause and the effect through the scientific method.

*correlation: occurring with, regardless of cause or effect
causation: the act of causing

Determining **Possible Causation**

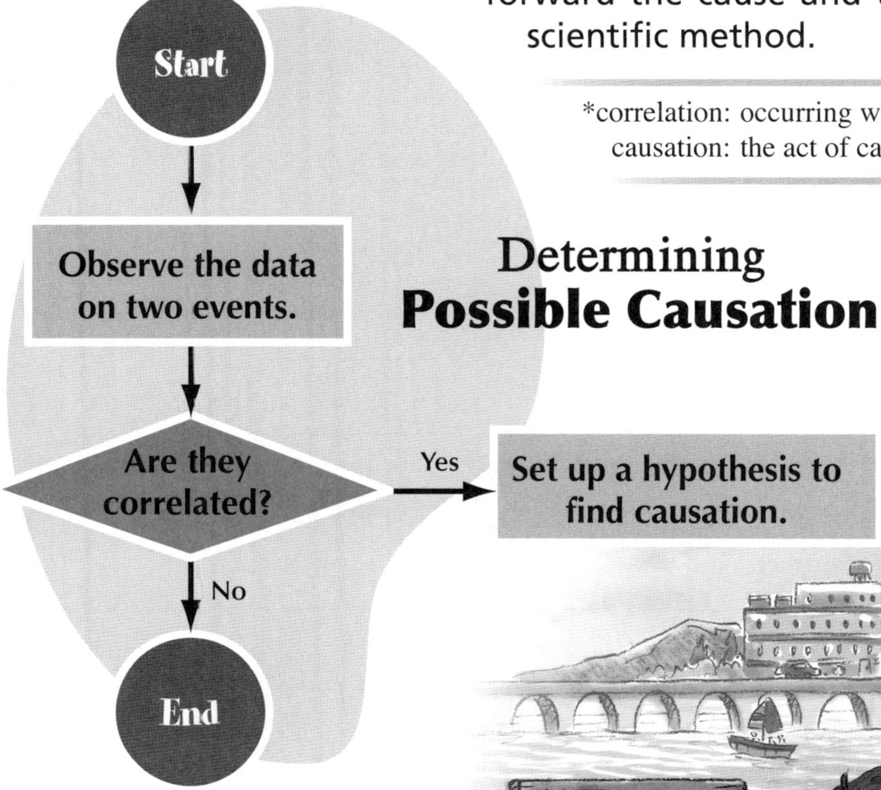

Case Study

The people in Tin Town want to know if the increase in the number of factories in their town has caused any changes. Therefore, Mr. Hudson, a scientist, gathered all the data he could find for the years since the first factory began operation, including the number of factories, the number of smog alerts, and the population numbers. A local flower shop also provided their own tally of yearly flower orders that they had diligently kept.

ISBN: 978-1-897457-80-1

Observational Studies (Check the relationships that the data show.)

Correlation

The data show a possible correlation between...

- ◯ the number of factories and the number of smog alerts.
- ◯ the number of factories and the population.
- ◯ the number of factories and the number of flower orders.
- ◯ the population and the number of flower orders.

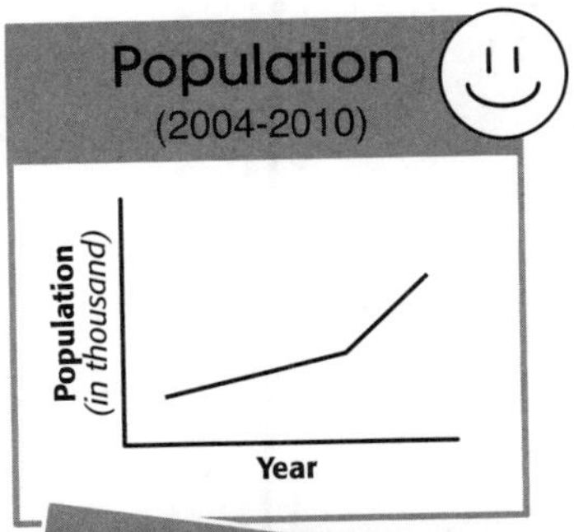

Causation

The data show that something is caused by...

- ◯ the number of factories.
- ◯ the number of smog alerts.
- ◯ the population.
- ◯ the number of flower orders.

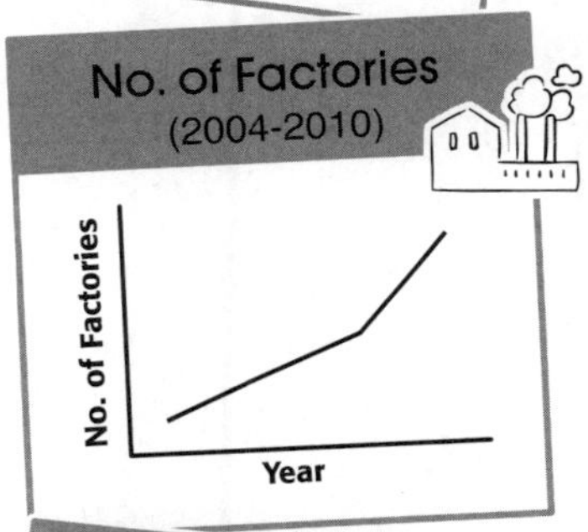

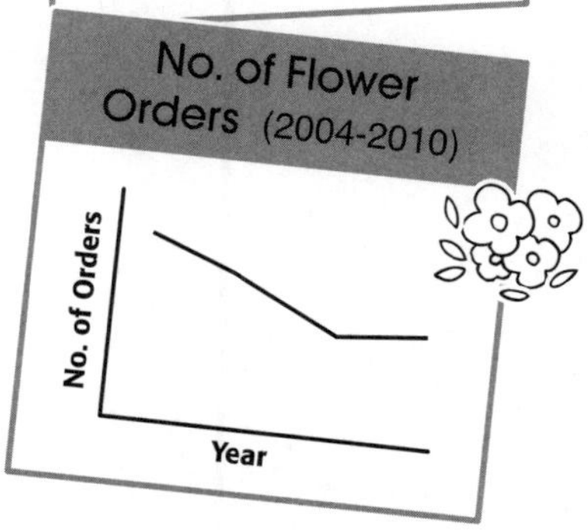

Observational Studies:

- ____________ show correlation
  can/cannot
- ____________ show causation
  can/cannot

Hypothesis

Help me set up a hypothesis for a further study on any one of the sets of correlated data.

____

____

ISBN: 978-1-897457-80-1

4 Work and Mechanical Advantage

Would it be better to carry your own groceries to the car or use a shopping cart? Mechanical systems are helpful to us. Scientists use formulas to determine how much work mechanical systems do. In this unit, you will examine how work and force are measured, and learn to find the mechanical advantages of some simple machines.

After completing this unit, you will

- understand how formulas help determine how much work simple machines do.
- know how mechanical advantage is calculated.
- be able to calculate the amount of work and force required, and the mechanical advantage of simple machines.

Vocabulary

newton (N): the unit of measurement of force

joule (J): the unit of measurement of work (1 joule = 1 newton-metre)

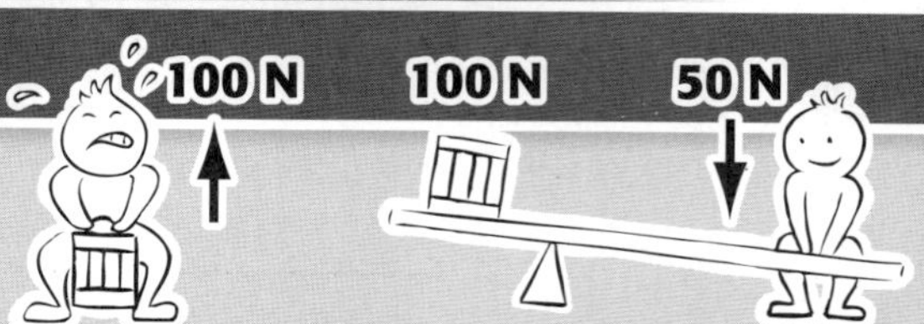

$$MA = \frac{100\text{ N}}{50\text{ N}} = 2$$

ISBN: 978-1-897457-80-1

Extension

Do you know what "work" is in physics? Work is the transfer of energy.

If you apply a force on an object over a distance, you have done work. For example, if you push a box in the direction of your force, you have done work. If the box slides down and pushes you, the box does work on you. If you push an object and it does not move, no work is done.

A. Write the terms and complete the descriptions. Then identify the pictures.

joules newtons force work

1. a. ____________

- a push or a pull that causes an object to move
- measured in b. ____________

Identify each as "push" or "pull".

c. ____________

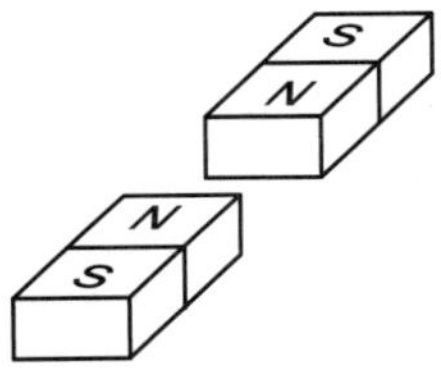

d. ____________

2. a. ____________

- the amount of effort made to move an object
- measured in b. ____________

Check the one that has done work.

ISBN: 978-1-897457-80-1

B. Read the hint and complete the formula for finding how much work is done. Draw a diagram to illustrate each question (like the one in question 2). Then solve the problems.

1. Work = ______________ x ______________
(Hint: distance moved is parallel to force)

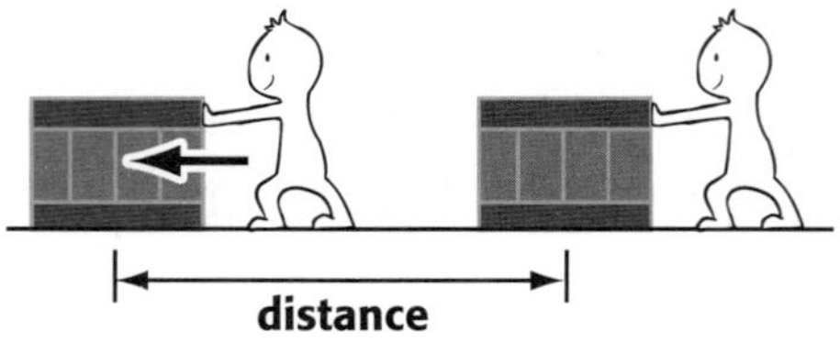

2. 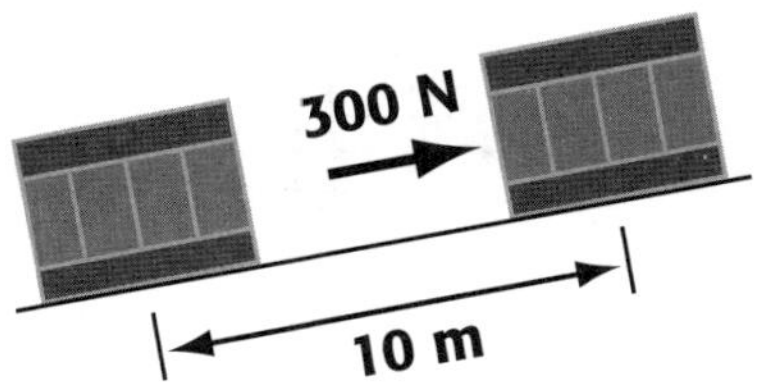

George applies a force of 300 N to move a box 10 m across the slope. Find the amount of work done.

____

3. Elaine and Greg apply a force of 600 N to move a piano 5 m across the room. Find the amount of work done.

____

4. A bucket was lifted 4 m up from the ground. If 800 J of work was done, what was the force applied?

____

5. Moise applied 200 N of force and did 1 kJ* of work to move a chair. How far was the chair moved?

____

*1 kJ = 1000 J

ISBN: 978-1-897457-80-1

C. Complete the formula for finding the mechanical advantage of a machine with the words in bold. Then solve the problems.

The mechanical advantage is the ratio ***(output force*** *to* ***input force)*** *that shows the number of times that a machine multiplies the input force.*

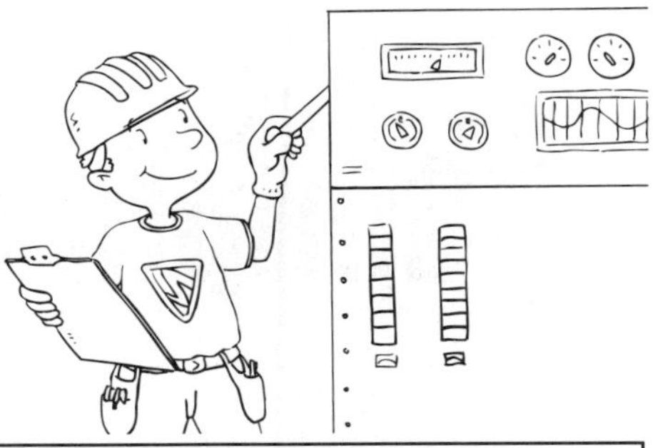

Mechanical Advantage (MA) = $\dfrac{\rule{3cm}{0.4pt}}{\rule{3cm}{0.4pt}}$

When MA is greater than 1, it means the machine can multiply the input force.

1. A car jack exerts a force of 4000 N when you crank it with 80 N of your force. What is the mechanical advantage of the jack?

   The MA is ______________ .

2. A machine is required to produce an output force of 600 N. If the machine has a MA of 5, what input force must be applied to the machine?

3. A force of 200 N is applied to a pulley system in order to lift a 1000-N load. What is the mechanical advantage of the system?

4. An input force of 35 N is applied to a machine with a mechanical advantage of 4. What is the maximum size of the load that this machine can lift?

ISBN: 978-1-897457-80-1

D. Read the letters to Machine Doctor. Then help Machine Doctor calculate the mechanical advantage of each machine and give advice.

Simple Machines Weekly

Dear Machine Doctor,

I will be moving into a new house next week and I need to get my piano up the front steps. The steps are 1 m high, so I won't be able to just lift it up there! I have two boards that I can use to make an inclined plane. One is 2 m long and the other is 4 m long. Which one should I use? I have to move all the rest of my stuff, too, so I need to conserve my energy!

Thanks so much,

Worried Musician

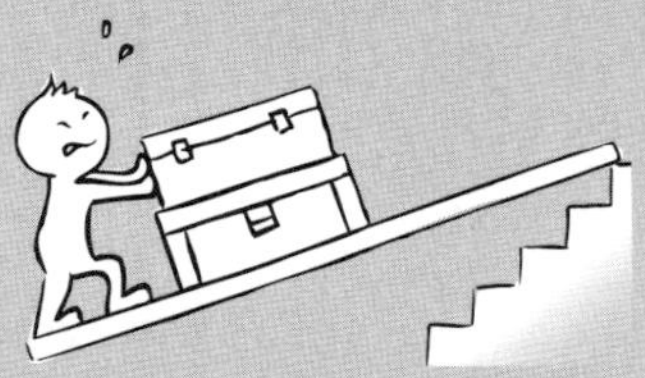

Dear Machine Doctor,

I store old things in heavy boxes in my basement, and I accidentally plopped one down onto my science notes! I want to lift up the box by making a lever with a 200-cm long stick and a ball. Could you tell me where to place the ball? Would it be better to place it in the middle of the lever or right next to the box?

Please reply soon,

Taking a Rest

Dear Machine Doctor,

I am starting my own house painting business and my first customer has a 4-storey house! I need to get the paint buckets up high when I am painting the upper floors and the roof. Which pulley system should I use?

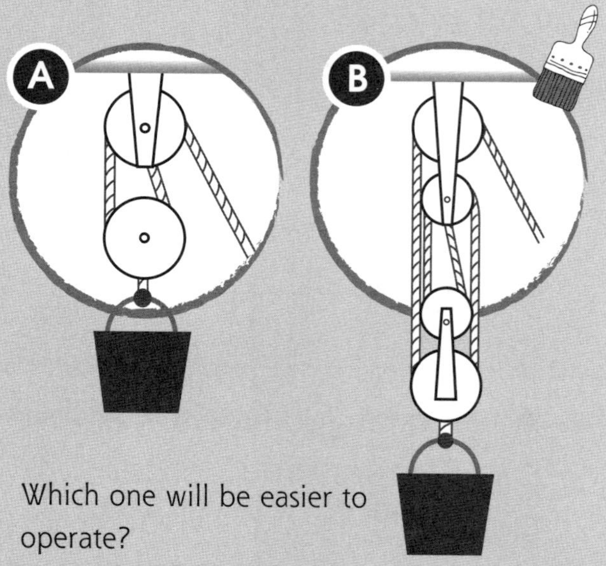

Which one will be easier to operate?

Would like to hear from you soon,

Lucky Painter

ISBN: 978-1-897457-80-1

To: Worried Musician

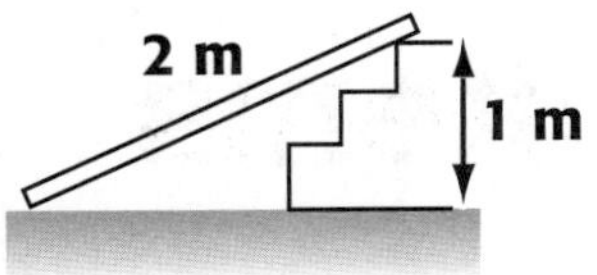

MA =

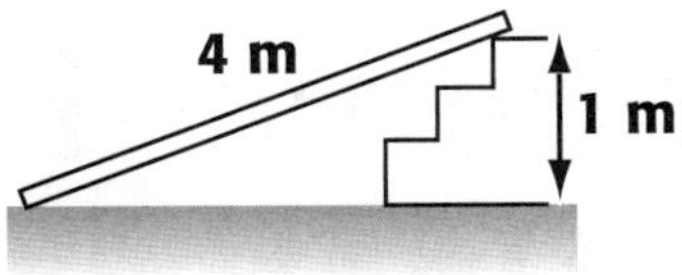

MA =

Machine Doctor's Advice

The MA of the **2-m / 4-m** board is

____

____

To: Taking a Rest

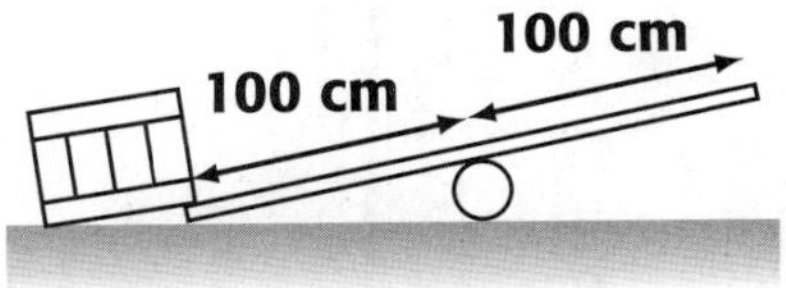

MA =

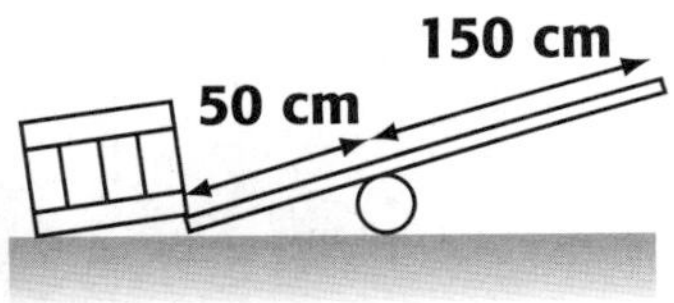

MA =

Machine Doctor's Advice

____

____

To: Lucky Painter

A: MA = ______ **B**: MA = ______

Machine Doctor's Advice

____

____

Machine Doctor's Note

Besides finding the ratio of output force to input force to figure out the mechanical advantage of a machine, we can also apply the formula below to find the MA of each kind of machine.

Inclined Plane

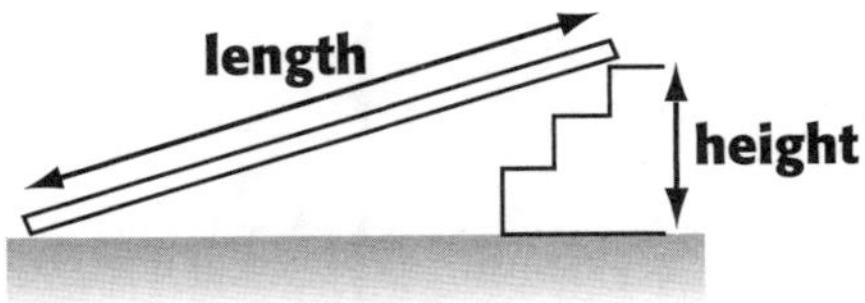

MA = length ÷ height

Lever

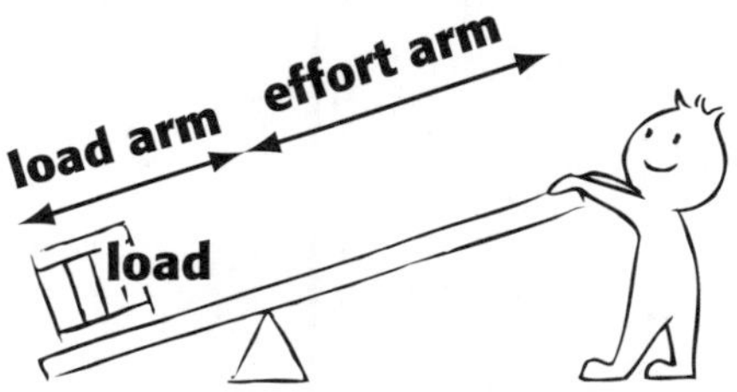

MA = length of effort arm ÷ length of load arm

Pulley

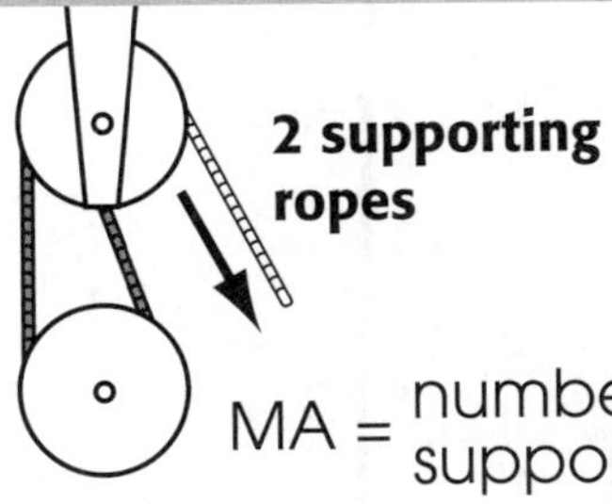

MA = number of supporting ropes

ISBN: 978-1-897457-80-1

5 Mechanical Systems and Heat

Mechanical systems produce heat. In a system, this is usually undesirable, as it represents energy loss. In this unit, you will examine some of the causes of heat in mechanical systems. Also, you will look at ways to avoid or minimize heat production in a mechanical system.

After completing this unit, you will

- understand the different ways mechanical systems produce heat.
- understand that heat due to friction can be minimized in different ways.

Vocabulary

friction: a slowing force caused by contact

compression: a reducing force caused by pressure

efficiency: maximal productivity with minimal waste

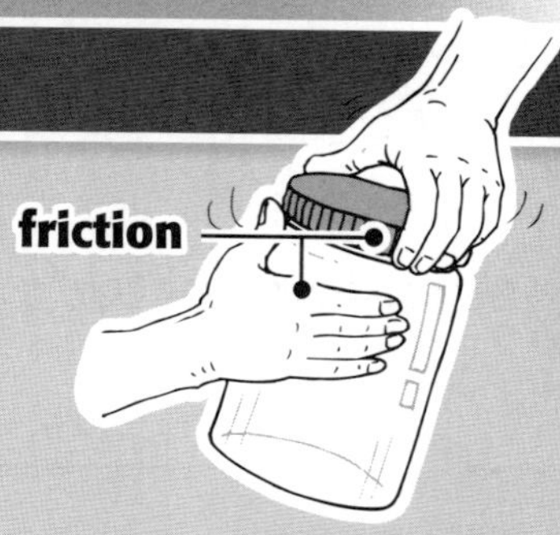

ISBN: 978-1-897457-80-1

Extension

The traditional light bulb contains a filament, which becomes hot and gives off a bright light when an electric current passes through it. The heat given off by this light bulb is wasteful. Therefore, scientists invented a more efficient light bulb – the fluorescent light bulb. Fluorescent light bulbs do not get as hot as filament light bulbs and they last much longer; they are also able to give off the same amount of light as filament light bulbs do.

Next time when your family needs new light bulbs, do not forget to look for the energy-efficient ones.

A. Fill in the blanks with the given words. Then name three common ways mechanical systems produce heat.

thermal	compression
contact	friction
energy	fluid resistance

Most mechanical systems, such as automobiles and power generators, contain many moving parts that are in 1.______________ with each other. In normal operation, mechanical systems generate 2.______________ energy in the form of heat. The heat is wasted 3.______________ that dissipates into the atmosphere.

Heat in Mechanical Systems Comes from:

4.______________ : the resistance that happens when a moving object is in contact with the surface of another object

5.______________ : the reduction in volume, and the resulting pressure of the squished molecules, of an object

6.______________ : the slowed movement, or resistance, that happens from contact with a gas or liquid

ISBN: 978-1-897457-80-1

B. Circle the correct words to complete the descriptions. Then name the ways that the mechanical systems produce heat.

Ways to Produce Heat:

friction compression fluid resistance

1. 

When you ride a bicycle, the chain and gears work together to generate **heat / electricity** .

The heat comes from ________________ .

2. 

When a space shuttle enters the atmosphere, the air moves very fast under the bottom of the shuttle to **slow it down / speed it up** . This generates heat.

The heat comes from ________________ .

3. 

When a basketball hits the ground on a bounce, the ball experiences the most **tension / compression** and heat upon contact.

The heat comes from ________________ .

4. 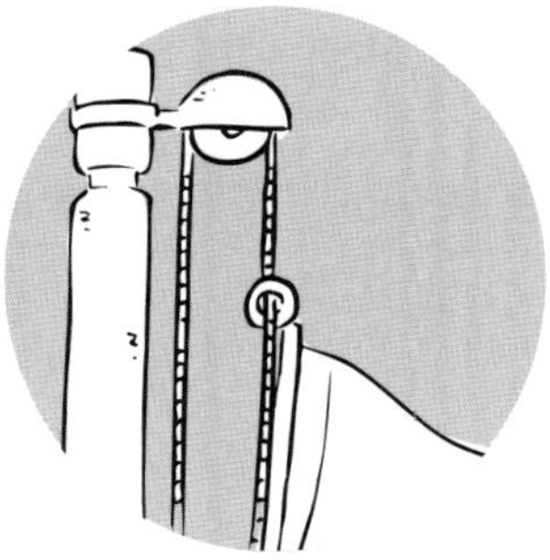

When a pulley turns on an axle, the axle rubs against the pulley, generating **friction / power** .

The heat comes from ________________ .

ISBN: 978-1-897457-80-1

C. Find the correct way to reduce friction in each mechanical system. Write the letters.

Ways to Reduce Friction

- **A** lubrication
- **B** heat resistant tiles
- **C** ball bearings
- **D** air cushion
- **E** physically separated using electromagnetic force

1.

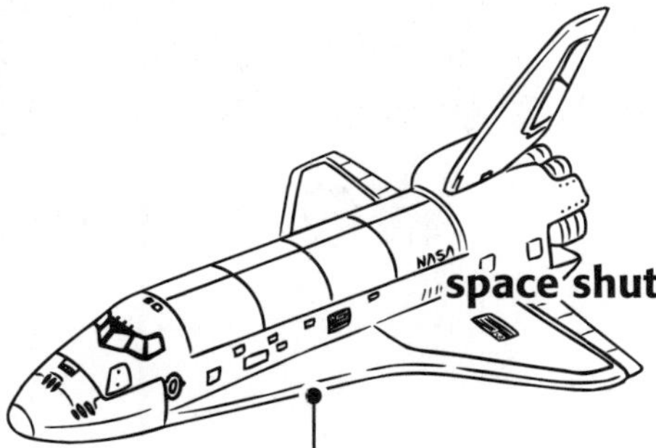

The bottom part has special materials to resist heat. ◯

2.

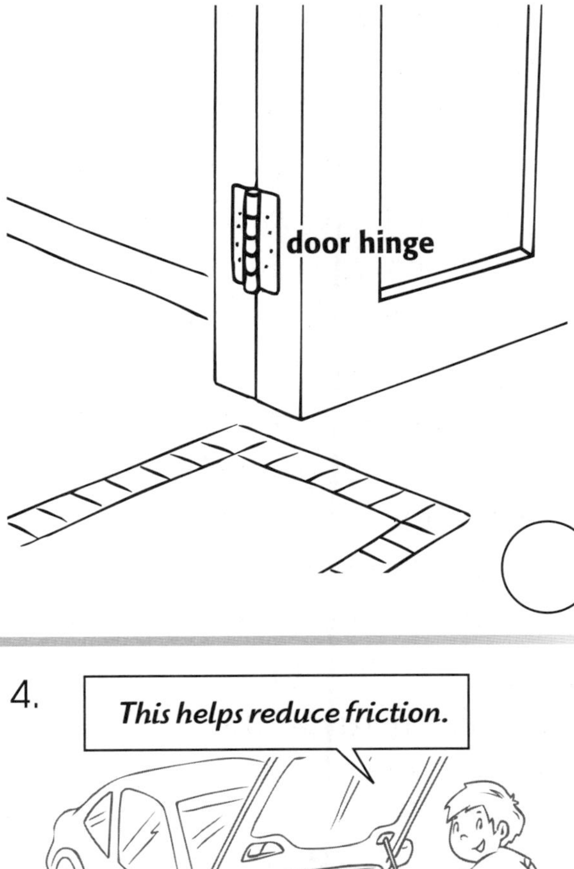

◯

3.

Magnetic fields keep the train from being in direct contact with the rail. ◯

4.

◯

5.

This craft glides across the surface on a cushion of air. ◯

ISBN: 978-1-897457-80-1

D. Read the passage. Then complete the path of energy conversion in a power plant and answer the questions.

People generate large amounts of heat energy, often referred to as waste heat. When we run electrical appliances, like air conditioners and computers, waste heat is generated. Even our bodies release waste heat when we pant and sweat. However, one source of waste heat trumps all others: the power stations that generate our electricity.

The Waste Heat We Create

Power stations turn one form of energy, such as gravitational energy from a hydroelectric dam or chemical energy from coal, into the electrical energy that we use in our homes and businesses. Transforming gravitational or chemical energy into electrical energy is actually accomplished through a series of transformations. For example, at a coal-fired station, coal is the chemical energy burned to heat water, which creates steam, or thermal energy. Steam is used to turn a turbine, which is mechanical energy, and the turbine generates electrical energy. During each transformation, energy is lost as heat.

You may be asking, "How much heat is lost?" At a coal power station, 45% of the energy from coal is transformed into electricity; the rest is lost as heat energy. This energy is lost as heat at many points: when valves open to release steam; if the pipes holding steam or water are not well insulated; and when moving parts heat up due to friction during the electricity generation process.

ISBN: 978-1-897457-80-1

1. a. **Making Electricity**

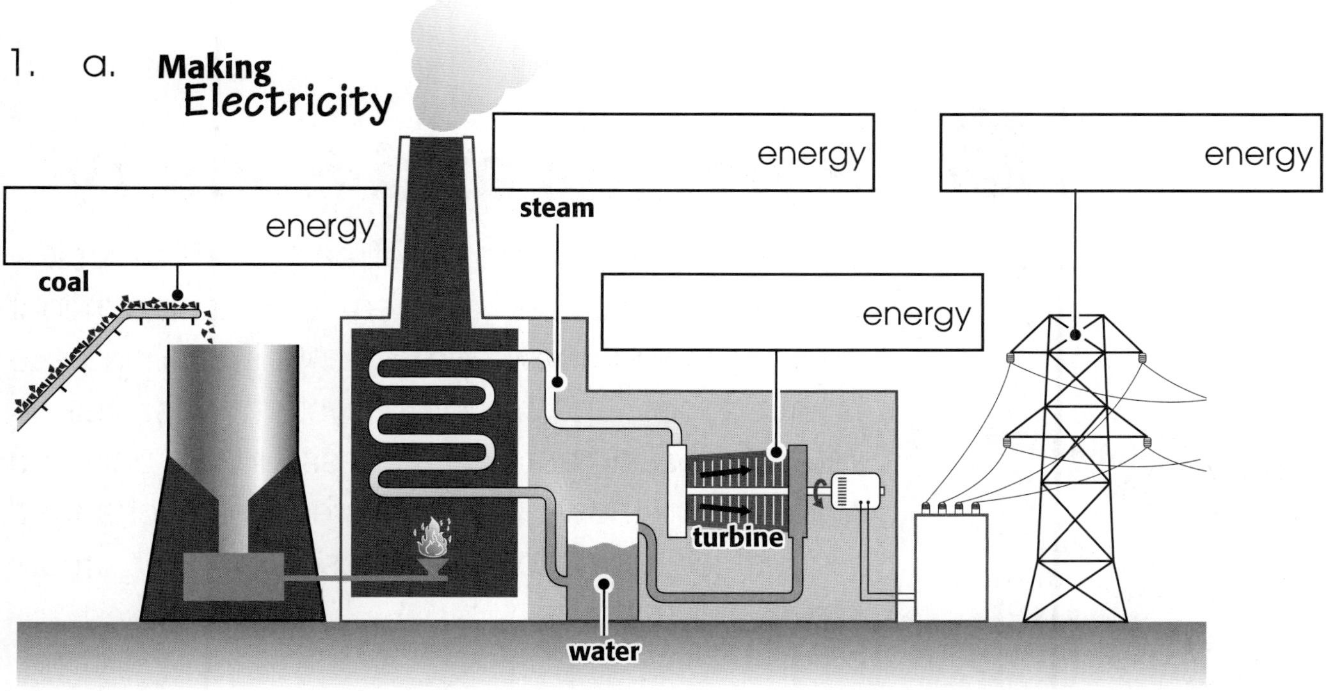

b. During each transformation of energy, what form of energy is lost? ____________

c. About how much energy is lost at a coal power station? ____________

2. Write three possible areas of heat loss in a power plant.

____

____

____

3. Put a checkmark in the circle if waste heat is generated in each situation. Then write one more example of generating waste heat.

Generating Heat as Waste

- ○ computer
- ○ cooler
- ○ tap
- ○ kettle
- ○ bookshelf
- ○ air conditioner
- ○ our body
- ○ ____________

ISBN: 978-1-897457-80-1

6 Systems and Society

Systems evolve for a variety of reasons. The medical emergency system of an area, for example, might grow to include new components if a mining site is introduced; the recycling system was created due to environmental awareness. In this unit, you will examine how different systems have changed industries, and how changes in society create evolving systems.

After completing this unit, you will

- understand that many systems have improved the productivity of industries.
- understand that social factors influence the evolution of a system.

Vocabulary

evolution: gradual development out of need

productivity: rate of production, ability to produce

criteria: standards of judging something

ISBN: 978-1-897457-80-1

Extension

In the past, without effective and quick communication systems, it would often take at least several days to pass a message from one part of a country to another. Imagine that you were a king during that time, how would you know what was going on in other parts of the country? To solve this problem, a king created a communication system. He appointed barons and gave each one a portion of his land, as well as the authority to rule over it. Each baron communicated the ongoings of his area to the king. Given this honour, barons had to support the king in other ways: they had to fight with the king's troops when needed, and pay the king taxes whenever he called for them.

Do you see the similarities and differences between society we are living in and society in the past?

A. Fill in the blanks with the words in the diagram to complete the descriptions.

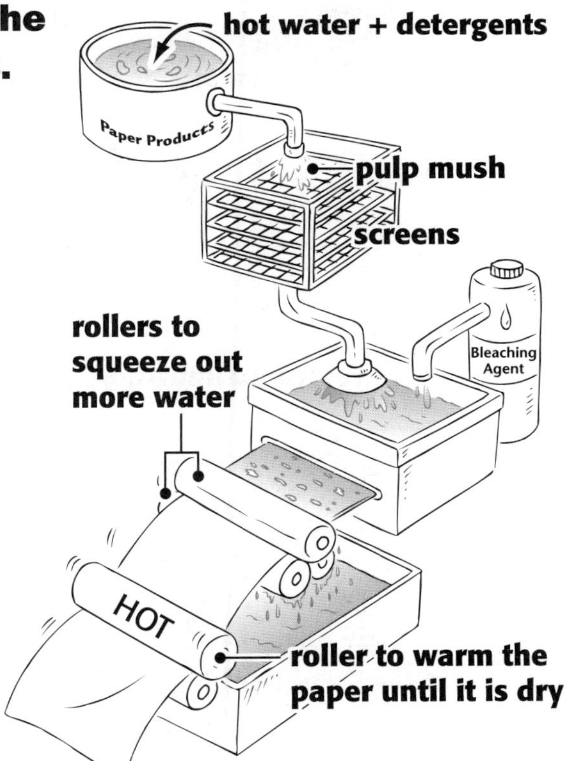

Paper Recycling System

Recyclable paper is mixed with detergents and 1.______________ in a huge mixing bowl. This process de-inks the paper products and turns them into a 2.______________ . The pulp mush passes through a series of different-sized 3.______________ to remove more elements, such as ink particles and glues. To bleach the pulp and make it bright white, a 4.______________ is added. Then the pulp is squeezed by rollers to remove 5.______________ . Finally, a heated roller presses and 6.______________ the paper sheet.

ISBN: 978-1-897457-80-1

B. Write the letters to match the industry with the system. Then describe one of the functions of each system.

A traffic control system **B** wireless system **C** checkout system

D automated teller system **E** transportation system

1.

____

____

2.

____

____

3.

____

____

4.

____

____

5.

____

____

 ISBN: 978-1-897457-80-1

C. Systems evolve according to social factors that change what we require from systems. The three systems in each group are affected by a social factor. Number the most affected system (1) to the least affected one (3).

1. **Birth Rate**

- ◯ school system
- ◯ food system
- ◯ home audio system

2. **Family**

- ◯ factory system
- ◯ medical system
- ◯ school system

3. **Literacy**

- ◯ food system
- ◯ school system
- ◯ public library system

4. **Environmental Awareness**

- ◯ marine antifouling system
- ◯ septic system
- ◯ school system

5. **Immigration**

- ◯ school system
- ◯ medical system
- ◯ factory system

6. **Economic Status**

- ◯ transportation system
- ◯ school system
- ◯ medical system

ISBN: 978-1-897457-80-1

D. Read the passage. Then answer the questions.

If you have kept fish as pets before, you should be familiar with the annoying film of slime that covers every pebble and every surface in the fish tank. This is actually a biofilm formed by bacteria or algae, and it is commonly found on anything immersed in water for a period of time. In fact, in oceans and lakes, a biofilm provides a foundation for the growth of large life forms, such as barnacles. The bottoms of ships, the bases of piers, and underwater pipes are all susceptible to this kind of biofouling.

Biofouling has long been a severe problem in the aquaculture industry. Additional labour is needed for the frequent and time-consuming cleaning of the nets to keep them free of blockage and allow water to flow through them easily, which is essential for the healthy growth of the raised fish. However, cleaning can be costly, so the aquaculture industry relies on technology to improve their net cleaning systems and maximize their profits. One method is to dip nets in copper paint. This antifouling coating makes nets more durable underwater and fewer cleanings are needed. Maintenance costs are thus reduced. Also, fish nets can stay clean for longer periods of time. This allows for better water flow and, thus, healthier fish.

No More Biofouling!

However, there are also disadvantages of using copper dipping on nets. The lifetime of the copper coating is limited and the application costs are high. The aquaculture industry is still looking for better ways and developing better systems to solve the biofouling problem.

ISBN: 978-1-897457-80-1

1. Check the pictures that show biofouling in progress. Then write what biofouling means.

Biofouling is ______________________________

____

2. What problems caused by biofouling do people have to cope with?

____

____

3. Describe how net cleaning systems help solve the biofouling problem.

____

____

4. Describe the method that is used to improve the net cleaning system. Write two disadvantages of using this method.

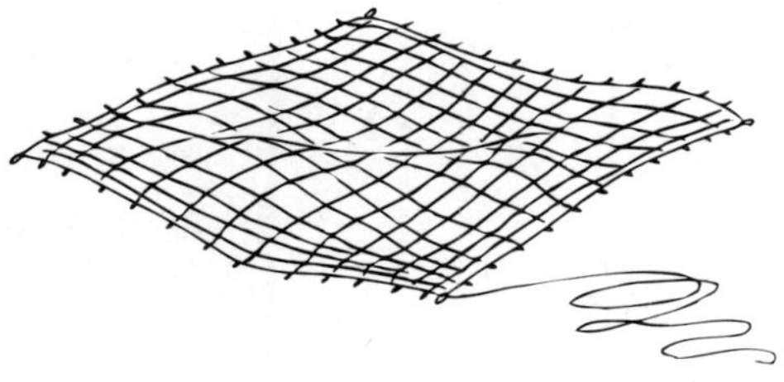

____

Disadvantages of using this method:

____

____

____

ISBN: 978-1-897457-80-1

Experiment

Introduction

Friction in the moving parts of a mechanical system causes heat and grip. It is the grip – the rubbing contact – that causes friction. Lubricants, in the form of oil or silicone, are often used to lessen friction. Will flour and oil have an effect on the friction between objects?

Hypothesis

Flour will increase / have no effect on / decrease and oil will increase / have no effect on / decrease the friction between two objects.

Materials

- *1 tablespoon of flour*
- *1 tablespoon of oil*
- *a beverage coaster*
- *a protractor*
- *a cutting board*

Steps

1. Place the coaster on one end of the cutting board.

2. Slowly raise the end of the cutting board and stop once the coaster starts to slide down.

3. Measure the angle of the board with the protractor at this point, and record it in the chart under "no lubricant".

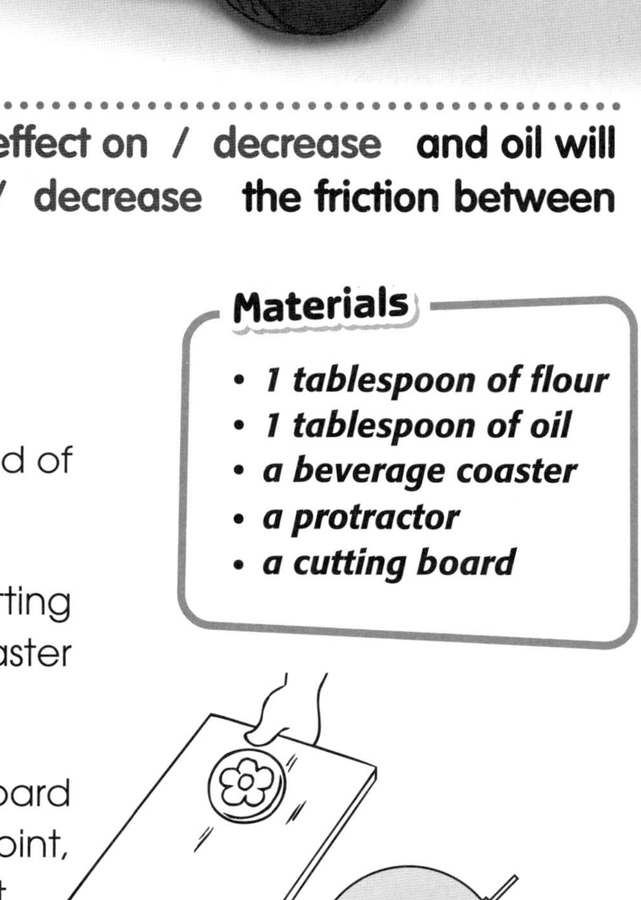

ISBN: 978-1-897457-80-1

4. Remove the coaster and sprinkle a little flour on the board.

5. Place the coaster on the flour.

6. Repeat steps 2 and 3.

7. Clean off the flour from the board and repeat the experiment with oil as a lubricant.

Result

Draw the cutting boards to show the angles and label them.

no lubricant	***flour***	***oil***

Conclusion

The hypothesis was: ______________________________

____

My experiment ______________________________ the hypothesis.
supported/did not support

ISBN: 978-1-897457-80-1

This review consists of five sections, from A to E. The marks for each question are shown in parentheses. The circle at the bottom right corner is for the marks you get in each section. An overall record is on the last page of the review.

A. Write T for true and F for false.

1. Systems can only be human-made. (**2**) ______

2. The greater the MA is, the less force is needed. (**2**) ______

3. Force is measured in joules and work is measured in newtons. (**2**) ______

4. A septic system generates electricity by using moving water. (**2**) ______

5. 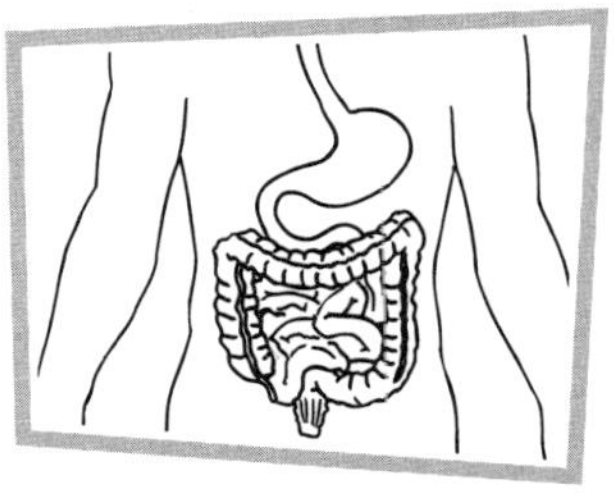

   The digestive system is the only subsystem in a human body. (**2**)

   ______

6. 

   Electricity is the input and wind is the output, whereas the fan is a system. (**2**)

   ______

12

ISBN: 978-1-897457-80-1

B. Do the matching.

1.

(3)

2.

(3)

3.

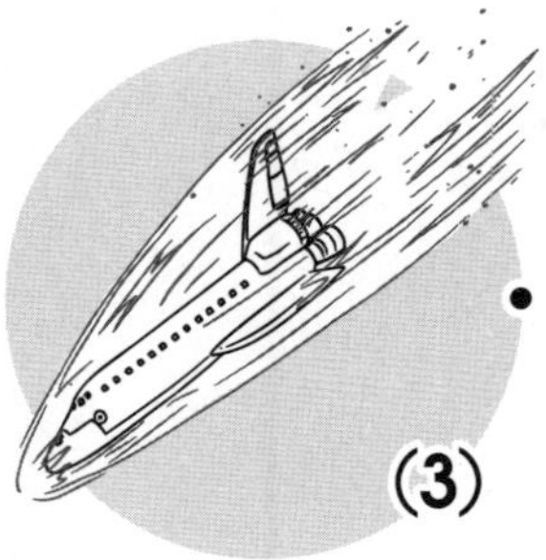

(3)

4.

(3)

5.

(3)

6.

(3)

- a subsystem of water transportation
- a component of a school system
- an example of fluid resistance in water
- heat resistant tiles are used to reduce heat
- wind is its input; electricity is its output
- is used to remove ink particles and glue in a paper recycling system

18

ISBN: 978-1-897457-80-1

C. Find how much work is done to move the box up the stairs by using different methods. Then answer the questions.

1. **Method 1** Lifting the box vertically **(4)**

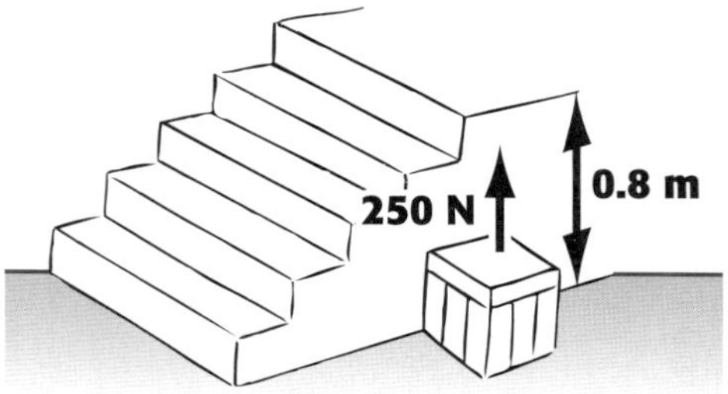

work done:

____

Method 2 Using an inclined plane **(4)**

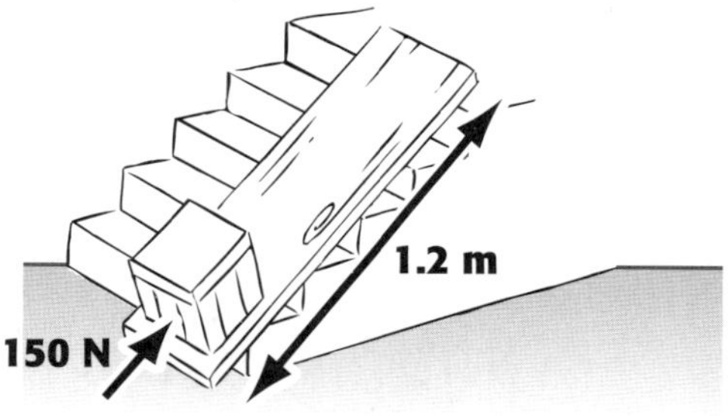

work done:

____

Method 3 Using a pulley **(4)**

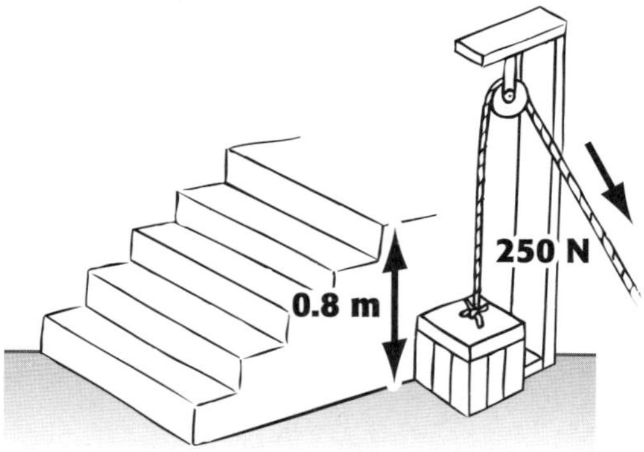

work done:

____

2. Which would be the best method to move the box up the stairs? Why? **(4)**

____

____

3. If the length of the inclined plane is doubled and the same amount of work is done, what is the force applied? **(4)**

____

20

ISBN: 978-1-897457-80-1

D. Define the term and check the correct formula for finding the MA of a machine. Then answer the questions.

1. Mechanical Advantage (MA) of a Machine

____

____

____

____________________ **(4)**

Formula for Finding MA: (2)

(A) $MA = \frac{\text{input force}}{\text{output force}}$

(B) $MA = \frac{\text{output force}}{\text{input force}}$

2. A force of 400 N is applied to a lever system in order to lift a 1800-N load.

   a. What is the mechanical advantage of the system? **(4)**

   ____

   b. If this lever system is used to lift a 2475-N load, what input force must be applied to the system? **(4)**

   ____

3. A wheelbarrow has a mechanical advantage of 2.5.

   a. If an input force of 200 N is applied to the wheelbarrow, how large is the output force that just lifts the load? **(4)**

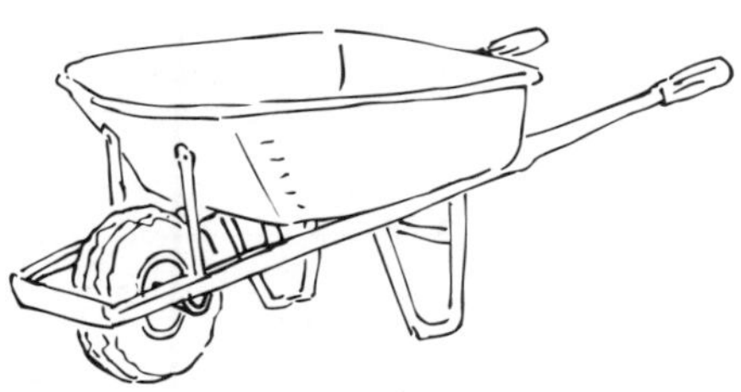

   ____

   b. Heat is generated at the wheel of the wheelbarrow when in use. What generates this heat? What can be done to reduce the amount of heat generated? **(4)**

   ____

   ____

22

ISBN: 978-1-897457-80-1

E. Look at the diagram of a home alarm system. Then answer the questions.

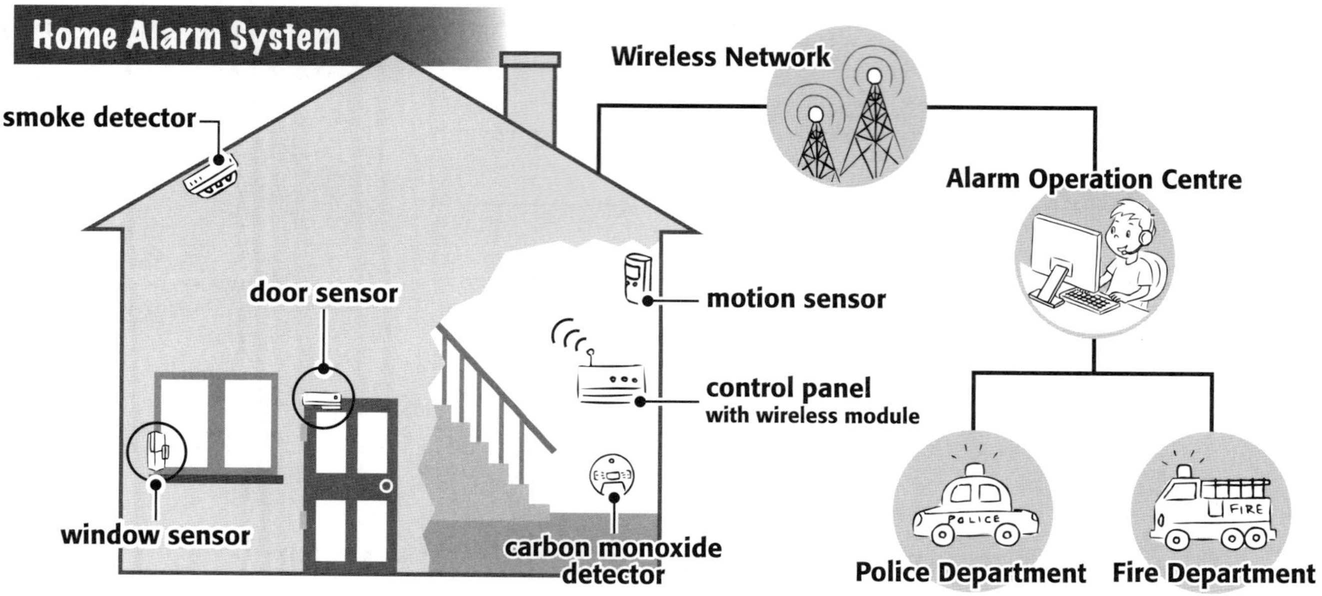

1. This is a **natural / human-made** system. **(2)**

2. Purpose of the System: ______________________ **(4)**

a. Name any four components of the system:

- ______________________ **(2)**
- ______________________ **(2)**
- ______________________ **(2)**
- ______________________ **(2)**

b. Give one example of input and output in the system.

input: ______________ **(3)**

output: ______________ **(3)**

3. What is the function of a smoke detector? **(4)**

____

4. If the wireless network of the home alarm system is inefficient, what will happen to the whole system? **(4)**

____

28

ISBN: 978-1-897457-80-1

My Record

Section A		12
Section B		18
Section C		20
Section D		22
Section E		28

Total	
	100

80-100

Great work! You really understand your science stuff! Research your favourite science topics at the library or on the Internet to find out more about the topics related to this section. Keep challenging yourself to learn more!

60-79

Good work! You understand some basic concepts, but try reading through the units again to see whether you can master the material! Go over the questions that you had trouble with to make sure you know the correct answers.

below 60

You can do much better! Try reading over the units again. Ask your parents or teachers any questions you might have. Once you feel confident that you know the material, try the review again. Science is exciting, so don't give up!

ISBN: 978-1-897457-80-1

The Mechanical Engineer

There are many locks in Ontario. No, we are not talking about locks we find in doors, but rather, locks for raising and lowering boats between stretches of water of different levels on river and canal waterways. A famous lock system is the Peterborough Lift Lock located on the Trent Canal in the city of Peterborough, Ontario. It is numbered Lock 21 on the Trent-Severn Waterway.

The Peterborough Lift Lock was designed by Richard Birdsall Rogers, a superintendent of the Trent-Severn Waterway. It was the first lock and at the time the largest structure in the world built with unreinforced concrete. The lock was named a Historic Mechanical Engineering Landmark by the American Society of Mechanical Engineers in 1987.

The dual lifts there were the highest hydraulic boat lifts in the world, with a lift of 19.8 metres. This was considered quite an accomplishment at the time when conventional locks usually had a 2-metre rise. Today, though, it is no longer the highest boat lift in the world. The lift at Strépy-Thieu in Belgium has a greater capacity (1350 tonnes) and height (73.15 metres) than the Peterborough Lift Lock.

ISBN: 978-1-897457-80-1

Cool Science Facts

ISBN: 978-1-897457-80-1

1. How can you build a structure out of water?

2. When you are on the top floor of a skyscraper on a windy day, you might feel that the building is swaying. What do scientists do to avoid tall buildings from swaying too much?

3. What is a foam cup made of?

4. What plant gave insight to the inventor of hook-and-loop fasteners?

Find the answers on the next page.

Cool Science Facts

1

Freeze the water! The ice hotel in Quebec, called Hôtel de Glace, is made of ice and snow. Despite the extremely low temperature outside, the thick wall keeps the hotel well insulated. Inside, the temperature varies only by a few degrees between 3°C and -5°C. Every year, the hotel gets demolished by the warm weather in late spring and is then rebuilt in the winter.

2

To limit the amount of wind drift in a skyscraper, scientists sometimes put a giant concrete block weighing a few hundred tonnes on the roof or mount it inside the building. This block is called a tuned mass damper. The Taipei 101 located in Taipei, Taiwan has a 730-tonne tuned mass damper suspended from level 92 to level 88. This giant tuned mass damper sways to counteract the building's movement and helps protect the building from any structural damage.

ISBN: 978-1-897457-80-1

3 Most foam cups are made of a plastic called polystyrene. The beads of polystyrene are placed in a mould. Then hot steam is forced into the mould, causing the beads to swell up into tiny balls. As the beads expand, they fill the mould and attach themselves to one another.

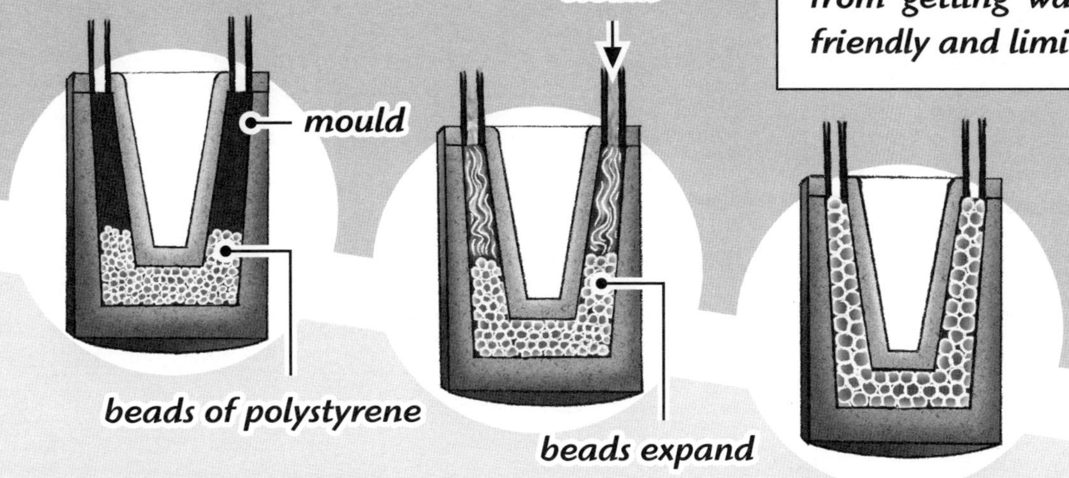

4 The seeds of burdock take the credit. One day, George de Mestral, a Swiss engineer, noticed that some seeds were sticking to his clothes. After examining them under a microscope, he found that these seeds had hundreds of "hooks" catching on the "loops" on his clothing. Then he came up with the idea of binding two materials with hooks and loops. That was where the invention of hook-and-loop fasteners began.

ISBN: 978-1-897457-80-1

ISBN: 978-1-897457-80-1

Section 3

Understanding Matter and Energy

ISBN: 978-1-897457-80-1

1 Fluids and Viscosity

You should have known fluids by certain characteristics – their ability to flow and their lack of a fixed shape. In this unit, you will identify different fluids by these characteristics, and examine another property of fluids – viscosity.

After completing this unit, you will

- understand the characteristics of fluids.
- understand how viscosity affects the flow rate of fluids.
- understand that temperature can affect a fluid's viscosity.

Vocabulary

fluid: any substance that flows

viscosity: thickness of a fluid

friction: resistance of movement when an object is in contact with another

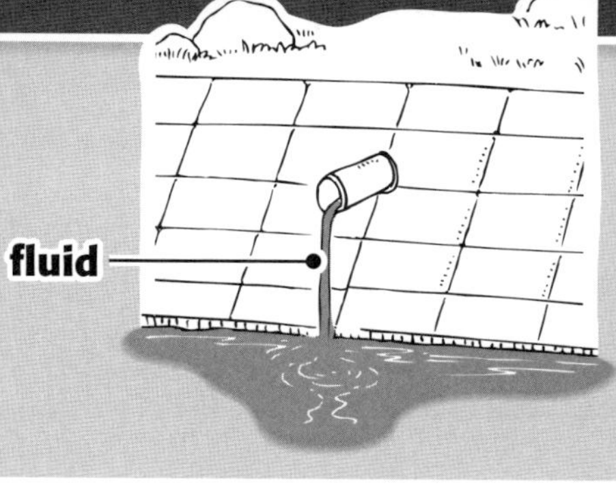

ISBN: 978-1-897457-80-1

Extension

You are surely familiar with these everyday words: thick, sticky, runny, gooey, stiff, and watery, which you use to describe the thickness of drinks, soup, and other fluids. Some fluids flow fast, but some do not. Do you know what makes fluids flow at different speeds? Do fluids that flow slowly have anything in common?

Check the ones that flow slowly. Do you think they have high viscosity? Which one do you think has the highest viscosity?

Fluids

- ◯ air
- ◯ melted butter
- ◯ oil
- ◯ juice
- ◯ liquid soap
- ◯ lava
- ◯ honey
- ◯ helium
- ◯ egg
- ◯ condensed soup

A. Fill in the blanks to complete the paragraph about fluids. Then circle the correct word.

The Viscosity of Fluids

Fluids 1. ________ (flow/stay) and do not have a fixed 2. ________ (shape/volume). Each fluid has its own viscosity that affects its 3. ________ (way/rate) of flow. Viscosity is not only a measure of a fluid's 4. ________ (thickness/taste) or thinness, but also a measure of its inner 5. ________ (air/friction), that is, its 6. ________ (resistance/reluctance) to flow, and how other substances 7. ________ (float/move) through it.

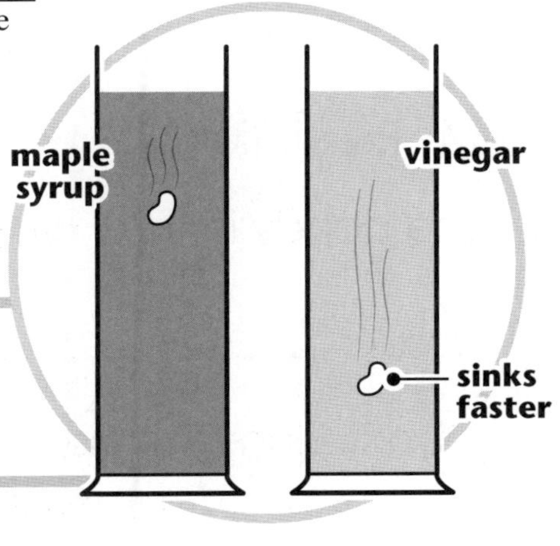

The inner friction of maple syrup is **greater / smaller** than that of vinegar.

ISBN: 978-1-897457-80-1

B. Make predictions. Then try out the experiments and record the results. Complete the conclusion.

Experiment 1: Comparing the Viscosity of Different Fluids

Put 1 teaspoon of each liquid on the cardboard.

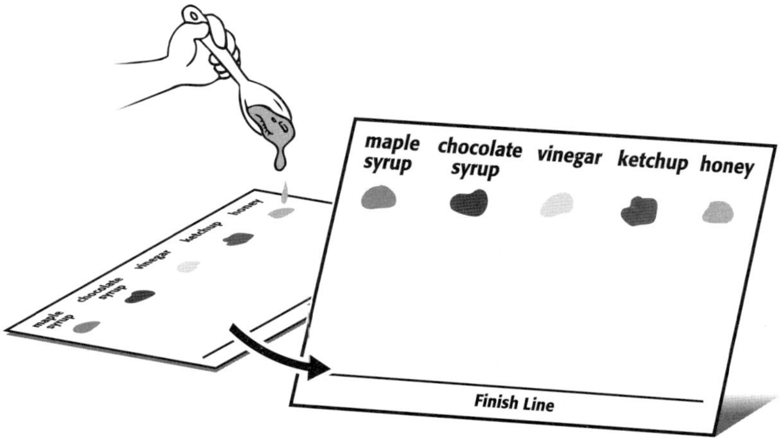

My Prediction	Result
Lowest Viscosity	
Highest Viscosity	

Then hold up the cardboard like this and see which fluid reaches the finish line first.

Conclusion: ______________ has the highest viscosity.

Experiment 2: Comparing the Viscosity of a Fluid at Different Temperatures

Put a candy each in a glass of refrigerated honey and a glass of warm honey to see which candy reaches the bottom first.

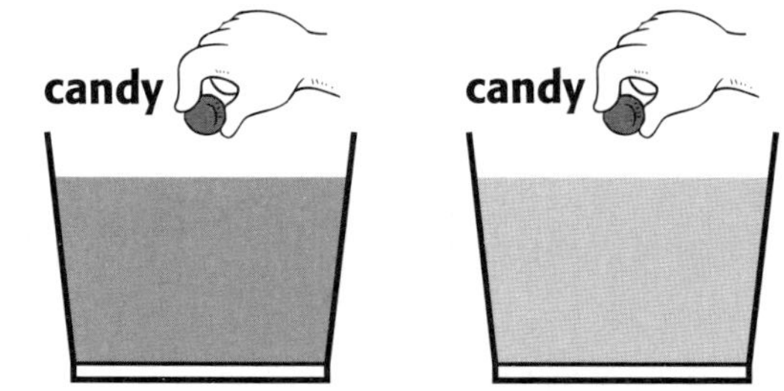

My Prediction:

The candy in the **refrigerated / warm** honey reaches the bottom first.

Result: ______________________________

Conclusion: The viscosity of a fluid **increases / decreases** with a rise in temperature.

ISBN: 978-1-897457-80-1

C. Read the paragraph. Then circle the correct words and answer the question.

Did you know that it is the viscosity of magma that determines the type of volcanic eruption that will occur and the shape of the volcano to be formed? Magma that is less viscous is more likely to cause volcanic eruptions because gases in it can be easily released, so these eruptions are usually less violent and are characterized by lava flows. As a result, the volcano develops gentle sloping sides. Magma with higher viscosity causes less frequent volcanic eruptions because gases in it are not easily released. However, as pressure builds, a really explosive eruption can occur, and this results in a higher volcano with steeper slopes.

1. **A Volcano Formed...**

- from a **less / very** violent volcanic eruption
- from magma with **high / low** viscosity
- with **gentle / steep** slopes

- from a **less / very** violent volcanic eruption
- from magma with **high / low** viscosity
- with **gentle / steep** slopes

2. How does the viscosity of magma affect the probability of volcanic eruptions?

____

____

ISBN: 978-1-897457-80-1

2 Fluids and Density

In this unit, you will learn to explain the difference among solids, liquids, and gases in terms of density using the particle theory of matter. You will also learn to calculate the density of a fluid with its mass and volume.

After completing this unit, you will

- understand that the particle theory of matter explains how different states of matter vary in density.
- understand the relationships among the mass, volume, and density of a fluid.

Vocabulary

density: the amount of mass per unit volume

mass: the amount of matter in a substance

volume: the amount of space a substance takes up

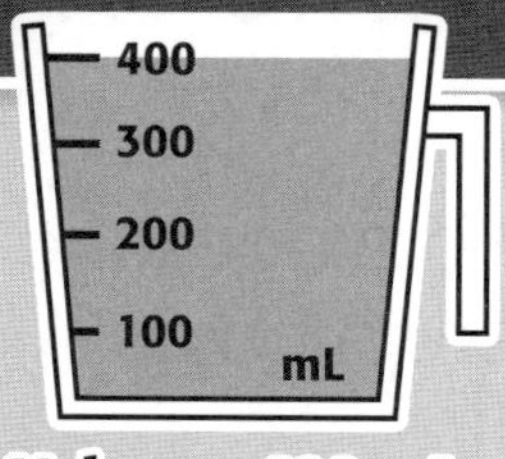

Volume: 400 mL

 ISBN: 978-1-897457-80-1

Extension

Water and oil are liquids that cannot be mixed, but why is oil always on top of water no matter which one you pour into a container first? It is because they differ in density.

Can you guess which liquid, oil or water, has a higher density?

Answer: Water has a higher density.

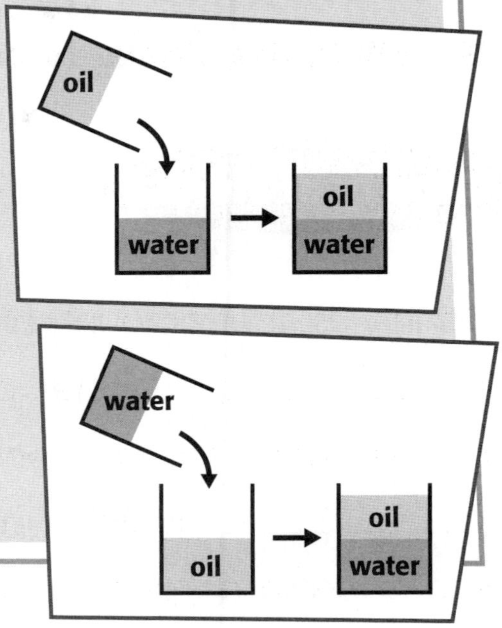

A. Circle the correct words to complete the description. Then draw particles to complete the diagrams and put ">" or "<" in the circles.

According to the particle theory of matter, particles in **solids / gases** are closely packed, while particles in **liquids / solids** are more loosely packed, but they still remain together, and particles in **liquids / gases** spread the farthest apart. Therefore, in general, solids are **denser / less dense** than liquids, which are in turn **denser / less dense** than gases.

Note

- density of a solid ◯ density of a liquid
- density of a liquid ◯ density of a gas
- density of a gas ◯ density of a solid

Density of the
Three States of Matter

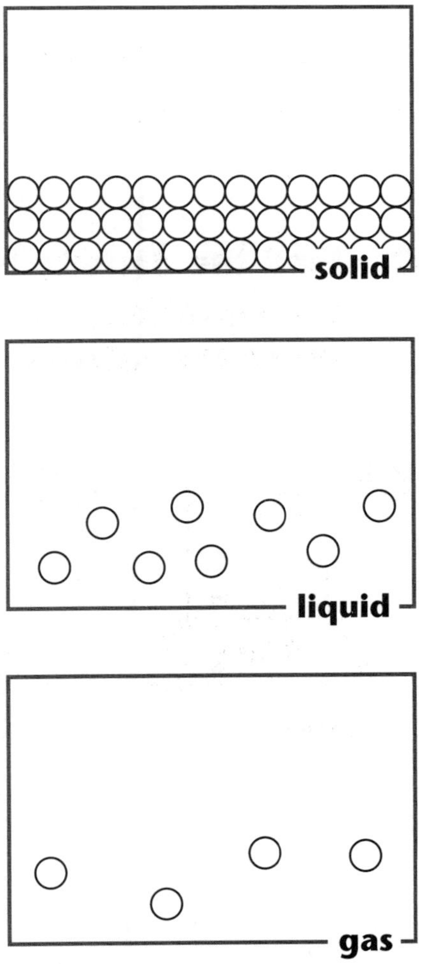

ISBN: 978-1-897457-80-1

B. Fill in the blanks to complete the paragraph.

Density of Fluids

same more less ratio volume mass

Density is the amount of mass in a given 1. ____________ . The particle theory of matter states that a denser substance has 2. ____________ particles and 3. ____________ space between particles in a given volume than a substance that is less dense. However, every fluid has a characteristic density that does not change with a change in volume or a change in 4. ____________ . For example, a glass of juice has the 5. ____________ density as a drop of juice. In fact, a fluid's density can be measured by the fluid's mass to volume 6. ____________ .

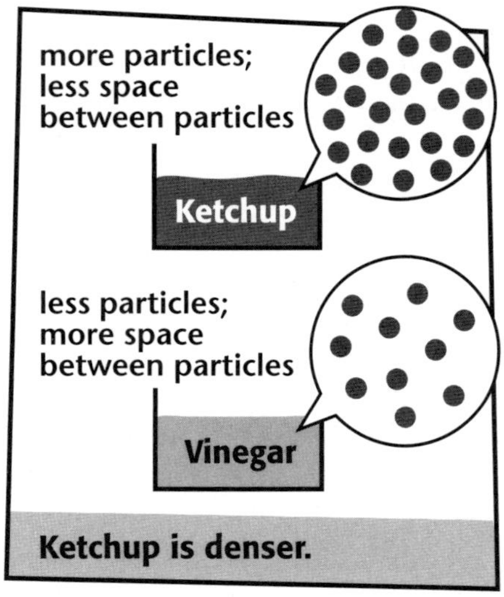

C. Find the density of each cake batter with the equation. Then put the batter in order. Write the letters. (The cup weighs 50 g.)

$$\text{density} = \frac{\text{mass}}{\text{volume}}$$

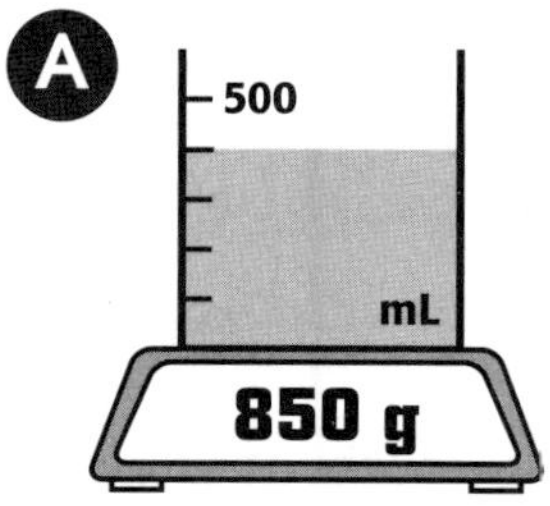

Density:

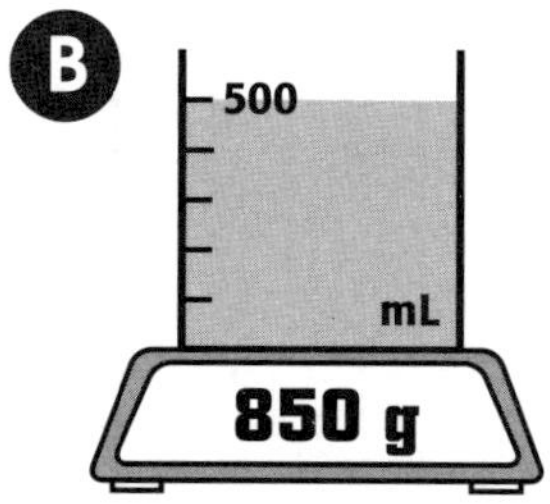

Density:

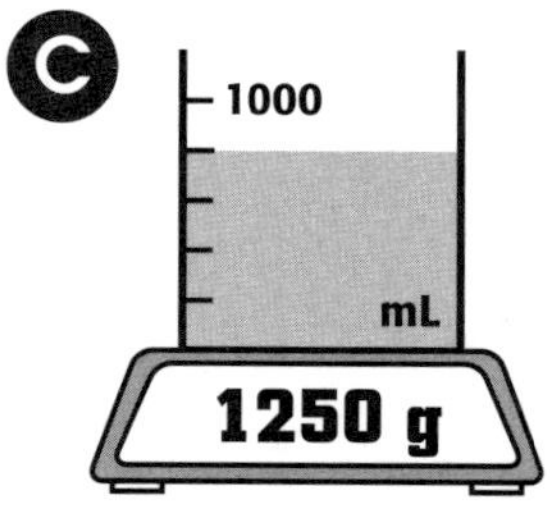

Density:

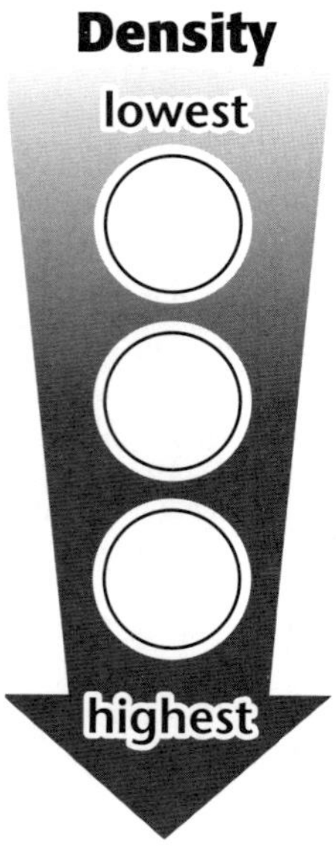

ISBN: 978-1-897457-80-1

D. Read the paragraph. Then answer the questions.

Most materials contract when they get colder. The colder a liquid is, the denser it becomes. However, water expands as it freezes to ice. It means that particles in liquid water are more closely packed than those in the solid state of water. This makes ice less dense than water and so it floats on water. Since water has this special property, we can find icebergs as heavy as 180 000 000 kg floating around in Antarctica.

A Huge Iceberg

1. Label the diagrams as "water in its liquid state" and "water in its solid state". Then explain your answer.

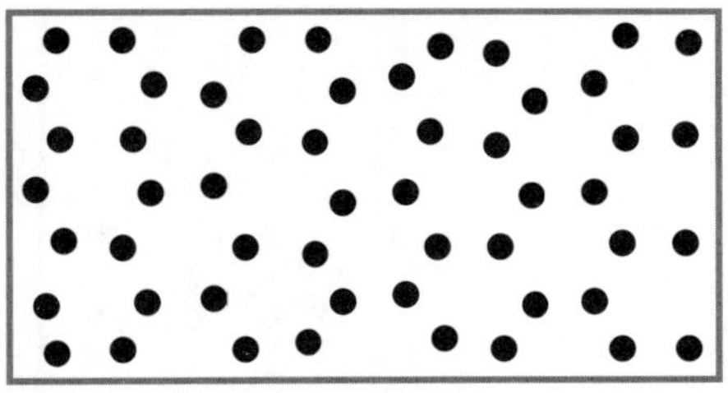

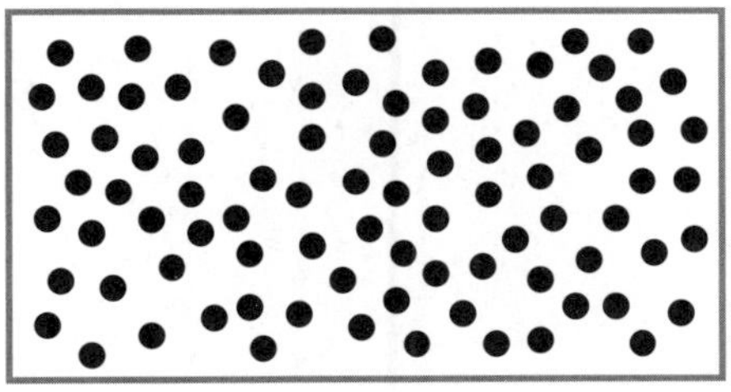

a. ____________________ b. ____________________

Explain: ______________________________

____

2. Why do huge and heavy icebergs formed from water float on water?

____

____

ISBN: 978-1-897457-80-1

3 Buoyancy

Some objects float in liquids or gases because of the force of buoyancy. Others do not. This is due to the difference in density of the objects and the fluids. In this unit, you will examine the relationship between buoyancy and density.

After completing this unit, you will

- understand that buoyancy is a force caused by the pressure exerted by fluids.
- understand the relationship between buoyancy and density.

The density of helium is lower than that of air. It makes the balloon rise.

Vocabulary

buoyancy: a property of fluids that causes some objects to float

density: the mass per unit volume of a substance

ISBN: 978-1-897457-80-1

Extension

You should have noticed that when you add an object to the water in a container, no matter whether the object floats or sinks, the water level rises. Why does this happen? Archimedes, a Greek mathematician, found the answer to this question when he was taking a bath in a bathtub. It all has to do with the relationship between density and buoyancy. Trace the correct lines to show the water levels of the two containers with different objects.

A. Fill in the blanks to complete the description. Then record the measurements.

displaces weight fluid =

Archimedes's Principle

Any object, fully or partially immersed in a 1. ____________, is buoyed up by a force equal to the 2. ____________ of the fluid it 3. ____________ .

4. buoyant force ◯ weight of the water displaced

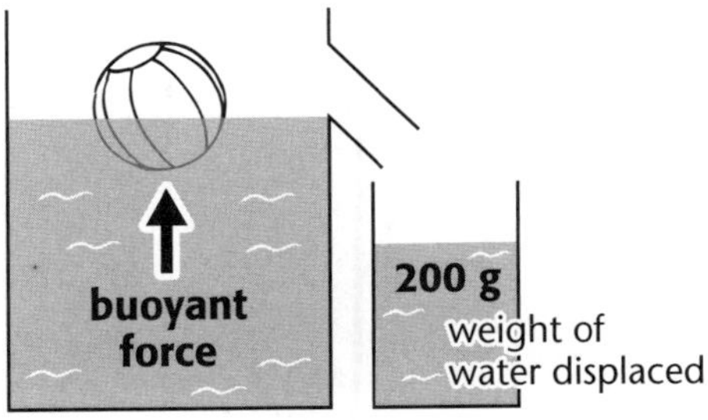

buoyant force: 5. ____________

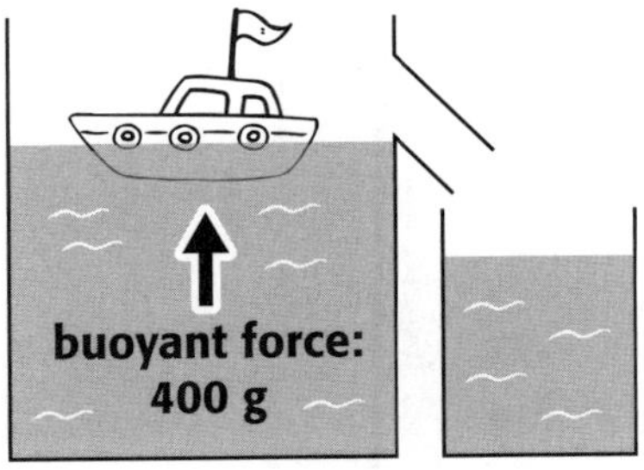

weight of water displaced:

6. ____________

ISBN: 978-1-897457-80-1

B. Choose the correct words to complete the description of buoyancy. Then draw arrows in the diagrams to show the directions of the forces, put ">" or "<" in the circles, and fill in the blanks.

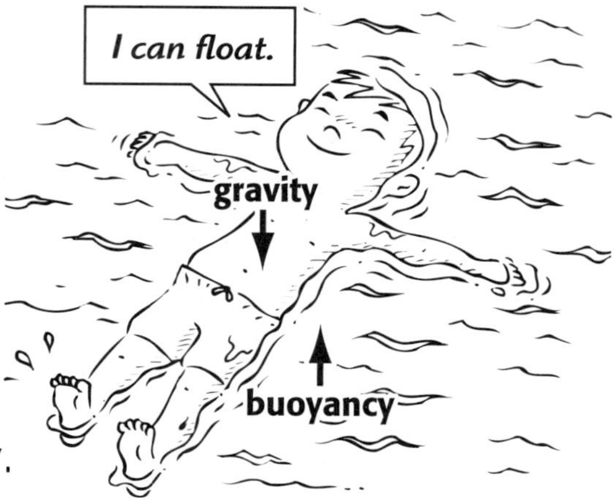

Buoyancy is a property of 1. ______________ (fluids/solids). It is a 2. ______________ (law/force) of fluids that opposes gravity. When the force of 3. ______________ (friction/gravity) pulls an object down on a fluid, the fluid pushes it back up with the force of buoyancy. When the force of buoyancy is 4. ______________ (greater/smaller) than the force of gravity, the object floats. What causes one of the forces to be greater than the other? It is 5. ______________ (colour/density). The density of a fluid, as well as the density of an object placed in the fluid, affects the 6. ______________ (length/strength) of the opposing forces. Therefore, buoyancy is determined by the 7. ______________ (difference/body) in density between the fluid and the object placed in it.

8.

force of gravity ◯ force of buoyancy

➡ The balloon ______________ (sinks/floats).

9.

force of gravity ◯ force of buoyancy

➡ The anchor ______________ (sinks/floats).

ISBN: 978-1-897457-80-1

C. Read the paragraph. Then draw eggs in the pictures and answer the questions.

How can you tell whether an egg is fresh or rotten without breaking it open? Simply put it in water. If it sinks, it is fresh; if it floats, it has gone rotten. Why is this so? When an egg is fresh, its density is greater than that of water, so it sinks. However, as the egg ages, air from outside enters the air pocket at the large end of the egg through the porous eggshell. When the egg is rotten, the air pocket becomes larger. Since air is less dense than water, the larger air pocket reduces the overall density of the egg. The egg becomes less dense than water, so it floats.

1. 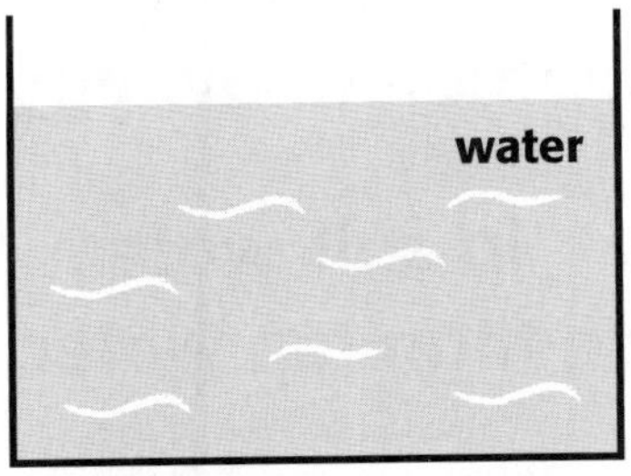

a fresh egg

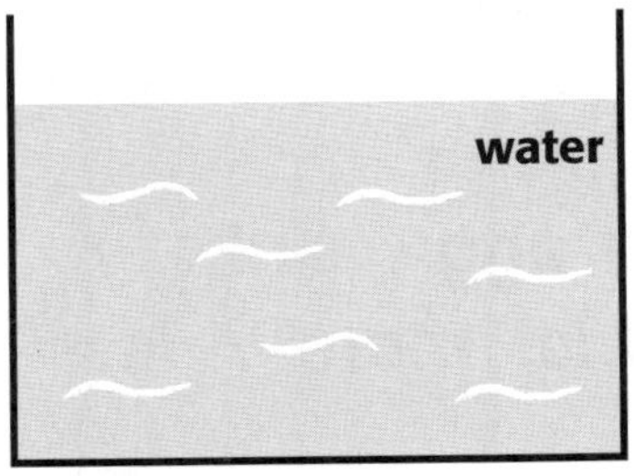

a rotten egg

2. Explain why an egg floats in water.

____

____

3. 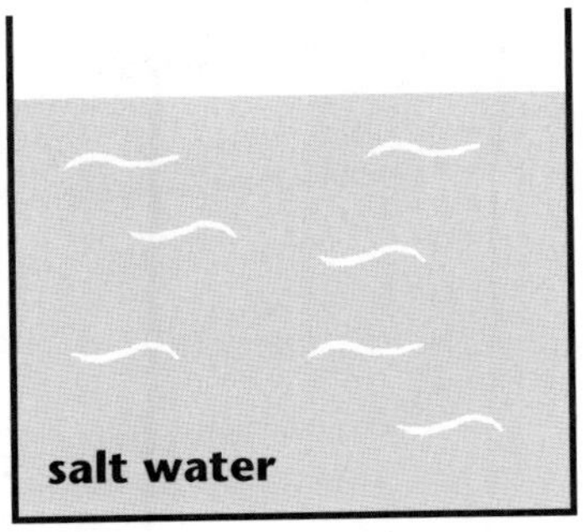

Salt water is denser than fresh water. If a rotten egg is put in salt water, will it float or sink? Draw it in the picture and explain.

____

____

ISBN: 978-1-897457-80-1

Experiment

Introduction

All solids and fluids have density. Whether a solid floats or sinks in a fluid depends on its density in relation to that of the fluid it is in. In this experiment, you'll compare the density of an egg and tap water, and the density of tap water and salt water.

Hypothesis

Circle the words to complete each hypothesis.

Experiment A A raw egg sinks / floats in warm tap water. Tap water is more / less dense than a raw egg.

Experiment B A raw egg sinks / floats in salt water. Salt water is more / less dense than tap water.

Steps For Experiment A

1. Put the raw egg in the cup of warm tap water.
2. Record your observation.

Materials

- *a raw egg*
- *a cup of warm tap water*
- *salt*
- *a teaspoon*

Which has greater density – a raw egg or tap water?

____

ISBN: 978-1-897457-80-1

Steps For Experiment B

1. Put the raw egg in the cup of warm water.
2. Add ¼ teaspoon of salt into the cup and observe the egg's movement.
3. Repeat step 2 until the egg moves significantly.
4. Record how much salt you added and what you observed.

   Amount of salt added: ____________________

   Observation: ____

Which has greater density – tap water or salt water? How do you know?

____

____

Result

Compare the density of a raw egg, tap water, and salt water. Which one has the highest density? Which one has the lowest?

____

Conclusion

Experiment A

The hypothesis was: ____

____

My experiment ____________________ the hypothesis.
supported/did not support

Experiment B

The hypothesis was: ____

____

My experiment ____________________ the hypothesis.
supported/did not support

ISBN: 978-1-897457-80-1

4 Compressible Fluids

The compressibility of fluids can make work easier for us. In this unit, you will look at the difference in compressibility of liquids and gases. You will also learn how hydraulic systems and pneumatic systems work.

After completing this unit, you will

- understand the difference between the compressibility of liquids and the compressibility of gases.
- understand how we make use of the compressibility of liquids and gases.

Vocabulary

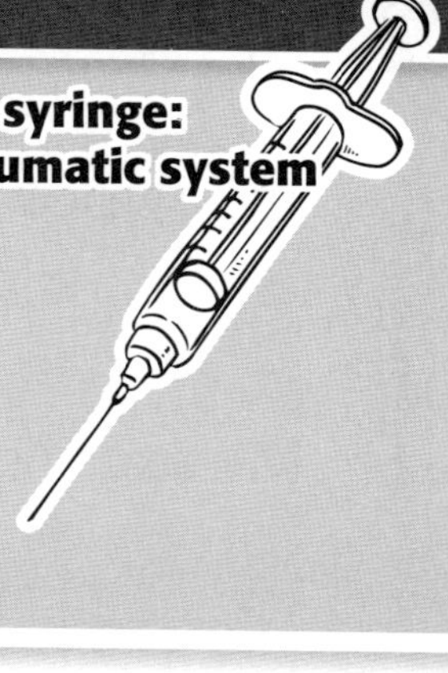

compressible: able to be made more compact by pressure

hydraulic system: a system that makes use of the pressure of a liquid

pneumatic system: a system that makes use of the pressure of a gas

ISBN: 978-1-897457-80-1

Extension

It is easy to inflate a balloon by blowing air into it with your mouth, but is it possible to inflate a flat bike tire in the same way? It would be quite impossible, but even if it is possible, it would definitely take you much more time and effort to get the job done. Then how can you inflate a bike tire easily? You can use a pump. It is a device that multiplies a force applied using air pressure, so you can inflate a tire with minimal effort.

A. Identify the particles as "gas" or "liquid". Draw to show the particles under pressure. Then circle the correct words to complete the sentences.

1. ____________ Particles

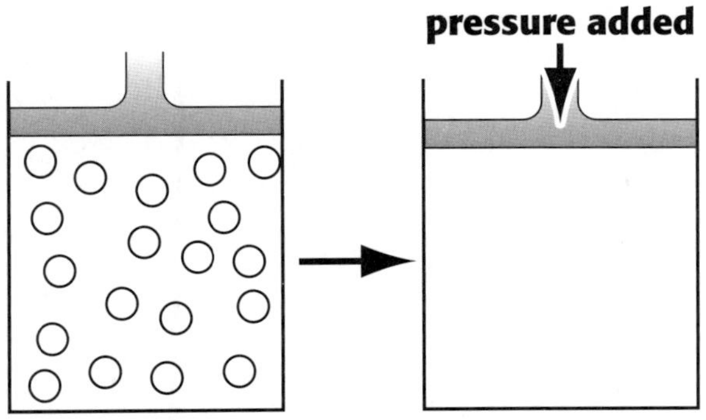

The compressed liquid particles

- have **a small / an obvious** change in volume.
- still have a **height / distance** apart.

2. ____________ Particles

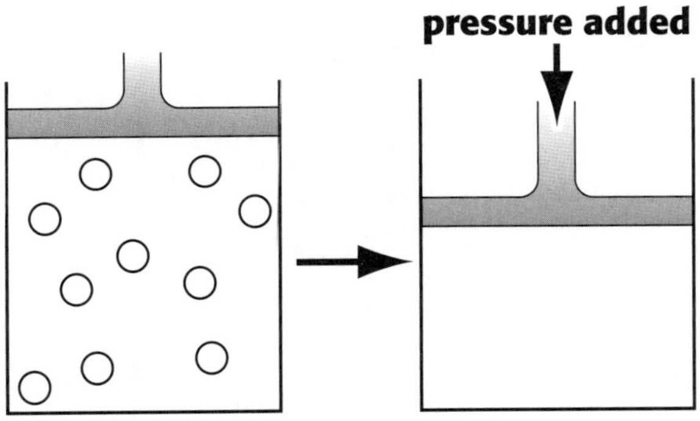

The compressed gas particles

- have a **smaller / greater** distance apart.
- have a noticeable **increase / decrease** in volume.

ISBN: 978-1-897457-80-1

B. Look at the Greek words from which "hydraulic" and "pneumatic" are derived. Draw lines to the correct meanings. Then fill in the blanks and draw arrows to show the small input forces and the great transmitted forces.

1.

hudro •	• wind (moving air)
pneuma •	• water

2.

Hydraulic and pneumatic systems use ______________ to transfer and ______________ an input force at a different ______________ .

small force: ⇨ great force: ⇨

3.

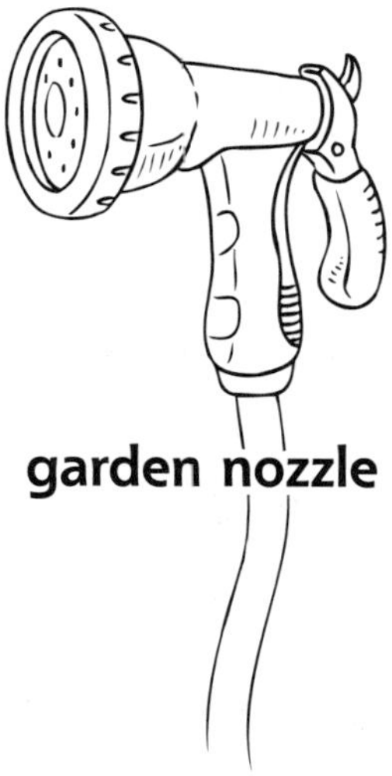

4.

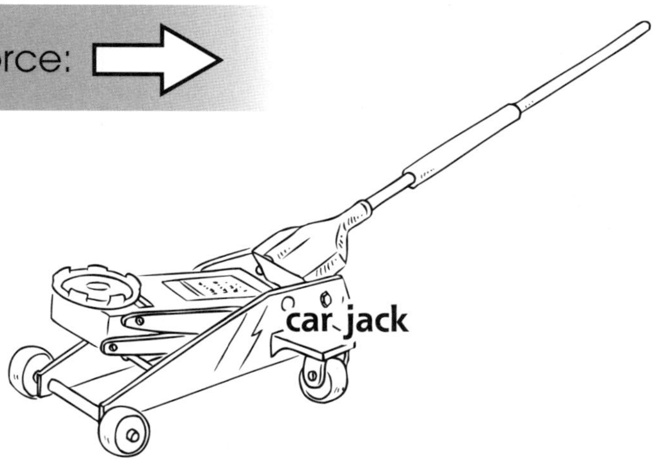

5.

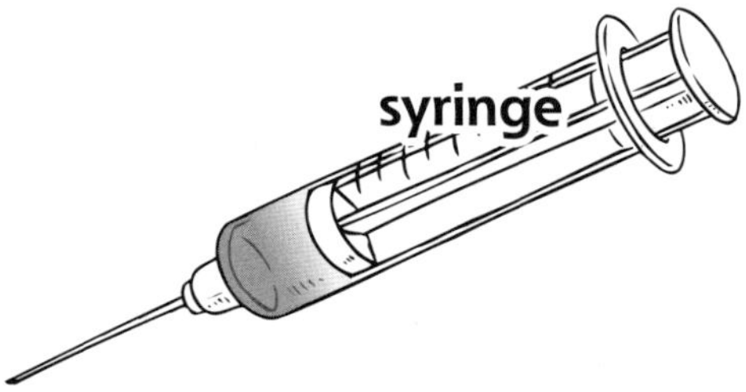

ISBN: 978-1-897457-80-1

C. Read the paragraph. Then answer the questions.

Liquids have much lower compressibility than gases because the particles of liquids are closer to one another than those in gases, so they have less room for compression. In fact, their compressibility is so low that they are even considered incompressible. However, the compressibility of both still allows us to use them to magnify a force applied so that work can be done easily. A hydraulic system uses a liquid as a source of power. When an input force is applied to the system, the output force at another part in the system will be much greater than the input force. A pneumatic system operates in a similar manner, but its source of power is the compressibility of a gas.

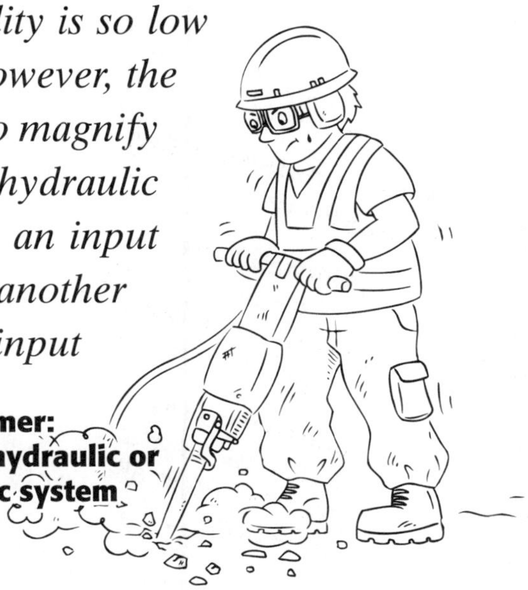

1. Which one has higher compressibility – a gas or a liquid? Why?

____

____

2. Why are solids incompressible?

____

____

3. How does a pneumatic system work?

____

____

4. The containers contain different kinds of gases. Put the gases in order.

Compressibility: ______________________________
highest lowest

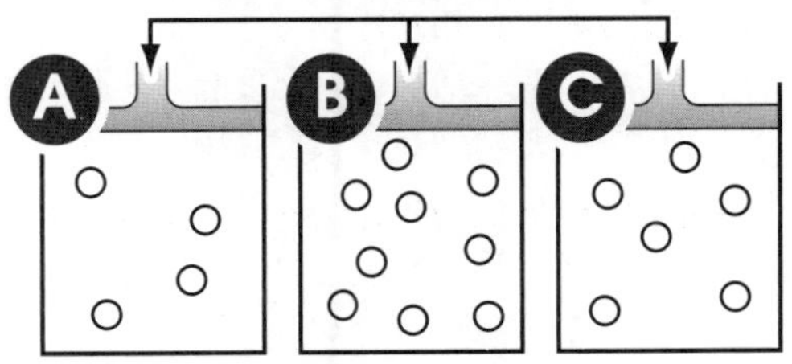

ISBN: 978-1-897457-80-1

5 Fluids and Pressure

Pressure on a fluid causes movement. Different systems take advantage of how fluids behave under pressure to make work easier. In this unit, you will examine the causes, as well as the results, of pressure in fluids.

After completing this unit, you will

- understand the relationships among pressure, volume, and temperature in fluids.
- understand that in fluids, forces are transferred in all directions.

- *The carbon dioxide dissolved in a bottle of soda creates a high pressure in the bottle.*
- *The pop is forced out through the small opening by the pressure.*

Vocabulary

pressure: a push

confined: fully enclosed

compressed: decrease in volume due to pressure

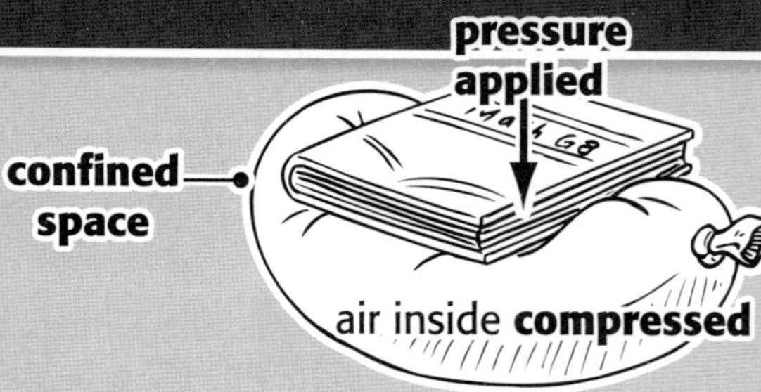

ISBN: 978-1-897457-80-1

Extension

Have you ever tried stepping on an air-filled balloon? Did you notice that when you stepped on it, it bulged out under your foot? Why did this happen? It was because when you stepped on the balloon, you were actually applying a force to the air confined in the balloon. The air was compressed, exerting pressure on the wall of the balloon, and so the balloon bulged out. Did you also notice that the balloon did not bulge out on one side only but on all sides? Why?

A. Fill in the blanks to complete the Pascal's law. Then check the correct pictures.

Pascal's Law

pressure undiminished directions confined

Pascal's law states that 1. ______________ exerted anywhere on a 2. ______________ fluid is transferred equally in all 3. ______________ and is 4. ______________ to every point of the fluid.

5. Pressing an inflated balloon

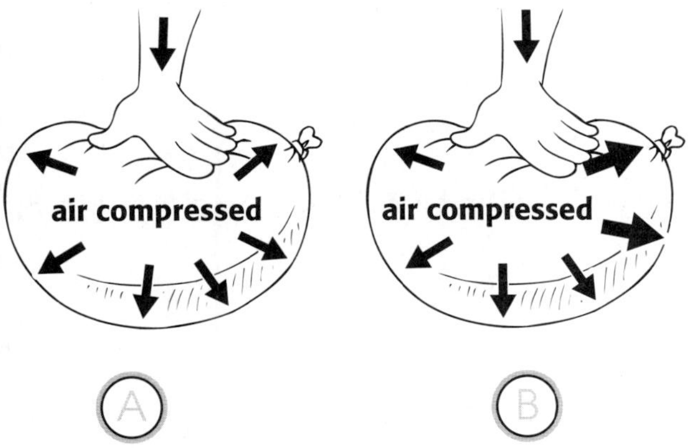

6. Pressing the top of a jar filled with water

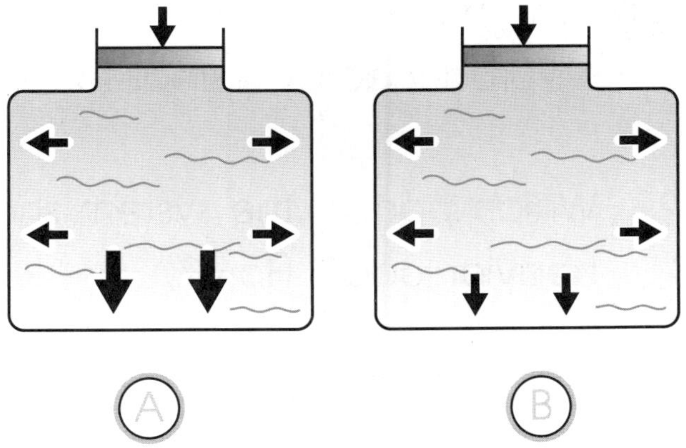

ISBN: 978-1-897457-80-1

B. Look at the diagram that shows how a hydraulic system works. Fill in the blanks to complete the descriptions. Then answer the question.

movement	greater	force	pressure	transmitted	initial	load

1. **A Hydraulic System:** uses a liquid to transfer a force between pistons

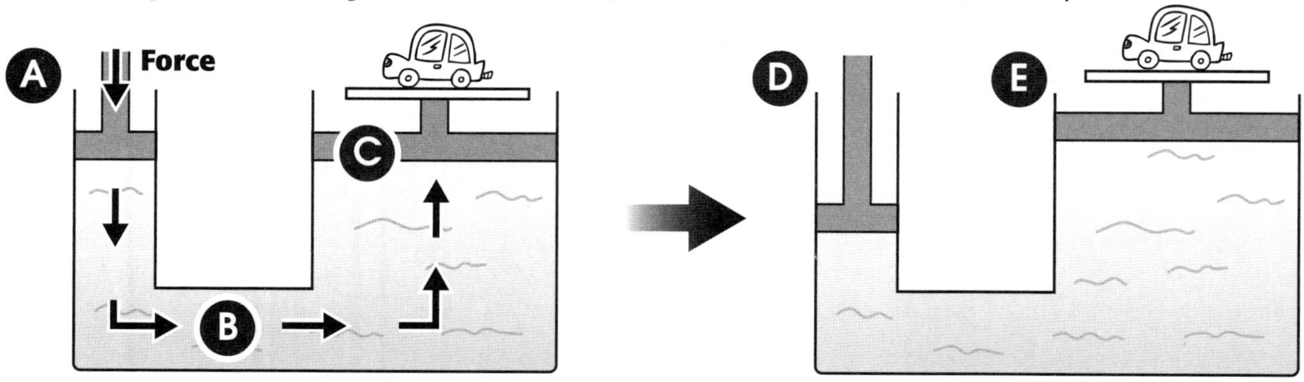

A A ________________ is applied to a small piston in the small cylinder.

B The pressure is ________________ through a liquid to a larger piston, causing ________________ .

C Since the ________________ is the same on both sides, the force on the large piston is a few times greater than the ________________ force applied.

D The small piston moves a ________________ distance than the large piston.

E The heavy ________________ is lifted. This shows that a large force is produced by a small force.

2. Which part of the system should be modified if it is used to lift a heavier load? How?

____

____

ISBN: 978-1-897457-80-1

C. Fill in the blanks to complete the sentences. Then write the meanings of the highlighted sentences.

Pressure in Fluids

expands	less	pressure	more
faster	decreased	rises	

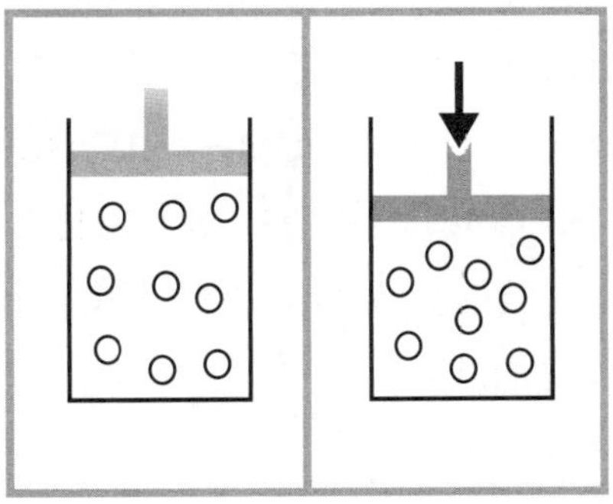

1. When a fluid is compressed, the particles are forced closer together to take up ____________ space.

   → The volume of the fluid is ____________ .

   → The fluid exerts more ____________ .

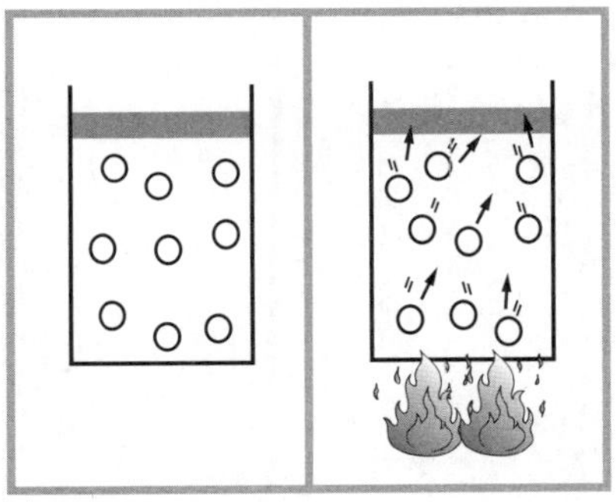

2. When heat is applied, the fluid temperature ____________ . The particles move ____________ and take up more space.

   → The fluid ____________ and has a greater volume.

   → The expanded fluid exerts ____________ pressure.

3.

Caution: *Keep out of reach of children.*

(A) Contents under pressure. Store in a cool place. (B) Do not leave it in direct sunlight, an enclosed vehicle, or expose it to temperatures above 45°C. Container may explode if heated.

Explanation:

(A) ____

____

(B) ____

____

ISBN: 978-1-897457-80-1

6 Fluids and Society

Fluids are widely used and controlled in our everyday lives. In this unit, you will compare the use and control of fluids in living things with the ways they are used and controlled in manufactured devices. You will also examine the properties of fluids that enable us to use and control them, and the impacts of fluid technology on our world.

After completing this unit, you will

- know the similarities between the use and control of fluids in living things and in manufactured devices.
- understand how the properties of fluids affect our use and control of them.
- understand the social, economic, and environmental impacts of fluid technology.

Vocabulary

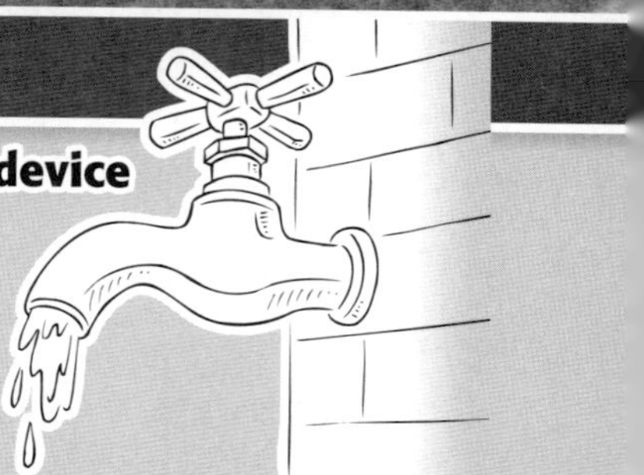

manufactured: made by machines

valve: device that opens and closes to control fluid flow

ISBN: 978-1-897457-80-1

Extension

Fluids are everywhere around us, and we use and control them in our daily lives. Water is probably the most common fluid we use and control at home. How do we control water at home? We use faucets and take advantage of the flow property of water. Did you know that a faucet is actually a valve? We use it to control the release of water and adjust water flow.

Can you name one more example of the use and control of a fluid that can be found at home?

A. Fill in the blanks to show how fluids are used for their properties.

shape density compressibility buoyancy flow

1. Liquid concrete takes the ____________ of the container it is in, allowing us to make strong and useful forms like concrete pillars.

2. The ____________ of air inside a hot-air balloon is increased or decreased in order to use the property of ____________ outside the balloon.

3. Fluids ____________ and can take solids and other fluids with them the way our blood carries oxygen and nutrients to all the cells in our bodies.

4. The ____________ of air allows divers to carry tanks much smaller than they otherwise would.

ISBN: 978-1-897457-80-1

B. Match the use and control of fluids in living things with the similar use and control in manufactured devices. Write the letters.

In Living Things

- [ ] The arteries and veins must be free of blockage for blood flow.
- [ ] A hollow coconut floats on water as an efficient dispersion method.
- [ ] The heart pumps blood quickly and efficiently using the circulatory system.
- [ ] A fish controls its depth in water by increasing or decreasing the amount of air in its swim bladder.

In Manufactured Devices

A. Log booms allow logs to flow across water to sawmills.

B. A submarine can dive or surface, depending on the level of water in its ballast tank.

C. Perimeter drains around buildings must be kept clear of silt and debris.

D. Piston pumps move liquids in hydraulic systems, such as windmills.

C. Find one positive impact and one negative impact of each fluid technology. Write the letters. Then write one more negative impact of your own for each case.

1. Oil Extraction and Transportation

☺ : ______

☹ : ______ ; ____________________

2. Heavy Machinery with Hydraulic and Pneumatic Systems

☺ : ______

☹ : ______ ; ____________________

3. Medical Innovation with Hydraulic and Pneumatic Systems

☺ : ______

☹ : ______ ; ____________________

Impacts of Fluid Technology

- **A** increases productivity
- **B** can be costly
- **C** saves more lives
- **D** creates new jobs
- **E** causes habitat destruction
- **F** leads to job loss for construction workers

ISBN: 978-1-897457-80-1

D. Read the paragraph. Then fill in the blanks to complete the diagram and answer the questions.

Many houses are now installed with low flow aerating shower heads instead of the traditional ones because they can help reduce water consumption. There is a built-in flow restrictor in a low flow shower head, and together with an aerating design that mixes air into the water stream, the amount of water coming through the shower head is greatly reduced, but a powerful stream of water can still be maintained. Some low flow shower heads are even equipped with a push-button cut-off valve so that the user can easily halt the flow of water while soaping up, and thus further reduces water consumption.

1.

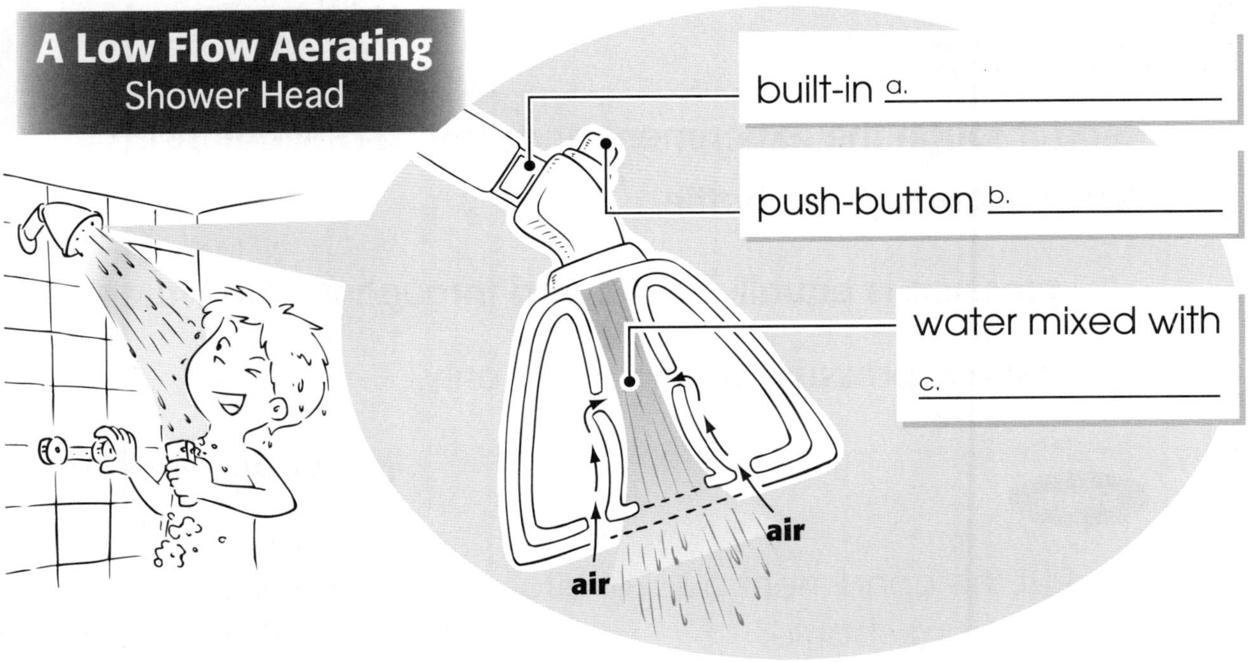

2. Why are low flow aerating shower heads widely used?

____

3. What is the use of a cut-off valve?

____

____

ISBN: 978-1-897457-80-1

Experiment

Introduction

When we squeeze a bottle of water, what will happen to the water in the bottle? Will the pressure be distributed throughout the water in the bottle? Let's put a condiment packet in a bottle of water to test this.

Hypothesis

Read through the experiment and choose a hypothesis.

When I squeeze the bottle,

- ◯ **pressure is equally distributed throughout the water.**
- ◯ **there is pressure on the bottle only.**

Materials

- ***1 plastic bottle***
- ***tap water***
- ***a small condiment packet of ketchup***
  (Put the condiment packet in water to see if it floats. Use one that floats for this experiment.)

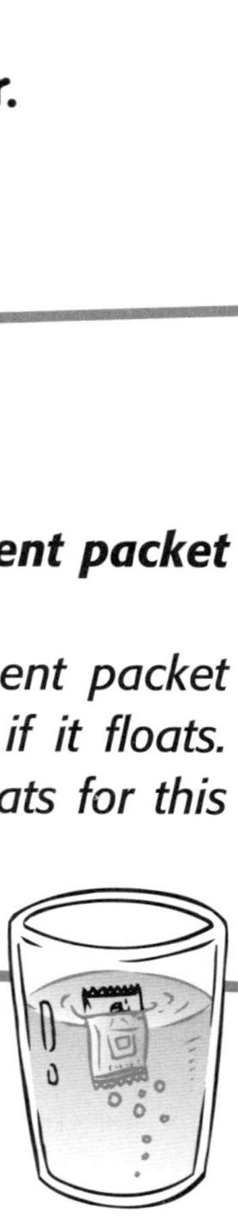

Steps

1. Put the condiment packet into the empty bottle.
2. Fill the bottle to the top with water and screw the lid tight.
3. Squeeze the bottle with your hands and then release. Observe what happens.
4. Record what happens.

ISBN: 978-1-897457-80-1

Result

Draw pictures to show what happened when you squeezed and released the bottle.

When squeezed
(with pressure)

When released
(without pressure)

Circle the correct words to complete the explanation of the experiment when the bottle is squeezed.

- The pressure **is / is not** distributed through the water to the condiment packet.
- The air in the condiment packet **is / is not** compressed.
- The density of the air in the packet **increases / remains the same** .
- The condiment packet **sinks / remains floating** .

Conclusion

The hypothesis was: ______________________________________

____

My experiment ______________________________ the hypothesis.
supported/did not support

ISBN: 978-1-897457-80-1

Try to complete this review in **30 minutes**.

30 minutes

This review consists of five sections, from A to E. The marks for each question are shown in parentheses. The circle at the bottom right corner is for the marks you get in each section. An overall record is on the last page of the review.

A. Write T for true and F for false.

1. The compressibility of a solid affects its rate of flow. **(2)** ______

2. Viscosity is a measure of a fluid's inner friction, that is, its resistance to flow. **(2)** ______

3. The density of a substance is the amount of space the substance takes up. **(2)** ______

4. Heavy machinery with hydraulic and pneumatic systems is used to save lives only. **(2)** ______

5. 

A carton of juice is denser than a teaspoon of juice. **(2)**

______

6. 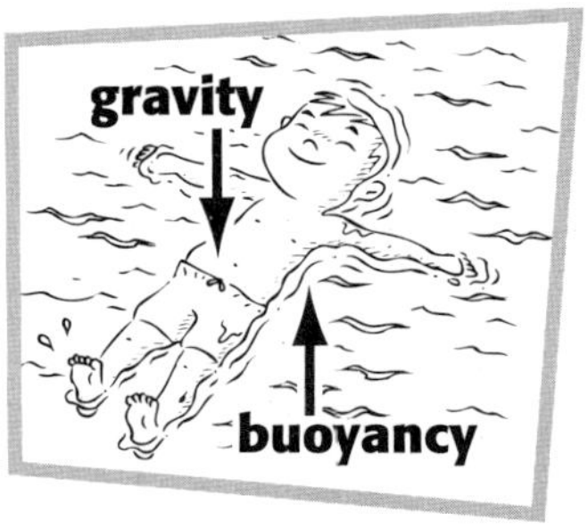

Buoyancy is a force of fluids that opposes gravity. **(2)**

______

12

ISBN: 978-1-897457-80-1

B. Do the matching.

1.

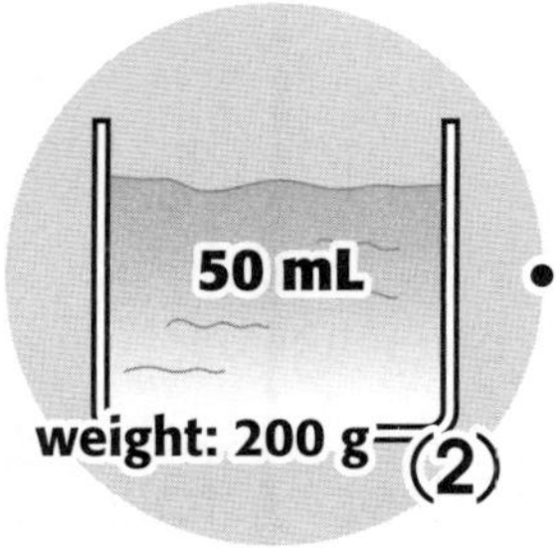

(2)

2.

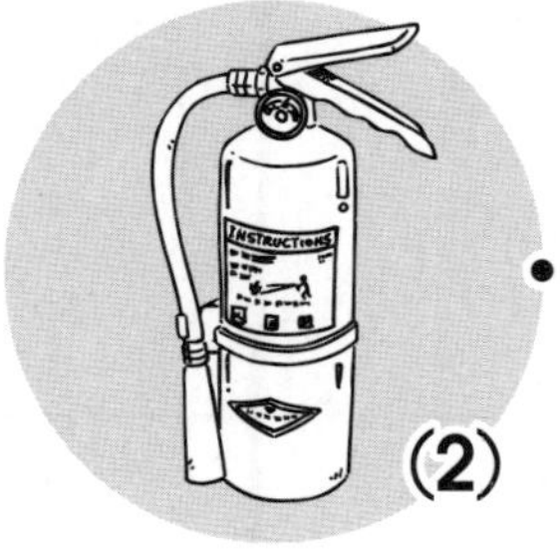

(2)

3.

(2)

4.

(2)

5.

(2)

6.

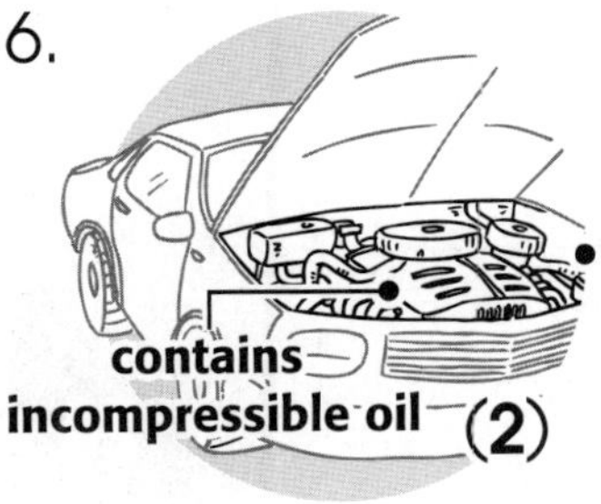

(2)

- has a density of 4 g/mL
- makes use of the compressibility of air
- use and control of water at home
- has lower viscosity than honey
- has a density lower than air
- a hydraulic system

12

ISBN: 978-1-897457-80-1

C. Look at the pictures. Circle the correct words and explain using the given terms.

1.

The helium balloon is let go.

The helium balloon **rises / falls** . (**2**)

Explain in terms of density: (**6**)

____

____

2.

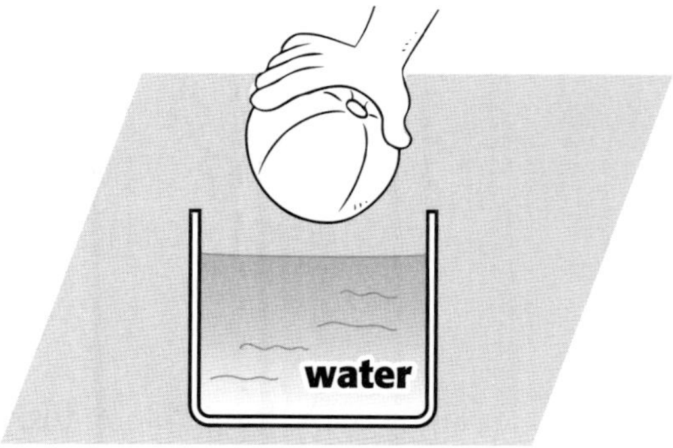

The ball is dropped into the water.

The ball **floats / sinks** . (**2**)

Explain in terms of buoyancy: (**6**)

____

____

3.

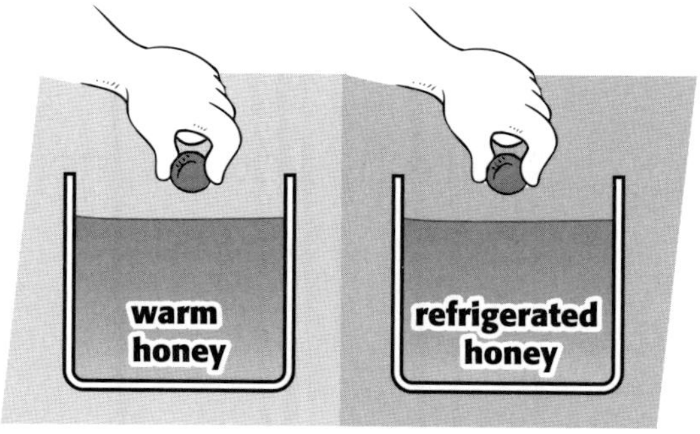

A candy is dropped into the honey.

The candy in the **warm / refrigerated** honey sinks to the bottom first. (**2**)

Explain in terms of viscosity: (**6**)

____

____

24

ISBN: 978-1-897457-80-1

D. Each container contains a special gas. Find the density of each gas. Then answer the questions.

1. Each container is filled with 0.2 m³ of gas.

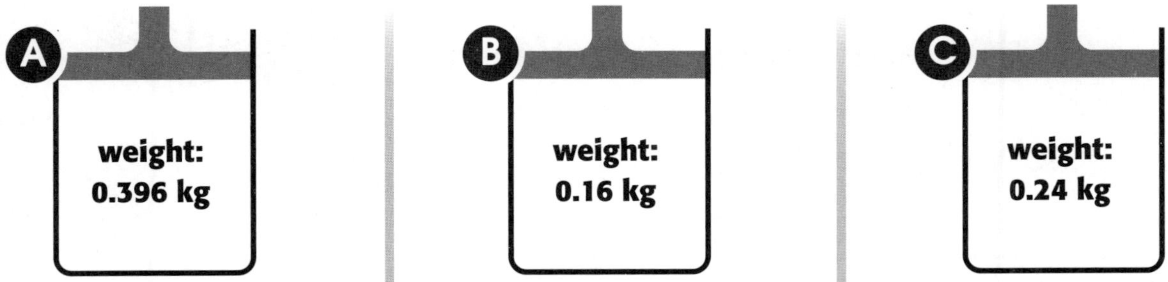

Density (**4**)

Density (**4**)

Density (**4**)

2. Which gas has the greatest density? (**2**)

____

3. How does the gas in each container react when a force is applied to the piston? How does the volume of the gas change? (**5**)

____

4. The same force is applied to each container. Identify the containers and explain your answer.

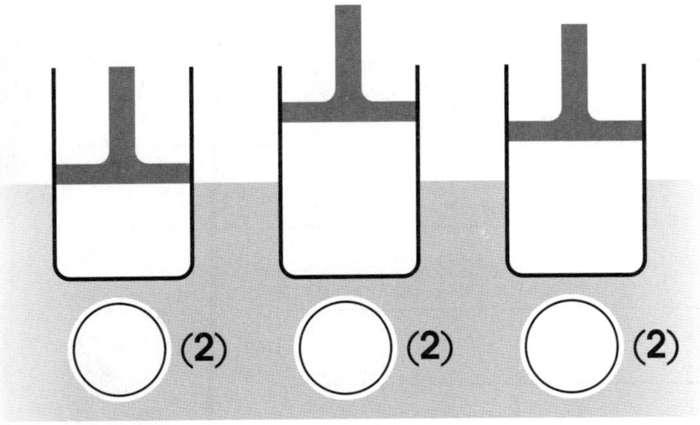

Explain: (**5**)

____

____

____

____

____

30

ISBN: 978-1-897457-80-1

E. Answer the questions.

1. a. Draw arrows to show the pressure inside the inflated balloon. **(2)**

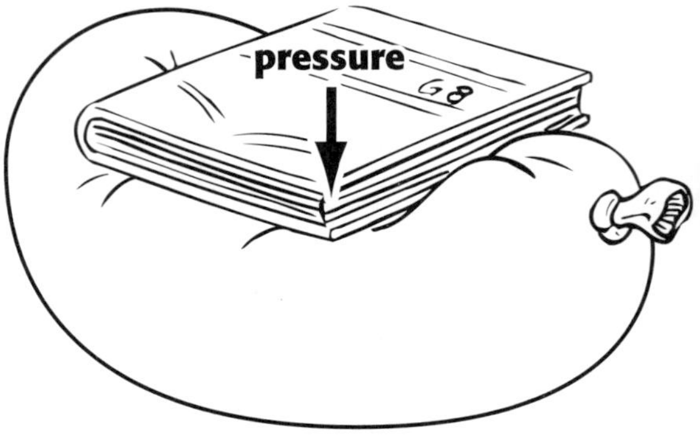

   b. Explain the distribution of pressure inside the balloon using the Pascal's law. **(5)**

____

____

____

2. Fill in the blanks to name the system and describe the input and output forces. Then explain how this system works in a car jack.

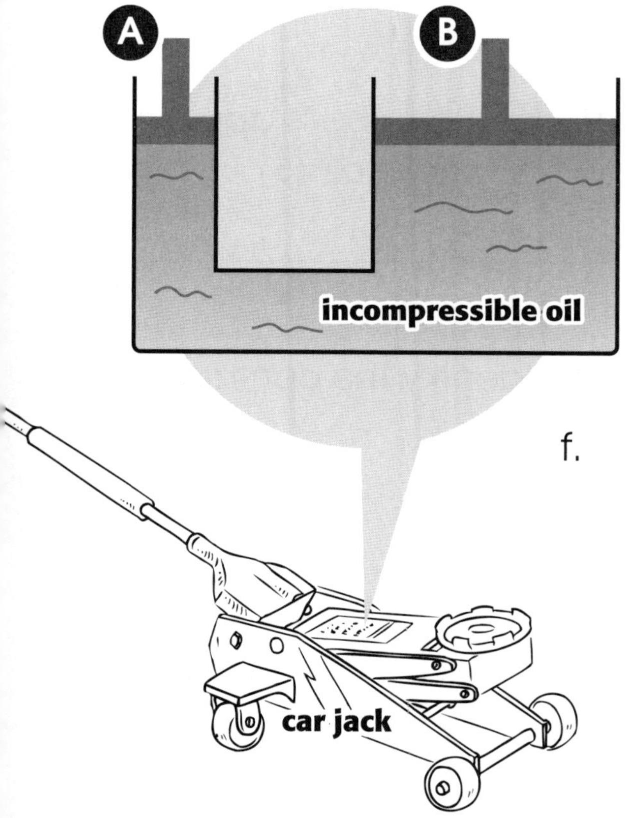

It is a a. ______________ **(2)** system.
(hydraulic/pneumatic)

- b. ______________ **(2)** input force at c. ______________ **(2)**
(great/small) (A/B)

- d. ______________ **(2)** output force at e. ______________ **(2)**
(great/small) (A/B)

f. How the system works in a car jack: **(5)**

____

____

____

____

____

22

ISBN: 978-1-897457-80-1

My Record

Section A	/12
Section B	/12
Section C	/24
Section D	/30
Section E	/22

Total /100

80-100

Great work! You really understand your science stuff! Research your favourite science topics at the library or on the Internet to find out more about the topics related to this section. Keep challenging yourself to learn more!

60-79

Good work! You understand some basic concepts, but try reading through the units again to see whether you can master the material! Go over the questions that you had trouble with to make sure you know the correct answers.

below 60

You can do much better! Try reading over the units again. Ask your parents or teachers any questions you might have. Once you feel confident that you know the material, try the review again. Science is exciting, so don't give up!

ISBN: 978-1-897457-80-1

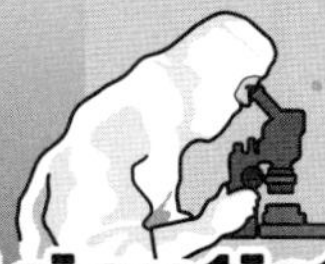

The Car Mechanic

Do you know that there are different kinds of fluids in a car? Fluids are the lifeblood of a car, and when we take the car to the garage for maintenance, the car mechanic often checks the fluids to see if they are in optimum condition.

The first kind of fluid the car mechanic checks is the engine oil. It is the lubricant that keeps the engine's moving parts friction-free. Without engine oil, the engine will break down. The next kind of fluid to check is the transmission fluid. It lubricates the car's gears that keep changing while the car is running. The third kind of fluid is the radiator coolant, which is a mixture of water with a chemical additive. The coolant has a higher boiling point and a lower freezing point than water. This compensates for the temperature extremes that the engine will experience. The fourth kind of fluid is the brake fluid. It provides hydraulic power to stop the car when the driver applies the brake. Without the brake fluid, the driver would need to exert a huge force to stop the car. The last kind of fluid in a car is the power steering fluid, which provides hydraulic power to make steering easy.

By checking these five kinds of fluids, the car mechanic ensures that your car stays fit and healthy.

ISBN: 978-1-897457-80-1

Cool Science Facts

ISBN: 978-1-897457-80-1

1 How does a ballpoint pen make use of a liquid's viscosity to work?

2 What is a supersaturated solution?

3 How does a submarine float and dive in the sea?

4 How does a perfume atomizer work?

Find the answers on the next page.

Cool Science Facts

1 A ballpoint pen has a narrow plastic tube filled with viscous ink. The high viscosity of the ink prevents it from spilling out from the small metal ball at the tip of the pen, while still allowing gravity to pull it down to the ball. As the ball rolls, the ink is transferred from the ball onto the paper.

2 A supersaturated solution is a solution that contains more solute than the amount of it that the solvent can dissolve. Rock candies are formed as a result of cooling a supersaturated solution of sugar. Water is heated to increase the solubility of sugar until no more sugar can dissolve. When this solution cools, the solubility of sugar decreases, making the solution supersaturated. The solution begins to crystallize and rock candies are formed.

ISBN: 978-1-897457-80-1

3 Most submarines have two hulls, one inside the other. The spaces between the two hulls, which are called ballast tanks, can be filled with air or water. There are valves in the tanks: the valves at the top allow air in the tanks to escape, while those at the bottom allow water to enter the tanks. When the ballast tanks are filled with air, the average density of the submarine is lower than that of water, so the submarine floats. When the submarine needs to dive, water is allowed into the ballast tanks to increase the density of the submarine, so it sinks.

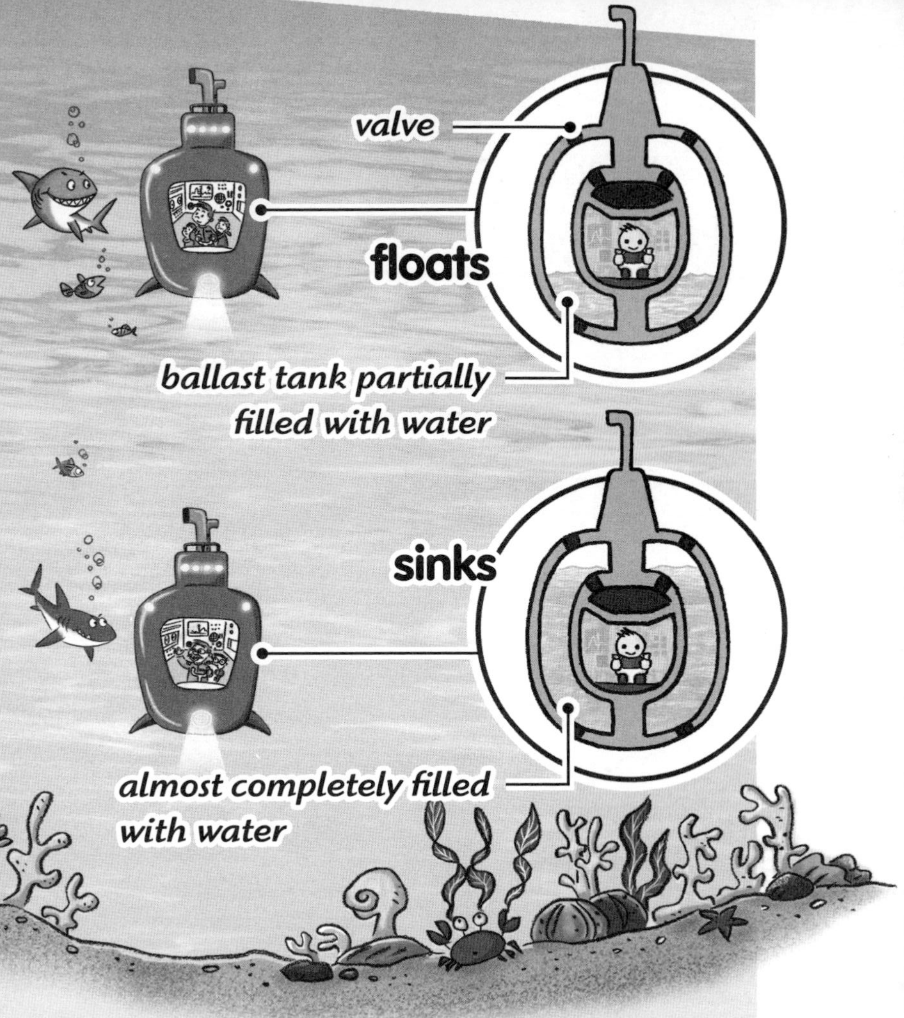

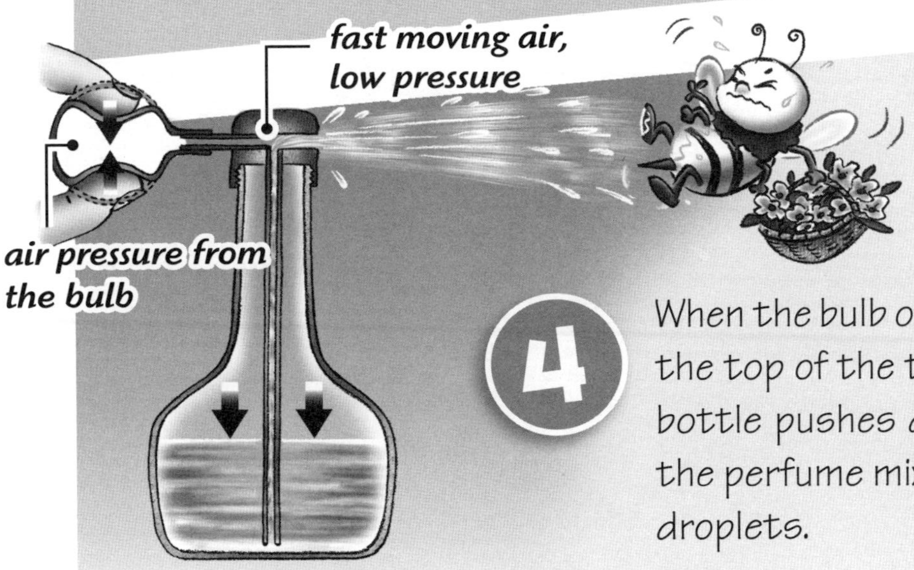

4 When the bulb of an atomizer is squeezed, fast moving air flows across the top of the tube, creating low pressure. The higher pressure in the bottle pushes down on the perfume and forces it up the tube, where the perfume mixes with the fast moving air and is sprayed out as tiny droplets.

ISBN: 978-1-897457-80-1

ISBN: 978-1-897457-80-1

Section 4

Understanding Earth and Space Systems

ISBN: 978-1-897457-80-1

1 Water on Earth

All living things need water, which can be found on Earth in the three states of matter. In this unit, you will examine how each state of water occurs on Earth and learn about the relative amounts of water in their storage places on Earth.

After completing this unit, you will

- understand the conditions under which each state of water exists.
- understand that water circulates around the Earth in a cycle.
- know the relative amounts of each state of water on Earth.

Vocabulary

transpiration: evaporation of water from living things, mainly plants

infiltration: process by which surface water enters the soil

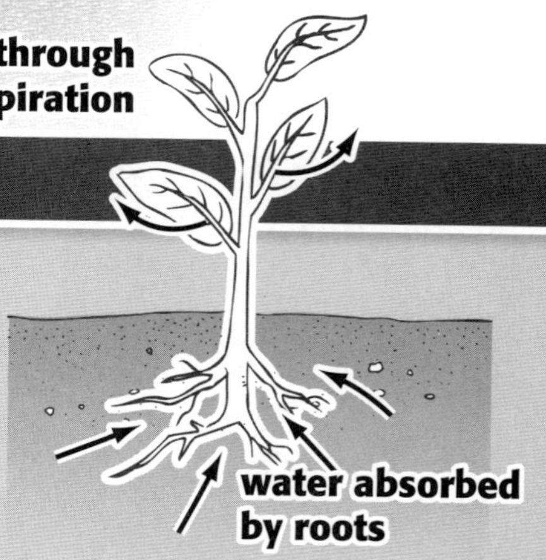

ISBN: 978-1-897457-80-1

Extension

When cloud particles become too heavy to remain suspended in the air, they fall to the Earth as precipitation. Precipitation occurs in different forms, but which form it is in when it reaches the ground depends completely on temperature.

Have you seen precipitation in these different forms?

Different Forms of Water:

A. Fill in the blanks to complete the description of water.

height   ice   evaporation   low   gas   water vapour
solid   steam   altitude   liquid   temperature

Water is the only substance that exists in three states of matter: 1. ________, 2. ________, and 3. ________ under the Earth's ordinary temperature conditions. There are two main conditions that determine which state water is in.

Condition 1: 4. ________

When the temperature is very 5. ________, water changes from liquid to solid, in the form of snow, frost, 6. ________, etc. When the temperature is high, water changes from liquid to gas, in the form of 7. ________. High temperatures also increase the rate of 8. ________, in which water changes to the gaseous state of 9. ________.

Condition 2: 10. ________

It is closely related to temperature. With an increase in 11. ________, temperature falls, and this in turn affects which state water is in.

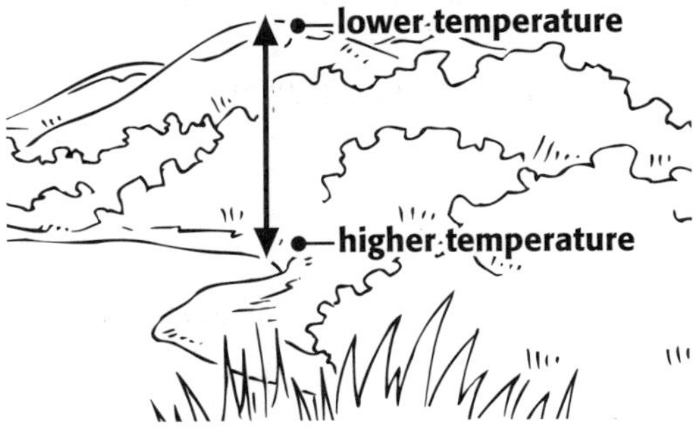

B. Fill in the blanks to complete the passage about the water cycle. Label the diagram. Then answer the questions.

states condensation infiltration groundwater
evaporation surface runoff precipitation
water transpiration recycled

The water on Earth now is the same 1. ____________ that has always been on Earth. No new water is made, but instead water is 2. ____________ around the Earth, changing into different 3. ____________ and moving through different places of storage in the water cycle. With the sun's heat, liquid water from water bodies, such as oceans and lakes, changes to water vapour through 4. ____________ . Water vapour also comes from 5. ____________ from living things. With cooler temperatures, water vapour becomes clouds through 6. ____________ . When the water droplets in clouds become too heavy for the clouds to hold, they fall back to the Earth's surface as 7. ____________ , usually in the form of snow and rain. Snow can accumulate to form glaciers and ice caps, while rain falls directly back to water bodies or on land as 8. ____________ , which enters water bodies through rivers and streams. Some rain gets into the ground through 9. ____________ and becomes 10. ____________ , which may take millions of years to find its way back to the surface again.

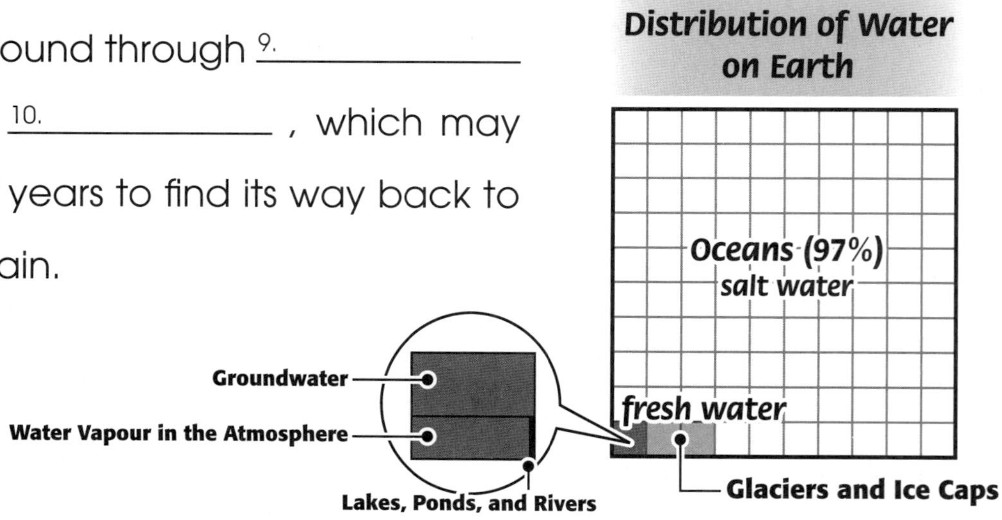

ISBN: 978-1-897457-80-1

11.

12. Is groundwater fresh water or salt water? Where does it come from?

____

____

13. Describe the journey of water starting from precipitation.

____

____

____

____

14. Humans can only drink unfrozen fresh water. ________ % of all the water on Earth is available for us to use.

15. A far greater variety of plants and animals live in salt water than in fresh water. Some living things spend part of their lives in salt water and part in fresh water. Write one example for each.

salt water: ____________

fresh water: ____________

both: ____________

2 The Watershed

Knowing where a watershed is means knowing where water comes from and where it moves to. In this unit, you will learn about watersheds and examine why watersheds are taken into account in water management.

After completing this unit, you will

- understand that the watershed is a fundamental geographical unit.
- know how the watershed relates to water management and planning.

Vocabulary

riparian: of or related to the banks of a river or a stream

aquatic: growing or living in or near water

ecosystem: a complex system of living organisms and their environment that function as a unit

 ISBN: 978-1-897457-80-1

Extension

You should have seen many maps before, and they were probably political maps that showed the territorial borders of different countries. Do you know that there are also physical maps that show different features of geography? There is one type that shows all the lines that follow the highest geographical parts of the world. The lines do not separate countries, like those on a political map, but they separate different areas known as watersheds.

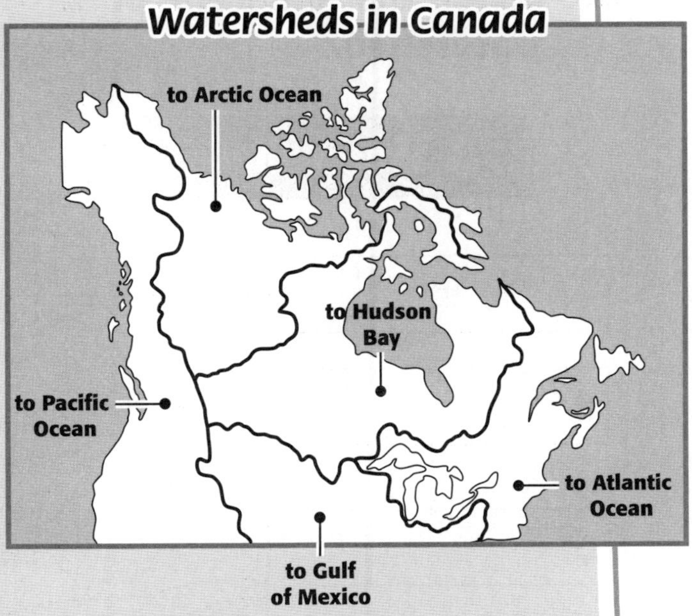

A. Circle the correct words to describe a watershed.

The Watershed

A watershed is a geographical area within which all **water / waste** from precipitation and melted ice and snow drains **uphill / downhill** into the same body of water. The water moves through a **network / source** of drainage pathways, both underground and on the **snow / surface**, which includes all the streams and **houses / rivers**. Watersheds are separated by areas of **high / low** elevation, such as **ridges / valleys** and mountains. These dividing lines are called water **basins / divides**.

ISBN: 978-1-897457-80-1

B. Label the diagram of a watershed.

lake | precipitation | water divide | groundwater | stream | river

A Watershed

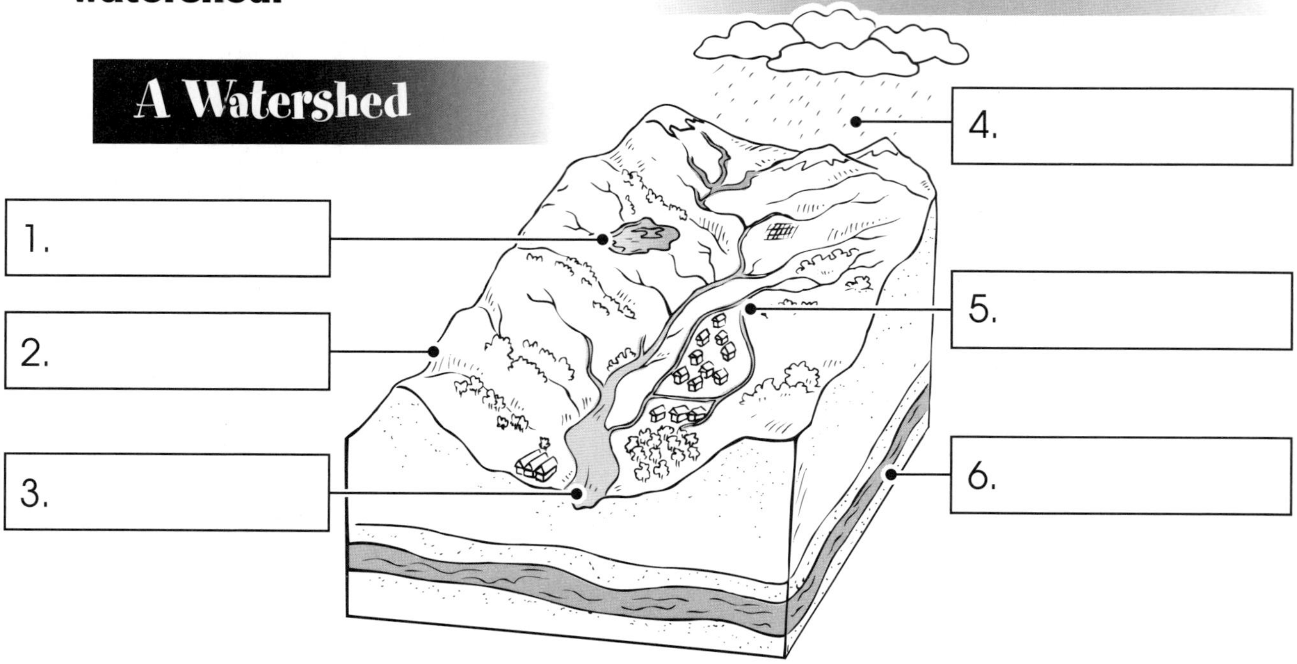

C. Sort the things that watershed-based water management has to consider.

human population
aquatic ecosystems
recreational activity
land animals and plants
climate/weather condition in the watershed

Things to Consider in Watershed-based Water Management

1 ecosystems within the watershed

- riparian ecosystems
- ____________________

2 human activity in the watershed

- industrial activity
- forestry activity
- agricultural activity
- ____________________

3 ____

- snow accumulation
- amount of precipitation

4 water requirements of all living things within the watershed

- aquatic animals and plants
- ____________________
- ____________________

ISBN: 978-1-897457-80-1

D. Read the paragraph. Complete the descriptions about phosphorus and the Lake Simcoe Protection Plan.

Since June, 2009, the Lake Simcoe Protection Plan has taken effect. It is the most comprehensive watershed-based legislated plan in Canada. One of the plan's main objectives is to improve water quality by reducing the loading of phosphorus to the lake. Phosphorus is found in many things, including toothpaste, detergents, household cleaning products, pesticides, and fertilizers. While some phosphorus is natural and necessary to support a healthy aquatic ecosystem, too much of it causes excessive algae growth, which in turn leads to the depletion of dissolved oxygen necessary for sustaining other aquatic species, such as coldwater fish. Major sources of phosphorus include effluent from municipal and industrial sewage treatment plants, septic systems, stormwater runoff, and airborne dust. The government is taking action to limit phosphorus discharges from sewage treatment plants to the lake. However, a collective effort which involves everyone in the community is required to protect the Lake Simcoe watershed.

1. **Phosphorus** (a mineral)
   - can be found ______________ (naturally/occasionally)
   - can be found in human-made products, such as

   ____

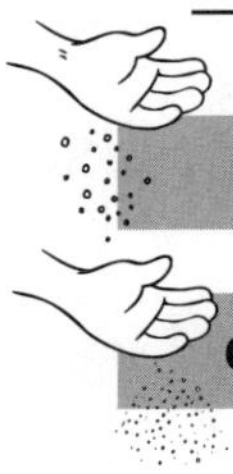

right amount : ______________________________

excessive amount : ______________________________

2. 

One of the main objectives: ______________________________

____

Major sources of phosphorus: ______________________________

____

Action taken: ______________________________

____

ISBN: 978-1-897457-80-1

3 The Water Table

People living in areas that do not have sufficient precipitation or surface water rely heavily on groundwater. The levels of water tables affect the amount of groundwater available for human use. In this unit, you will examine the water table and how natural events and human activity affect it.

After completing this unit, you will

- understand what the water table is.
- know that both natural and human factors cause changes in the water table.

Vocabulary

porous rock

impermeable: does not allow something to pass through

saturated: full; unable to hold more

porous: with holes big enough for a substance to pass through

 ISBN: 978-1-897457-80-1

Extension

Try to fill a clear cup with sand and pour some water into it. You will find that the water seeps into the sand and disappears from the surface. However, if you observe the cup from its side, you will see the top level of the water in the sand. Below this level, the water is confined within the impermeable wall and the bottom of the cup, and the sand below this top level is saturated with water.

Did you know that water in nature is trapped underground in a similar way?

A. Fill in the blanks to complete the paragraph with the help of the diagram.

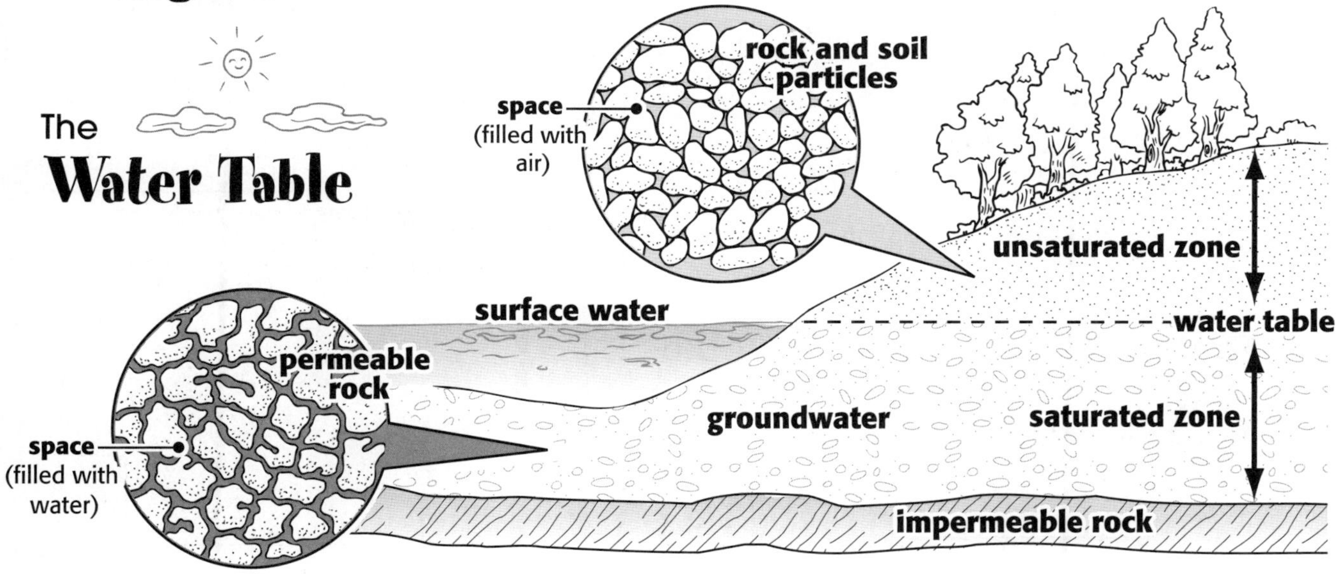

Water which has soaked through the ground from the last rainfall, last winter's snowmelt, or which has been trapped underground for thousands of years is called 1.____________ . 2.____________ rock and 3.____________ between particles of rock and soil allow surface water to penetrate until it reaches a layer of 4.____________ rock. A water table is the upper surface of the 5.____________ zone, where all the space between rock and soil particles are filled with 6.____________ .

ISBN: 978-1-897457-80-1

B. Label the diagram. Identify the factors that cause a water table to rise and fall. Then write "N" for natural factors and "H" for human factors in the boxes.

saturated zone unsaturated zone water table surface water impermeable rock	• heavy rainfall • persistent drought • lake seepage • groundwater mining • structural change in soil due to construction	• bottled water industry • inefficient showers and toilets • melted snow and glaciers • removal of deep-rooted trees

1.

a. ______

b. ______

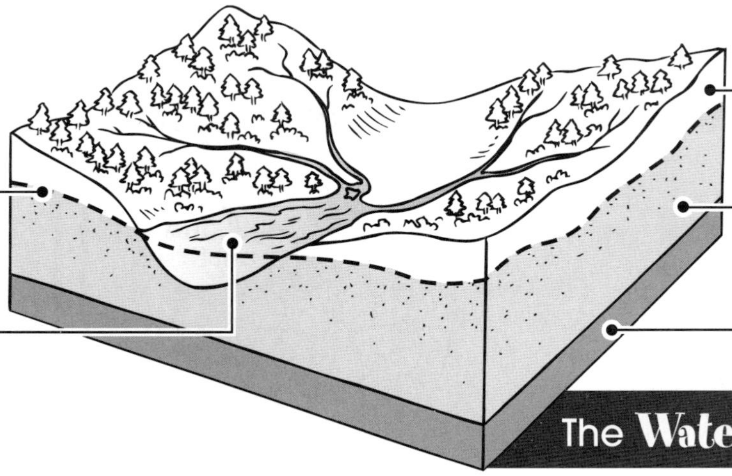

c. ______

d. ______

e. ______

The Water Table

2. **Factors Affecting a Water Table**

Rises due to...

- ______ ☐
- ______ ☐
- ______ ☐
- ______ ☐

Falls due to...

- ______ ☐
- ______ ☐
- ______ ☐
- ______ ☐
- ______ ☐

 ISBN: 978-1-897457-80-1

C. Read the paragraph. Then answer the questions.

An underground storage of water is called an aquifer. Aquifers can be found all over the world. People have been tapping groundwater off these underground reservoirs using wells since long ago. Did you know that the oldest known well dates back to 8100 BCE? In the past, water from aquifers was much cleaner and safer for drinking than surface water because as water seeped through the soil to aquifers, many pollutants were filtered out. However, nowadays, many aquifers have been polluted and water from these aquifers has become unsafe for drinking. Agricultural chemicals, such as fertilizers and pesticides, landfills, leaking oil tanks, and accidental spills are some sources of pollution.

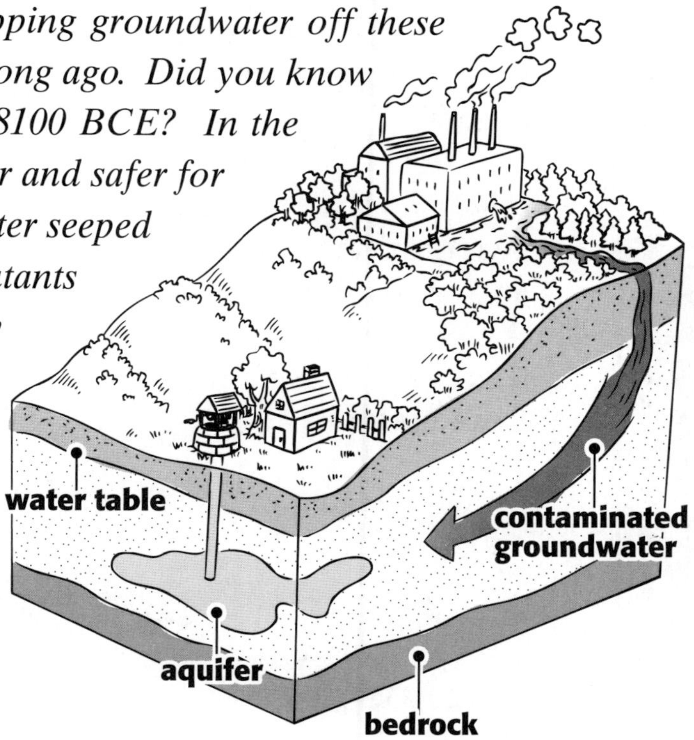

1. What is an aquifer?

   ____

2. Why was water from aquifers cleaner and safer for drinking than surface water in the past?

   ____

   ____

3. What causes the pollution of aquifers?

   ____

   ____

4. Write one more source of pollution besides those mentioned in the paragraph.

   ____

Experiment

Introduction

Most of all the water on Earth is salt water in the oceans. Since salt water is not drinkable, we rely on the processes of evaporation, condensation, and precipitation, that is, the water cycle to ensure that we have drinkable fresh water.

Hypothesis

Fresh water can / cannot be obtained from salt water.

Steps

1. Place the bowl in the centre of the box.
2. Pour water into the box around the bowl until it reaches about 2 cm below the bowl's height.
3. Remove the bowl and add salt to the water. Stir until the salt dissolves.
4. Place the bowl back in the centre of the box.
5. Cover the box loosely with plastic wrap.
6. Secure the plastic wrap with string.

Materials

- *a plastic box*
- *a plastic bag*
- *a heavy bowl*
- *plastic wrap*
- *ice cubes*
- *tap water*
- *salt*
- *a string*
- *a spoon*

ISBN: 978-1-897457-80-1

7. Put the ice cubes in the plastic bag and seal.
8. Place the bag of ice cubes on the plastic wrap directly above the bowl.
9. Let the box sit in the sun for 2 hours.

Result

Describe what happened at different stages of your experiment with the words – evaporation, condensation, precipitation, liquid, and gas.

Beginning: ____________________

____

After 1 hour: ____________________

____

After 2 hours: ____________________

____

Conclusion

The hypothesis was: ____________________

____

My experiment ____________________ the hypothesis.
supported/did not support

ISBN: 978-1-897457-80-1

4 Glaciers and Polar Ice Caps

Glaciers and polar ice caps hold most of the fresh water on Earth. They play an important role in the water cycle and affect both local and global water systems. In this unit, you will look at the characteristics of glaciers and polar ice caps, and examine the effects of the changes they go through.

After completing this unit, you will

- know some of the characteristics of glaciers and polar ice caps.
- understand the factors that affect the size of glaciers and polar ice caps.
- understand the effects of changes in glaciers.

Vocabulary

glacier: large mass of accumulated ice on land that moves slowly downhill due to its own weight

polar ice caps: ice that covers large areas of land in the polar regions

ISBN: 978-1-897457-80-1

Extension

Icebergs are huge pieces of ice from fresh water floating in the sea. They are ice pieces that broke off from glaciers and polar ice caps. As the density of ice is just slightly lower than the density of sea water, only a small part of an iceberg, about one-seventh to one-tenth of its total volume, is visible above the water. Icebergs are generally 1 to 75 metres above sea level, but how big and how deep their bottom portions can reach is hard to predict, which makes them extremely dangerous to ships.

A. Fill in the blanks with the given words to complete the descriptions.

Glaciers and Polar Ice Caps

equator
polar
downhill
size

All glaciers and polar ice caps are dynamic; they change in ______________ seasonally or over years.

Glaciers

- They move slowly ______________ and outwards in all directions due to their own weight.
- They can be found in different parts of the world, even near the ______________ .

Polar Ice Caps

- They cover both ______________ regions.

B. Look at the picture clues to write the climatic factors that affect the size of glaciers and polar ice caps. Then fill in the blanks.

1. 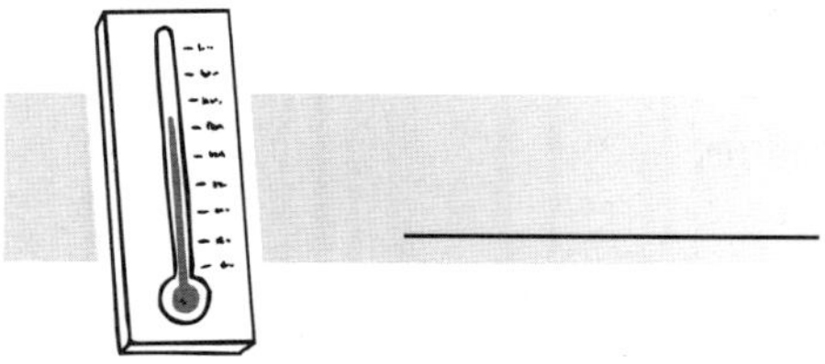 ____________

As it increases, ice size decreases; as it decreases, ice size ____________ .
increases/decreases

2.  ____________

With more of it, ice size increases; with less of it, ice size ____________ .
increases/decreases

C. Complete the flow chart to show the cause and effect of glacier change.

flooding fresh water disappear warmer hydroelectric rivers lakes

The
Cause and Effect of
Glacier Change

1. ____________ than average temperatures cause glaciers to melt faster.

Too much water supply at once causes 2. ____________ .

The glacier gets smaller and smaller and may eventually 3. ____________ .

4. ____________ and 5. ____________ that have the glacier as their water source have diminished water supply.

Living things that depend on 6. ____________ lose their water supply.

Water flows for 7. ____________ power plants is diminished.

ISBN: 978-1-897457-80-1

D. Read the paragraphs. Then answer the questions.

The geological history of the Earth includes long periods of low temperatures – low enough that ice caps were ice sheets that reached far past the Arctic and Antarctic circles, and glaciers very likely covered the land that we now inhabit.

The process of the growth and establishment of glaciers is known as glaciation. An ice age is a geological period of major glaciation. Evidence of glaciation can be seen in smoothed mountains and boulders, as well as moraines, which are accumulations of silt to boulder-sized rock deposits. These deposits were rock and soil picked up by a glacier as it advanced, and got transported and deposited as the glaciers retreated and melted.

Lake Louise, Alberta

1. Why might the place where you live now be covered by glaciers in the past?

____

____

2. Write about each term.

glaciation: ____________________

____

____

moraines: ____________________

____

____

3. Write 1 to 3 to show the formation of a moraine.

Rock and soil are deposited and accumulated as the glacier retreats and melts. (A)

Rock and soil are picked up by a glacier. (B)

Rock and soil move along with the glacier as it moves downhill. (C)

5 Water Systems and Climate

A large body of water influences the condition of the atmosphere around it. In this unit, you will examine the effect of a large body of water on the climate of an area.

After completing this unit, you will

- understand that large bodies of water affect atmospheric conditions.
- understand that the effects of large bodies of water on atmospheric conditions contribute to climate and weather patterns.

Vocabulary

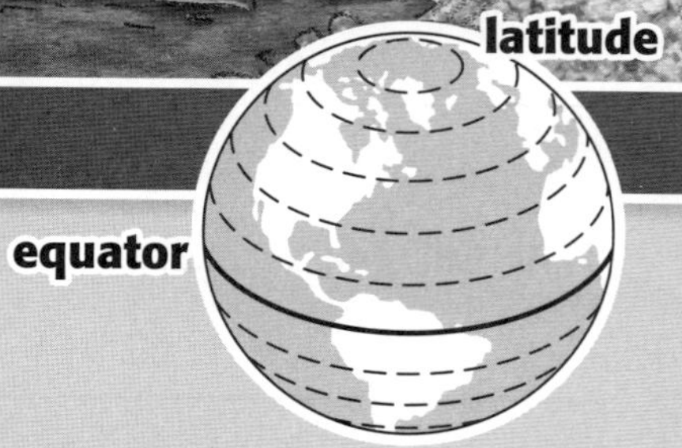

latitude: imaginary horizontal line that indicates distance from the equator

topography: features of a landscape

ISBN: 978-1-897457-80-1

Extension

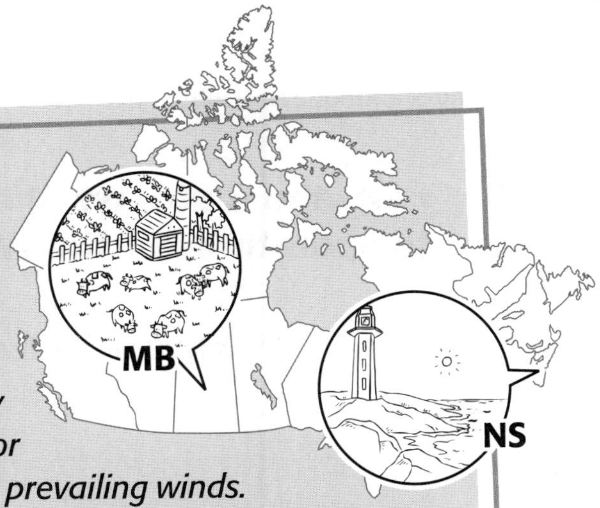

Canada is such a big country that it spans the North American continent from east to west. In a country this big, it would not be a surprise to know that different provinces and territories have very different climates. The climate of each province or territory is affected by its latitude, topography, and prevailing winds. Whether or not it is near a large body of water also makes great differences to its climatic conditions.

Can you think of some climatic differences between a coastal Atlantic province, like Nova Scotia, and a Prairie province, like Manitoba?

A. Fill in the blanks to complete the descriptions and show the factors affecting air temperature.

longer　extreme　Prince Rupert　slower　mild　Winnipeg

1. While water heats up and cools down at a a. ____________ rate than land, water holds onto its absorbed heat b. ____________ than land.

 **Continental Climate**

c. ____________ temperatures

e.g. d. ____________, Manitoba

 **Marine Climate**

e. ____________ temperatures

e.g. f. ____________, British Columbia

2. Factors that affect **Air Temperature**:

-  large bodies of a. ____________
-  b. ____________ mountains and plains
-  prevailing c. ____________
-  d. ____________

latitude
water
topography
winds

ISBN: 978-1-897457-80-1

B. Plot the data on the graph to compare the average daily temperatures of the two cities. Then answer the questions.

1. ***Average Daily Temperature***

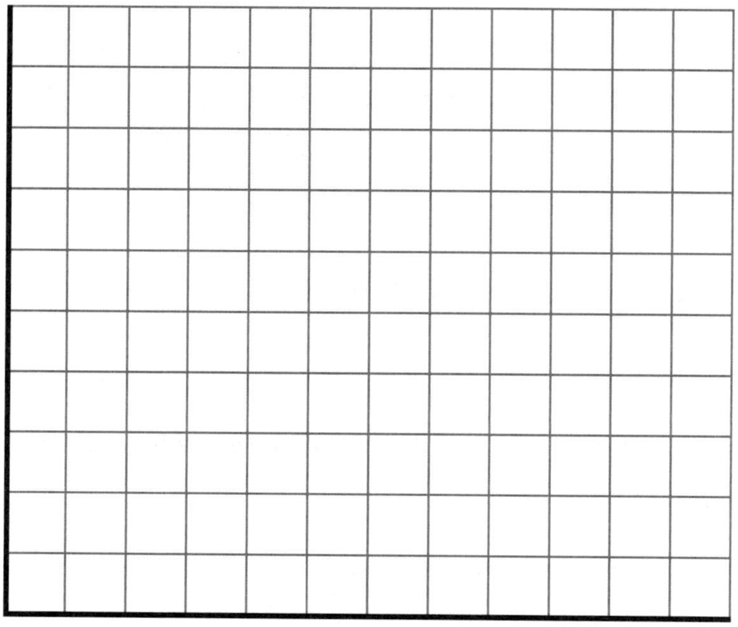

Average Daily Temp.	City A	City B
Jan	3°C	-18°C
Feb	5°C	-14°C
Mar	7°C	-6°C
Apr	9°C	4°C
May	13°C	12°C
Jun	15°C	17°C
Jul	17°C	20°C
Aug	18°C	19°C
Sep	15°C	12°C
Oct	10°C	5°C
Nov	6°C	-5°C
Dec	4°C	-14°C

2. Find the range* of the average daily temperatures of each city.

City **A**: ____________

City **B**: ____________

**range:* *the difference between the greatest and smallest numbers in a set of data*

3. Determine the city that has a "continental" or "marine" climate. Then write the characteristic of each climate.

City **A**: ____________ climate; ______________________________

City **B**: ____________ climate; ______________________________

4. Which city would be Vancouver, BC? Why?

____

____

ISBN: 978-1-897457-80-1

C. Read the paragraph. Complete the diagram with the words in bold and draw arrows to show the wind direction. Then answer the questions.

The prevailing winds – winds that blow most frequently across a region – in Canada are westerly winds. They are winds that blow from the west. A westerly wind from the Pacific Ocean is laden with moisture when it reaches the west coast of Canada. It is forced to rise on the ***windward*** *side (the side of a mountain facing the wind) of the Canadian Rockies, and moisture in the wind is lost through precipitation. The wind then descends on the other side (the* ***leeward*** *side) of the Rockies and becomes dry and warm. This wind is known as a Chinook, and can bring to places east of the Rockies what seems like a summer day even in the middle of winter.*

1. **Westerly Wind**

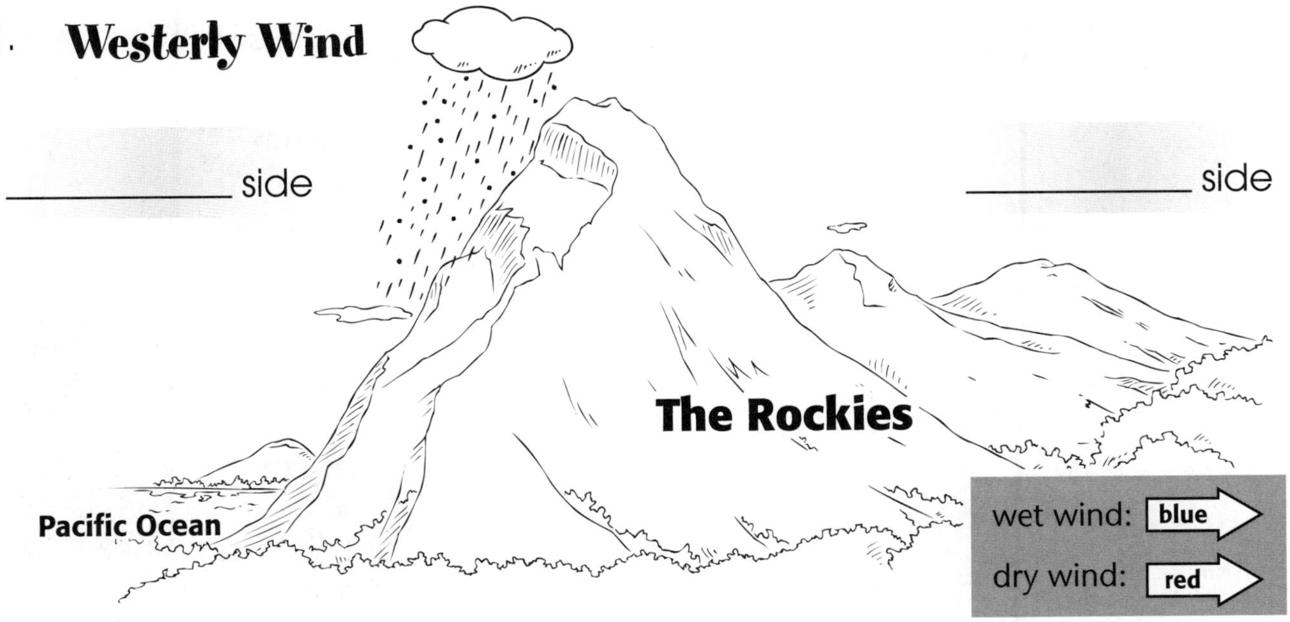

2. What is a Chinook?

____

____

3. Why does the western side of the Rockies receive more precipitation than the eastern side?

____

____

____

ISBN: 978-1-897457-80-1

6 Society and Water Systems

We have many uses for water, but the most important is the one that sustains our lives: drinking. In this unit, you will examine some issues regarding the delivery of the valuable resource, that is, our water supply.

After completing this unit, you will

- know some issues regarding local water supplies.
- understand how fresh water is treated to become potable water for citizens.
- understand how the use of water and other activities in a community affect local water supplies.

Vocabulary

sedimentation: process of depositing sediment

potable: drinkable for humans

desalinate: separate salt from water

fluoridate: add fluoride

ISBN: 978-1-897457-80-1

Extension

Since water is crucial to life and it affects us in many ways, there are many jobs and branches of science that are related to water. Here are three of them.

Glaciologists

- *take samples of ice from deep inside a glacier to understand more about the period of time the ice formed*
- *study how glaciers move*

Water Treatment Plant Operators

- *test water at every stage of water treatment*
- *add necessary chemicals to water*

Oceanographers

- *study the behaviour and happenings of oceans*
- *work with scientists from other branches of science*

Can you name one more job that is related to water and describe its work?

A. Circle the correct words to show what a community has to consider about its water supply.

Different places have different water supply issues, but the goal of every community is the same: to provide a continuous supply of potable water for its citizens.

What to Consider about Water Supply:

1. how to **measure / desalinate** sea water
2. how to control water **weight / pressure**
3. what type of **reservoir / well** to store it
4. where the waste water is **sold / discharged**
5. whether or not to **boil / fluoridate** the water
6. how to **distribute / obtain** water to households
7. how to **treat / consume** waste water

ISBN: 978-1-897457-80-1

B. Fill in the blanks. Then circle the correct words to show how water is processed.

wells | rural | distributing | cities

Residents of 1.__________ communities in Canada usually pump water right out of the ground from 2.__________ . People living in 3.__________ have water filtered before 4.__________ it to them for use.

Processing Water

1. Fresh water from a water source is screened to **add / remove** large particles.
2. Chemicals are added to water in a **tank / aquarium** to make small particles clump together.
3. Sedimentation occurs with the clumps of particles settling on the **left / bottom** of the tank.
4. The remaining tiny solids are removed when the water passes through a **door / filter** .
5. Chlorine, and sometimes **oxygen / fluoride** , is added to the filtered water.
6. The water is distributed to homes and businesses in the community through **pipes / streams** .
7. Water is flushed or drained to a **food / sewage** treatment plant.
8. The treated water is returned to the **natural / human-made** environment.

ISBN: 978-1-897457-80-1

C. Read the headlines and look at the pictures. Describe how each activity affects water supply.

How Each Activity Affects Water Supply:

A ______________________________

____

B ______________________________

____

C ______________________________

____

D ______________________________

____

Experiment

Introduction

> *The rise in global temperatures causes many icebergs and glaciers to melt. How does the melting of these huge ice masses affect the sea level?*

Hypothesis

Fill in the blanks with "raises", "lowers", or "does not affect".

The melting of icebergs ____________ the sea level, while the melting of glaciers ____________ the sea level.

Materials

- *a large glass*
- *a large container*
- *water*
- *a big, flat rock*
- *ice cubes*
- *tape*

Steps

Experiment 1 **(melting of icebergs)**

1. Fill the glass with as many ice cubes as you can fit.
2. Fill the glass with water right to the top.
3. Let the glass sit until all the ice cubes have melted.
4. Observe the water level and check the result.

ISBN: 978-1-897457-80-1

Experiment 2 (melting of glaciers)

1. Put the flat rock in the container and add water to about 1 cm below the rock's surface.
2. Mark the water level with a piece of tape.
3. Place some ice cubes on the rock.
4. Let the ice cubes melt and note the water level again.

Result

Experiment 1

◯ The water overflew after the ice cubes had melted.

◯ The water level stayed the same after the ice cubes had melted.

Experiment 2

◯ The water level rose after the ice cubes had melted.

◯ The water level stayed the same after the ice cubes had melted.

Conclusion

The hypothesis was: ______________________________

____

My experiment ______________________________ the hypothesis.
supported/did not support

ISBN: 978-1-897457-80-1

This review consists of five sections, from A to E. The marks for each question are shown in parentheses. The circle at the bottom right corner is for the marks you get in each section. An overall record is on the last page of the review.

A. Write T for true and F for false.

1. Water holds onto its absorbed heat longer than land. **(2)** ______

2. Altitude and air pressure determine which state water is in. **(2)** ______

3. There is only one river in a watershed. **(2)** ______

4. A marine climate has extreme temperatures while a continental climate has mild temperatures. **(2)** ______

5. 

   97% of the water on Earth is salt water; the remaining 3% is fresh water available for human use. **(2)**

   ______

6. 

   Glaciers can be found in places near the equator. **(2)**

   ______

12

ISBN: 978-1-897457-80-1

B. Do the matching.

1. 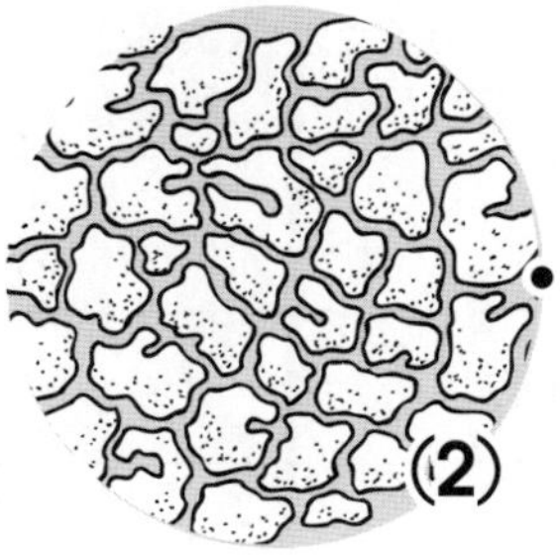

(2)

2. 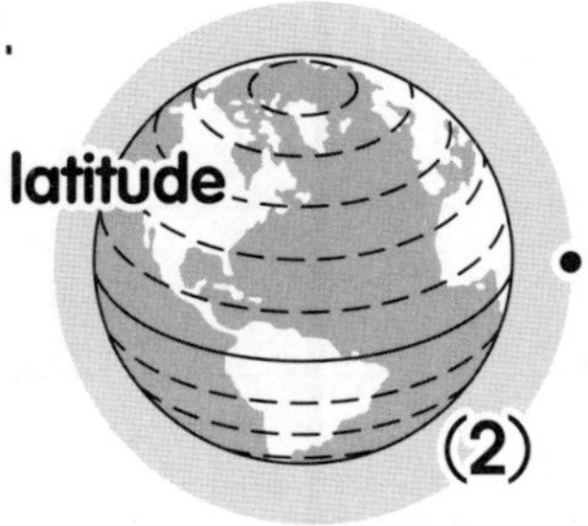

(2)

3. 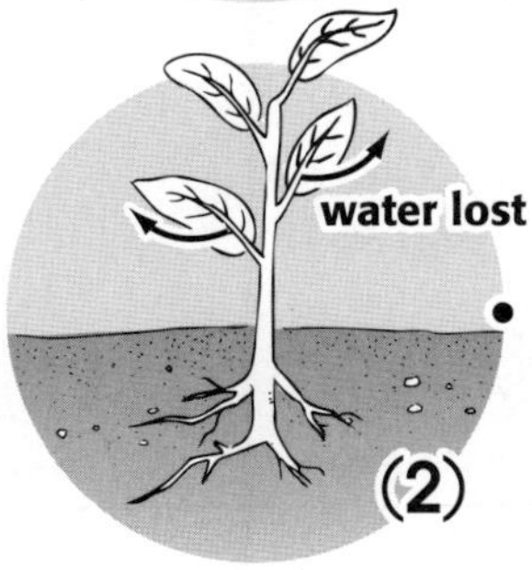

(2)

4. 

(2)

5. 

(2)

6. 

(2)

- people living in rural areas use this to get groundwater
- a province where there is a continental climate
- rock that allows water to penetrate
- one of the factors that determines air temperature
- ice size increases with more of it
- the evaporation of water from living things

12

ISBN: 978-1-897457-80-1

C. Label the diagram. Then answer the questions.

river	groundwater
stream	precipitation
lake	water divide

(12)

1.

A Watershed

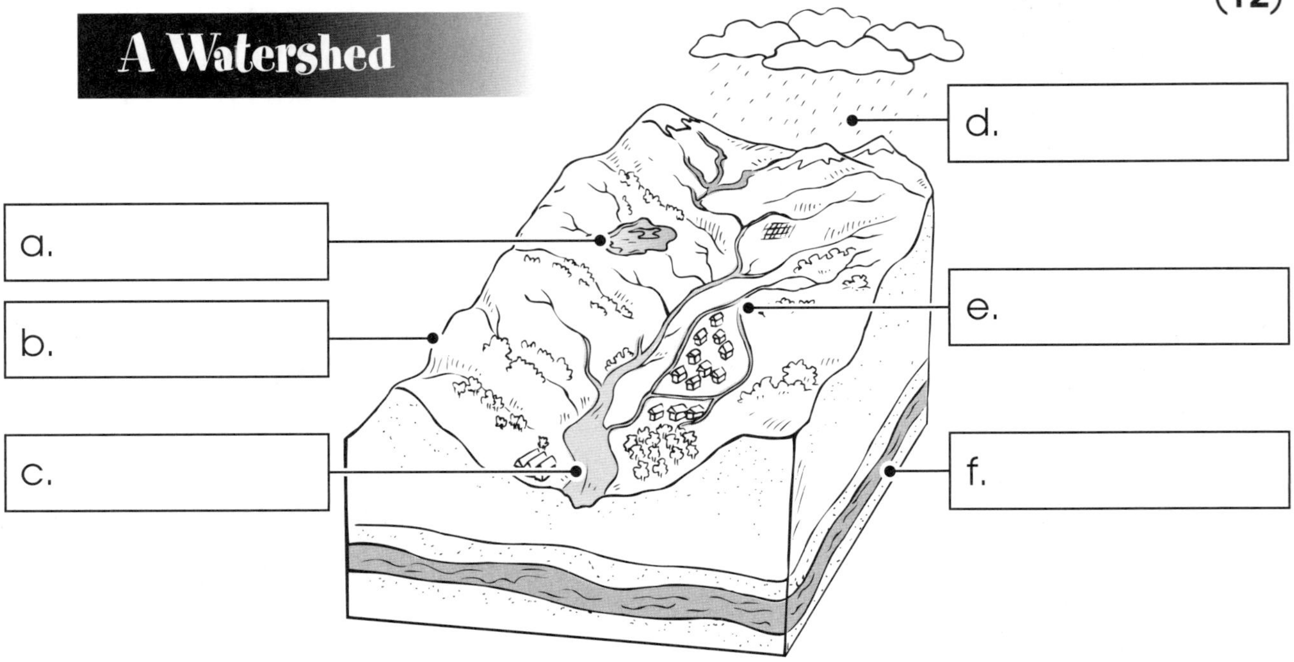

2. Explain these terms. **(6)**

watershed: ______________________________

____

water divide: ______________________________

____

3. Can groundwater be found in the saturated zone or unsaturated zone? What is the feature of that zone? **(4)**

____

____

4. Write the four types of human activities that affect the water in a watershed. **(4)**

____

____

____

26

ISBN: 978-1-897457-80-1

D. Label the diagram. Then answer the questions.

1.

saturated zone unsaturated zone water table surface water impermeable rock

(10)

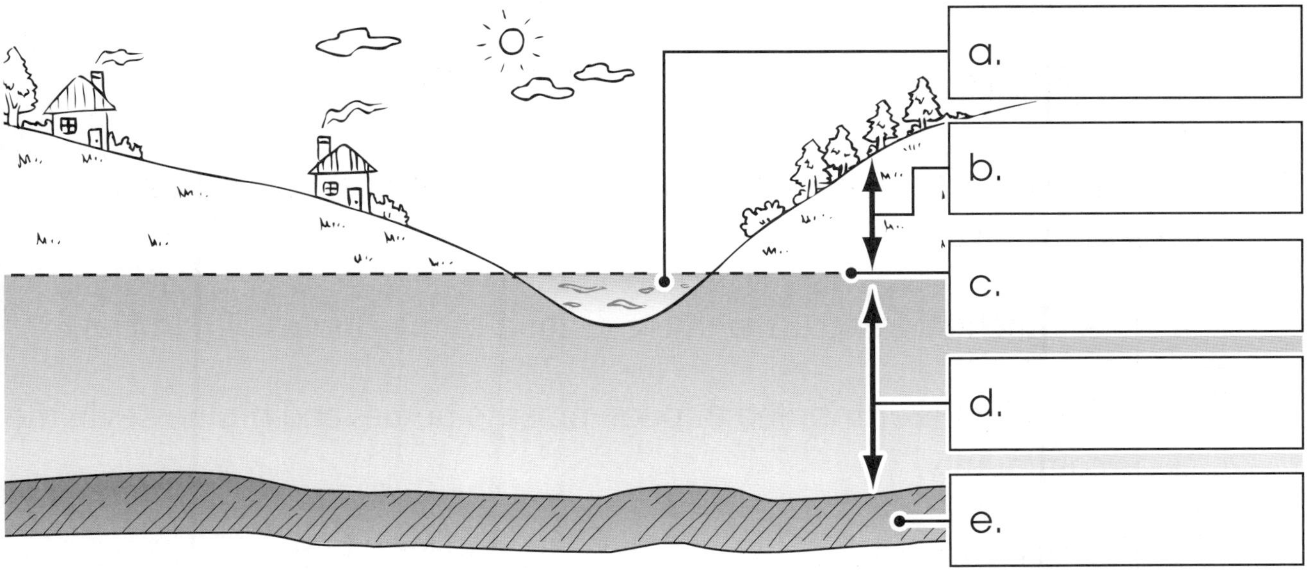

2. The residents want to build a well close to their houses. Draw to show where and how deep the well should be. Describe the water level in the well. **(4)**

____

3. It is found that the glacier in the mountain is melting. Write one cause and one effect of glacier change. **(4)**

cause: ______________________________________

effect: ______________________________________

4. As the glacier melts, what happens to the water table? Besides the melting of glaciers, write two more factors that cause the same change to the water table. **(6)**

____

____

24

ISBN: 978-1-897457-80-1

E. Answer the questions.

1. Check the factors that affect air temperature. **(8)**

   (A) latitude
   (B) groundwater
   (C) government policies
   (D) prevailing winds
   (E) topography
   (F) large bodies of water

2. Number the sentences to show how water is processed in a community. **(10)**

   ☐ Sedimentation occurs with the settling of the clumps of particles.

   ☐ The water is distributed through pipes to homes and businesses in the community.

   ☐ Water is drained to a sewage treatment plant and the treated water is returned to the natural environment.

   ☐ The remaining tiny solids are removed with a filter and chlorine or fluoride is added to the filtered water.

   ☐ Fresh water from a water source is screened to remove large particles and then chemicals are added to make small particles clump together.

3. Number the sentences to show the journey of water starting from precipitation. **(8)**

   ☐ Evaporation occurs in water bodies and transpiration takes place in living things.

   ☐ Water becomes water vapour and then condenses to form clouds.

   ☐ Water from precipitation falls directly to water bodies, and some infiltrates into the ground to become groundwater.

   ☐ With increased weight, water droplets fall back to the Earth as precipitation.

26

ISBN: 978-1-897457-80-1

My Record

	Score
Section A	/12
Section B	/12
Section C	/26
Section D	/24
Section E	/26

Total /100

80-100

Great work! You really understand your science stuff! Research your favourite science topics at the library or on the Internet to find out more about the topics related to this section. Keep challenging yourself to learn more!

60-79

Good work! You understand some basic concepts, but try reading through the units again to see whether you can master the material! Go over the questions that you had trouble with to make sure you know the correct answers.

below 60

You can do much better! Try reading over the units again. Ask your parents or teachers any questions you might have. Once you feel confident that you know the material, try the review again. Science is exciting, so don't give up!

ISBN: 978-1-897457-80-1

Scientists at Work

The Oceanographer

The oceans have significant effects on the biosphere. Oceanic evaporation is the source of most rainfall, and ocean temperatures determine climate and wind patterns that affect life on land. Ocean currents also affect the Earth's climate. They transfer heat from the tropics to the polar regions, and move warm or cold air and precipitation to coastal regions, where winds may carry them inland.

Thanks to oceanographers, we now know more about oceans and how they affect our lives. Oceanographers are scientists concerned with the physics, maths, chemistry, biology, and geology of the oceans. They observe and measure currents, tides and circulation, rocks under the sea, plants and animals, and how the sea and the atmosphere interact. They study how human activity and new developments at sea affect the environment, and they also research into things like improving weather forecasts, safe ways to dispose of waste, or how to harness the ocean as a source of renewable energy.

Because of the nature of their work, oceanographers often have to spend long stretches of time away at sea, sometimes in cramped conditions and in arduous weather conditions. However, most oceanographers view fieldwork as motivational, challenging, and exciting.

ISBN: 978-1-897457-80-1

Cool Science Facts

ISBN: 978-1-897457-80-1

1. What is hard water and soft water?

2. Is drinking water in Canada hard water or soft water?

3. Why do people find hard water a nuisance?

4. Where does the water over Niagara Falls come from? Where does it go?

Find the answers on the next page.

Cool Science Facts

1

All water, except distilled water, contains dissolved minerals, such as calcium and magnesium. Water with a high dissolved mineral content is known as hard water whereas water with a relatively low dissolved mineral content is soft water.

2

Drinking water in the prairie provinces, with groundwater as the main source, is hard water with very high contents of calcium and magnesium, while drinking water on the west coast, with glaciers and snowmelts as the main sources, is soft water with a very low mineral content.

ISBN: 978-1-897457-80-1

3 Hard water is a nuisance to people in many ways. The amount of minerals in water affects the amount of soap and detergent needed for cleaning. The minerals in water may combine with soap or detergent to form sticky soap curds. If sticky soap curds are left on our skin, it may cause irritation. In addition, hard water does harm to our hot water systems. Heated hard water forms a scale of minerals that builds up in hot water tanks and pipes, just as it does inside a kettle. The hot water pipes may be clogged as a result.

4 The water over Niagara Falls comes from four of the five Great Lakes – Lakes Superior, Michigan, Huron, and Erie. From Niagara Falls, water flows down the Niagara River, merges with the water of Lake Ontario, and then flows into the St. Lawrence River located in northeast Canada. There, fresh water eventually flows north into the Atlantic Ocean.

ISBN: 978-1-897457-80-1

ISBN: 978-1-897457-80-1

Answers

ISBN: 978-1-897457-80-1

Answers

Section 1

1 Postulates of the Cell Theory

A. 1. growth 2. respiration
3. movement 4. reproduction
5. feeding 6. excretion
7. sensitivity

B. Postulate 1: more
Postulate 2: unit
Postulate 3: cells
1. microscope 2. cells
3. living things 4. structure
5. functions 6. pre-existing
7. division 8. F
9. T 10. F

C. A: All cells come from pre-existing cells.
B: The cell is the basic unit of function in living things.
C: All living things are made up of one or more cells.

D. 1. C 2. B
3. A 4. A

E. 1. Zacharias Janssen
2. compound light microscope
3. 1663
4. Robert Hooke
5. bark
6. first
7. 1674
8. Anton van Leeuwenhoek
9. cell
10. light microscope
11. Charles-François Brisseau de Mirbel
12. continuous
13. 1824
14. Henri Dutrochet
15. cell
16. 1838
17. Theodor Schwann
18. Matthias Jakob Schleiden
19. cell products
20. Rudolph Virchow
21. other living cells

2 Parts of the Cell

A. 1a. cell membrane
b. encloses c. protects
d. cytoplasm e. membrane
f. nucleus g. chromosomes
h. controls
2. cell membrane, cytoplasm, nucleus

B. 1. nucleus 2. mitochondrion
3. ribosome 4. lysosome
5. golgi apparatus
6. endoplasmic reticulum
7. cytoplasm 8. cytosol
9. nucleus 10. energy
11. nucleus, mitochondrion, ribosome, lysosome, golgi apparatus, endoplasmic reticulum

C. 1. light microscope ; see ; parts ; A
2. electron microscope ; destroyed ; smaller ; organelles ; B
3a. light microscope
b. electron microscope
c. electron microscope

D. 1a. rotating nosepiece
b. objective lenses ; most
c. stage clips ; slide
d. diaphragm ; light
e. light source f. eyepiece ; eye
g. arm h. stage
i. coarse focus knob ; big
j. fine focus knob ; small
k. base
2. C
3. It uses light and multiple lenses to see cells.
4. diaphragm

ISBN: 978-1-897457-80-1

3 Animal Cells and Plant Cells

A. 1a. Animal b. cell membrane
c. nucleus d. cytoplasm
2a. Plant b. cell membrane
c. nucleus d. cytoplasm

B. 1.

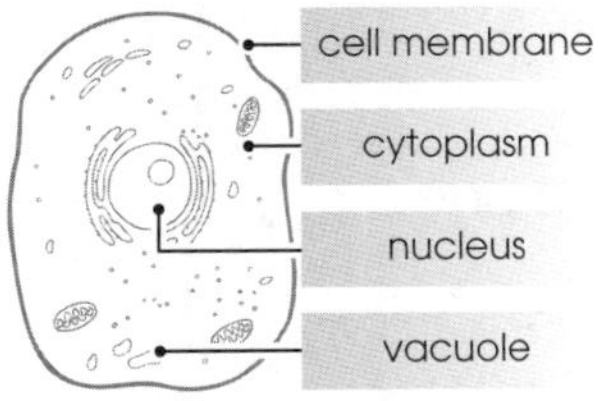

Check: nucleus ; cytoplasm ; cell membrane ; vacuoles: small

2.

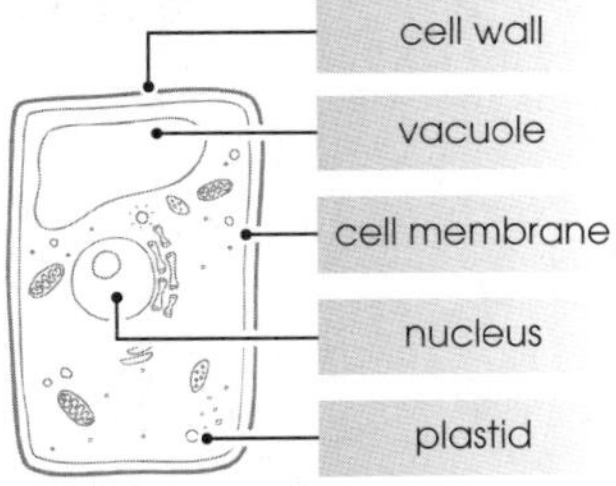

Check all. ;
vacuoles: large ; chloroplasts: green

3. A plant does not have a bony skeleton. The cell wall, which is just outside the cell membrane, supports the plant.

C.

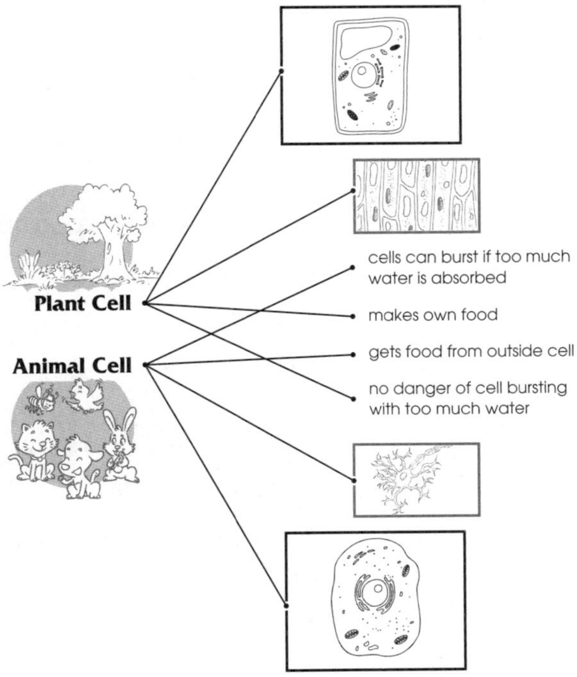

D. 1. Neurons ; Nerve ; to carry messages through the body
Check: cell membrane ; nucleus

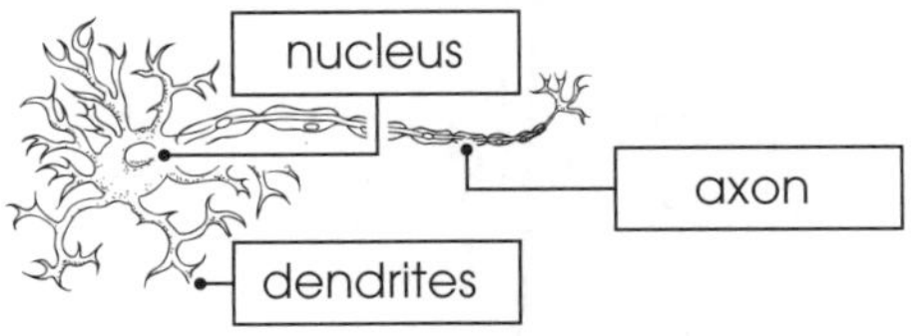

2. Muscle ; to contract, to stretch, and snap back into shape ; long and fibre-like

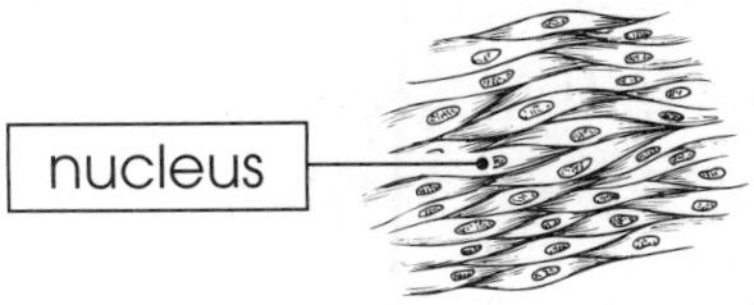

Check: cell membrane, nucleus

3. Red Blood ; to deliver oxygen to the body ; partially concave disc shape
Check: cell membrane
Cross out: nucleus

Experiment

(Individual experiment outcome)

4 Diffusion and Osmosis

A. 1. contents 2. out
3. substances 4. permeability
5. water 6. diffusion
7. osmosis 8. permeable
9. impermeable

B. 1. substance ; high ; low
2. A: B:

Check: C ; E
G: (Individual example)

ISBN: 978-1-897457-80-1

C. diffusion ; membrane
1. water 2. sugar
3. low 4. concentration
5. out

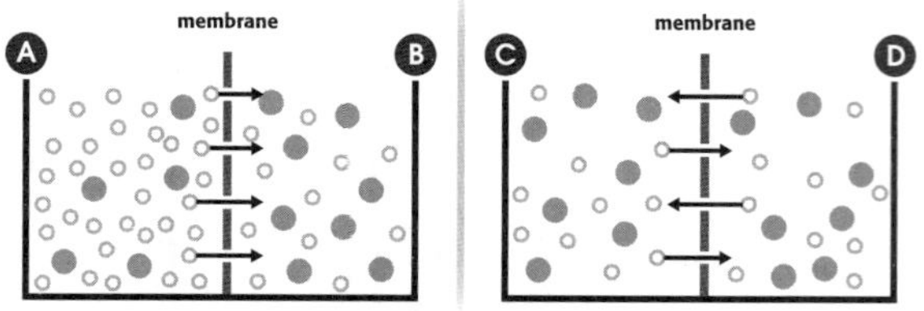

A has a high concentration of water and B has a low cocentration of water. ;
C and D have equal concentration of water.

D. 1. (Suggested examples)
heated ; cooked steak
frozen ; frozen fillet
smoked ; smoked chicken
chemically treated ; preserved canned fish

2. It is because salt and sugar kill micro-organisms. Their presence creates a lower concentration of water outside the cells of micro-organisms than inside their cells; osmosis then occurs, drawing water out of the micro-organisms until they are no longer functional.

The Cell of a Micro-organism

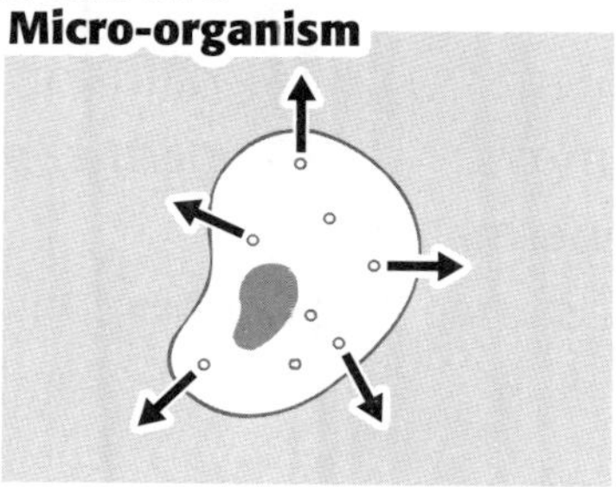

3.

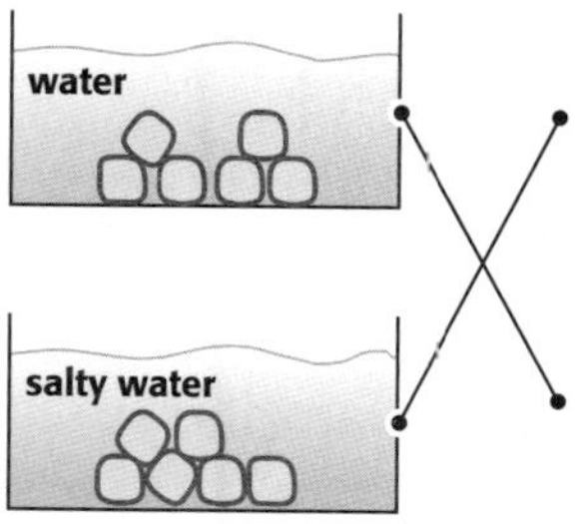

The potatoes will become softer than before.

The potatoes will become harder than before.

5 Unicellular and Multicellular Organisms

A. 1a. more b. one cell
2a. multicellular b. multicellular
c. unicellular d. multicellular
e. unicellular f. unicellular

B. 1. diffusion 2. Oxygen
3. carbon dioxide
4.

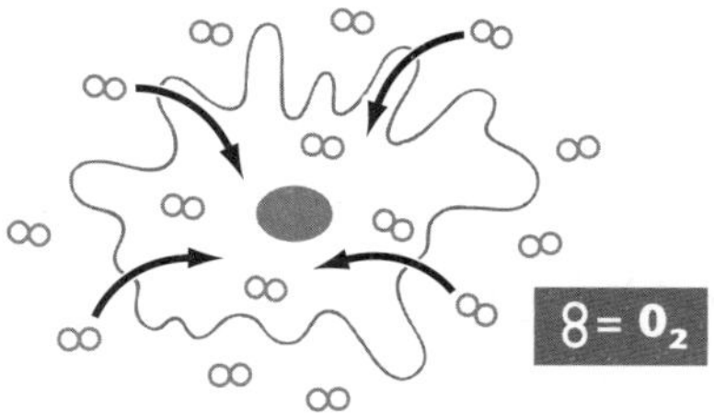

into

5.

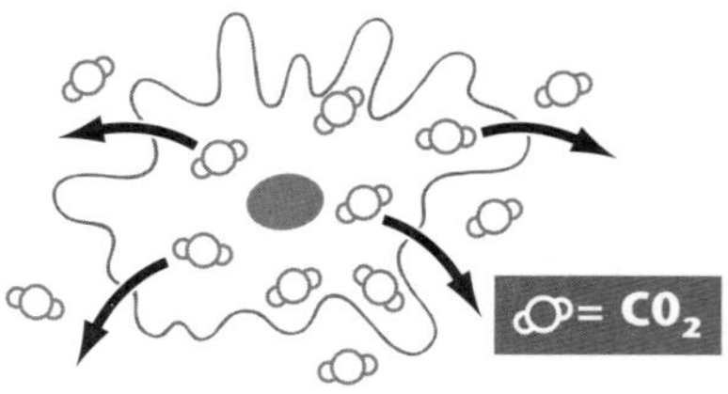

out of

C. 1. make 2. chloroplasts
3. photosynthesis
4. eat ; 1 ; 4 ; 2 ; 3

D. 1. shape 2. food
3. invader 4. locomotion
5. watery 6. spiral
7. tail 8. propel
9. Amoebae ; cytoplasmic streaming
10. Euglena ; flagellum
11. Paramecia ; cilia

E. 1. **Viruses:**
Size: 250
Life Processes: inside ; dormant
Reproduction: inside a living cell
Parts: three ; genes ; protein coat ; lipid envelope
Bacteria:
size: 1000
Life Processes: are

ISBN: 978-1-897457-80-1

Reproduction: independent of another organism
Parts: cell membrane ; cytoplasm ; nucleus

2a. T	b. F	c. F
d. T	e. T	f. F

6 Cells in Multicellular Organisms

A. 1. tissue ; 2 2. cells ; 1
3. organism ; 5 4. organ system ; 4
5. organ ; 3

B. 1. cell ; A ; E 2. tissue ; B ; G
3. organ ; C ; J 4. organ system ; D ; F
5. organism ; H ; I

C. 1. muscle 2. nervous
3. connective 4. epithelial

D. (Individual examples)
1. stomach 2. brain
3. bones 4. Muscular
5. Respiratory 6. Circulatory

E. 1a. mouth ; breaks food down into small pieces
b. esophagus ; pushes food pieces down to the stomach
c. stomach ; breaks down food with gastric juice
d. small intestine ; absorbs nutrients from food
e. large intestine ; absorbs water from the waste product
f. rectum ; stores solid waste

2a. 3 to 7 m b. 2.5 to 3 cm
c. epithelial d. folded
e. villi
f. the small intestine's surface area
g. more

Experiment

(Individual experiment outcome)

Review

A. 1. F	2. F	3. T
4. F	5. T	6. F

B. 1.
2.
3.
4.
5.
6.

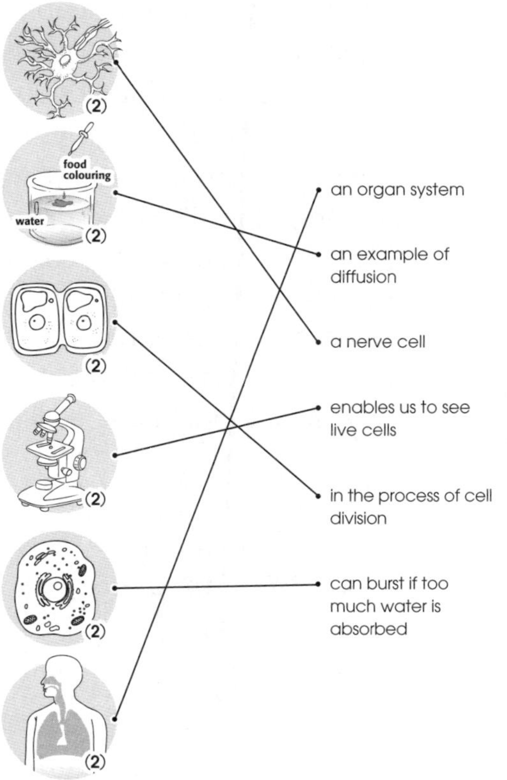

C. 1. All living things are made up of one or more cells. ;
The cell is the basic unit of function in living things. ;
All cells come from pre-existing cells.
2. Plant ;
a. cell wall ; provides structure for the plant
b. vacuole ; provides shape and stores food
c. cell membrane ; encloses and protects the cell
d. nucleus ; contains all of the cell's information
e. plastid ; makes food for the cell
3. (Suggested answer)
It has a cell wall and a large vacuole in proportion to its size.
4. cell membrane, cytoplasm, nucleus

ISBN: 978-1-897457-80-1

D. 1. A: high ; low
B: low ; high
2. The membrane is permeable to water molecules and impermeable to sugar molecules.
3. Osmosis occurs on either side of a cell's selectively permeable membrane.
4. When the water molecules are in high concentration, they are drawn to the side where there is a low concentration of water molecules. When the concentration is equal on both sides of the membrane, the water molecules move in and out at an equal rate.
5.

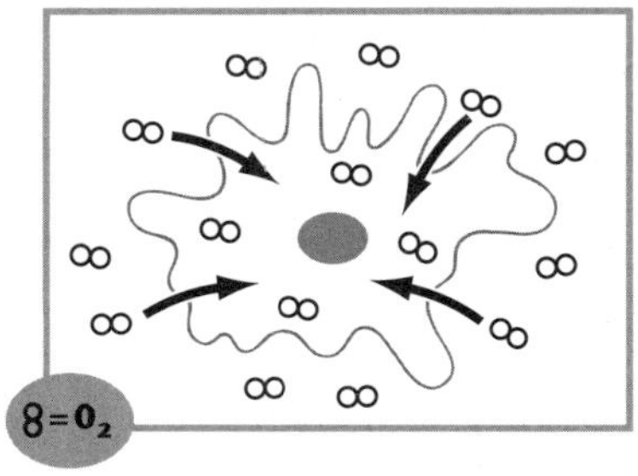

An amoeba gets oxygen from the outside through diffusion.

E. 1. A: mitochondrion ; controller of energy
B: endoplasmic reticulum ; canal that carries substances through the cytoplasm
2. Euglena are unicellular organisms. They contain chloroplasts to make their own food through photosynthesis.
3. (Suggested features)
A: light microscope ; allows us to see live cells
B: electron microscope ; cells and their organelles are visible
4. Cells make up tissue, which makes up an organ. Organs work together to make up an organ system and all organ systems make up an organism.

Section 2

1 Systems

A. 1. together 2. more
3. nature 4. subsystems
5. subsystem 6. system

B. (Individual examples)
1. digestive ; natural
components: esophagus ; stomach
2. ecosystem ; natural
components: trees ; lion
3. education ; human-made
components: school ; student
4. solar ; natural
components: Earth ; sun
5. electrical ; human-made
components: electricity ; wires

C. 1. land transportation:
subway ; horses ; cars ; buses ; railways ; trains ; bicycles
air transportation:
gliders ; hot-air balloons ; runways ; helicopters ; airplanes ; airports
water transportation:
lighthouses ; ships ; canoes ; cruise ships ; freighters ; locks ; barges ; ferries
2. land transportation ; air transporation ; water transportation
3. (Suggested answer)
road

D. 1a. screen b. aeration tank
2. ❶ Large objects are removed as the sewage passes through the screen.
❷ In the aeration tank, bacteria eat and digest the pollutants in the water.
❸ Any dirt that remains is filtered out here.
❹ Chlorine is added to disinfect the water.
3. The three components are: bacteria, air, and the aeration tank.

ISBN: 978-1-897457-80-1

4. The water would not be completely disinfected and would pollute the surface water.

2 More about Systems

A. existing ; achieves
   1. health ; illness
   2. factory ; goods
   3. political ; affairs
   4. hydraulic ; less
   5. gear ; speed

B. input ; output
   1. oxygen ; respiratory system
   2. night light ; light
   3. hydroelectric plant ; electricity
   4. ingredients ; cookies
   5. plant ; oxygen

C. **Septic System:**
purpose: to treat waste water and sewage
components: toilets ; sinks ; bathtubs ; drains ; drain pipes ; septic tank ; distribution box ; septic field
inputs: waste water ; sewage
output: clean water

Computer System:
purpose: to store and manipulate data
components: monitor ; tower ; mouse ; keyboard ; printer
input: data
output: processed information

D. 1. keyboard 2. microphone
3. electric guitar 4. input
5. mixer 6. amplifier
7. computer 8. output
9. CD 10. input
11. CD player 12. speaker system
13. output

3 Systems in Action

A.

Energy — the capacity to do work
- the capacity to do work
- something that helps you stay awake

Force — a push or pull that causes movement or stress on an object
- all of the police officers in the city
- a push or pull that causes movement or stress on an object

Work — the effort it takes to cause an object to move or change shape
- the effort it takes to cause an object to move or change shape
- what we do to make money

Efficiency — the ratio of useful work to the amount of energy it takes to do the work
- being organized
- the ratio of useful work to the amount of energy it takes to do the work

B. A: Yes, work is being done because effort is needed to move carbon dioxide out of the body.
B: No, no work is being done because the effort does not cause the wheelbarrow to move.
C: Car B is more efficient because it travels a longer distance than car A with the same amount of gas.
D: Peter exerted more force because his pull force causes Tom to move forwards.
E: Jim needs more energy because a trolley has less capacity to do work than a truck.

C. A: amount B: efficiency
C: safety D: ergonomic
E: necessary
D ; C ; E ; B ; A

D. 1. 2009 ; 1990 ; 1983 ; 2002
   a. A new cellphone offers greater efficiency.
   b. A new cellphone often has a more modern appearance.
2. Old cellphones should be disposed of in the recycling drop box in an electronics store or at a local Household Hazardous Waste Depot.

ISBN: 978-1-897457-80-1

3. Toxic Chemicals:
   be extracted and put into a secure landfill where they will not leak ; be recycled into new batteries
   Non-toxic Chemicals:
   plastics can be recycled to make CD cases or computer parts ; metals can be used in jewellery or industrial products

Experiment

Observational Studies: can ; cannot
(Suggested hypothesis)
As the number of factories increases, the number of smog alerts also increases.

4 Work and Mechanical Advantage

A. 1a. force b. newtons
c. pull d. push
2a. work b. joules
Check: A

B. 1. force ; distance
2. 300 x 10 = 3000 ;
3000 J of work is done.
3.

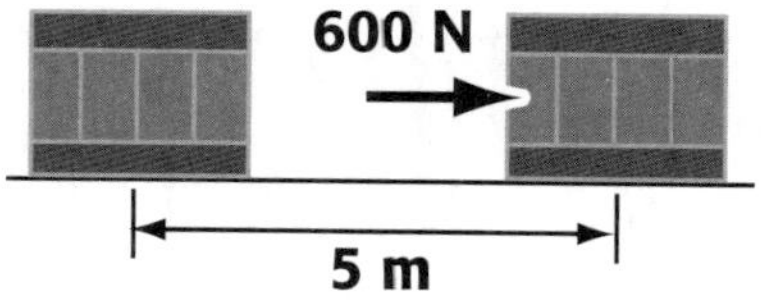

600 x 5 = 3000 ;
3000 J of work is done.

4.

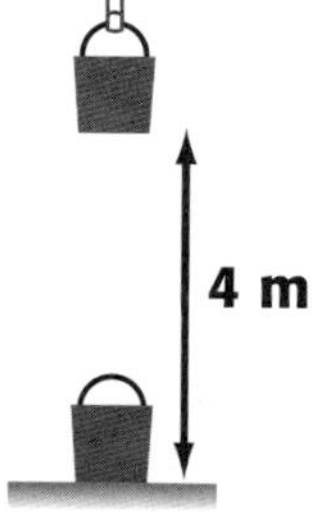

800 ÷ 4 = 200 ;
200 N of force was applied.

5.

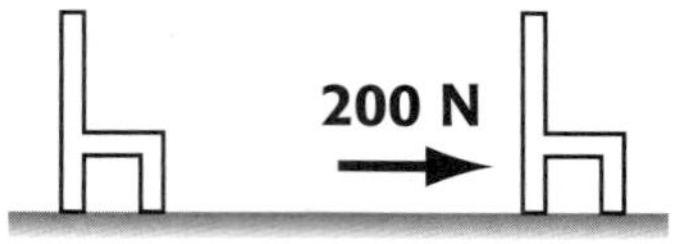

1000 ÷ 200 = 5 ;
The chair was moved 5 m across.

C.

$$\text{Mechanical Advantage (MA)} = \frac{\text{output force}}{\text{input force}}$$

1. $\frac{4000}{80} = 50$; 50
2. $\frac{600}{5} = 120$; The input force is 120 N.
3. $\frac{1000}{200} = 5$; The MA is 5.
4. 35 x 4 = 140 ; The maximum size of the load is 140 N.

D. Worried Musician:
MA = 2 ÷ 1 = 2
MA = 4 ÷ 1 = 4
4-m ; greater so the 4-m board should be used.
Taking a Rest:
MA = 100 ÷ 100 = 1
MA = 150 ÷ 50 = 3
Place the ball right next to the box because it gives the lever a greater MA.
Lucky Painter:
A: 2
B: 4
Use pulley system B because it has a greater MA.

5 Mechanical Systems and Heat

A. 1. contact 2. thermal
3. energy 4. friction
5. compression 6. fluid resistance

B. 1. heat ; friction
2. slow it down ; fluid resistance

ISBN: 978-1-897457-80-1

3. compression ; compression
4. friction ; friction

C. 1. B　　2. A　　3. E
4. C　　5. D

D. 1a. coal – chemical ; steam – thermal ; turbine – mechanical ; electrical
b. heat energy
c. about 55%
2. Heat loss may occur when valves open to release steam; if the pipes holding steam or water are not well insulated; and when moving parts heat up due to friction.
3. (Individual example)
Check: computer ; air conditioner ; tap ; our body ; kettle

6 Systems and Society

A. 1. hot water　　2. pulp mush
3. screens　　4. bleaching agent
5. water　　6. dries

B. (Suggested descriptions)
1. A ; to direct aircraft to prevent collisions
2. C ; to check out items for consumers
3. B ; to allow for communication globally without long wires
4. D ; to provide clients of a bank with access to financial transactions without a bank teller
5. E ; to provide transportation services by air, land, and water

C. (Suggested answers)
1. 1 ; 2 ; 3　　2. 3 ; 1 ; 2
3. 3 ; 1 ; 2　　4. 2 ; 1 ; 3
5. 2 ; 1 ; 3　　6. 1 ; 3 ; 2

D. 1. Check: A ; B ; D
the build up of a biofilm formed by bacteria or algae, which is commonly found on anything immersed in water for a period of time.
2. Biofouling poses problems in the aquaculture industry because biofouling blocks nets, making it difficult for water to flow through.
3. Nets are cleaned frequently so that they are free of blockages and allow water to flow through, which is essential for the healthy growth of the raised fish.
4. dip nets in copper paint ;
The lifetime of the copper coating is limited and the application costs are high.

Experiment

(Individual experiment outcome)

Review

A. 1. F　　2. T　　3. F
4. F　　5. F　　6. T

B.
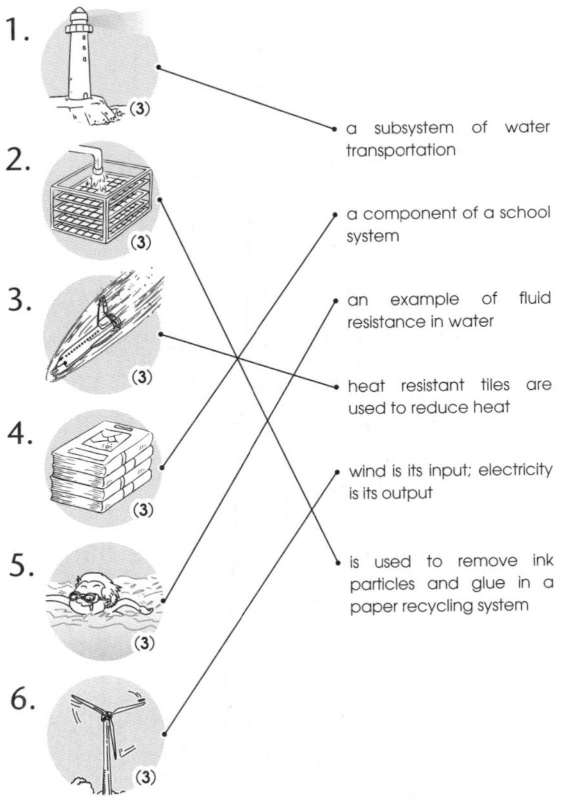

ISBN: 978-1-897457-80-1

C. 1. Method 1:
250 x 0.8 = 200 ;
200 J of work is done.
Method 2:
150 x 1.2 = 180 ;
180 J of work is done.
Method 3:
250 x 0.8 = 200 ;
200 J of work is done.
2. Method 2 would be the best because it requires the least amount of force and the least amount of work to do the same job.
3. 180 ÷ (1.2 x 2) = 75 ;
The force applied is 75 N.

D. 1. The MA of a machine is the ratio that shows how many times the machine multiplies the input force. A MA greater than 1 means that the machine can multiply the input force.
Check: B
2. $\frac{1800}{400} = 4.5$
The MA is 4.5.

3. $\frac{2475}{4.5} = 550$
The input force is 550 N.

3a. 200 x 2.5 = 500 ;
500 N of output force lifts the load.
b. Friction generates heat. Reducing friction by using lubricants can reduce the amount of heat generated.

E. 1. human-made
2. (Suggested answers)
to alert user to possible danger and notify the control centre which determines whether or not further assistance is needed
a. door sensor ; motion sensor ; wireless network ; police department
b. motion ; sound
3. It sounds an alarm when smoke is detected.
4. The required assistance may not be provided immediately.

Section 3

1 Fluids and Viscosity

A. 1. flow 2. shape
3. rate 4. thickness
5. friction 6. resistance
7. move
greater

B. (Individual predictions)
Experiment 1:
(Suggested result)
Result: vinegar ; maple syrup ; chocolate syrup ; honey ; ketchup
Conclusion: Ketchup
Experiment 2:
Result: The candy in the warm honey reaches the bottom first.
Conclusion: decreases

C. 1. very ; high ; steep
less ; low ; gentle
2. The less viscous the magma is, the more likely it is for volcanic eruptions to take place.

2 Fluids and Density

A. solids ; liquids ; gases ; denser ; denser
> ; > ; <

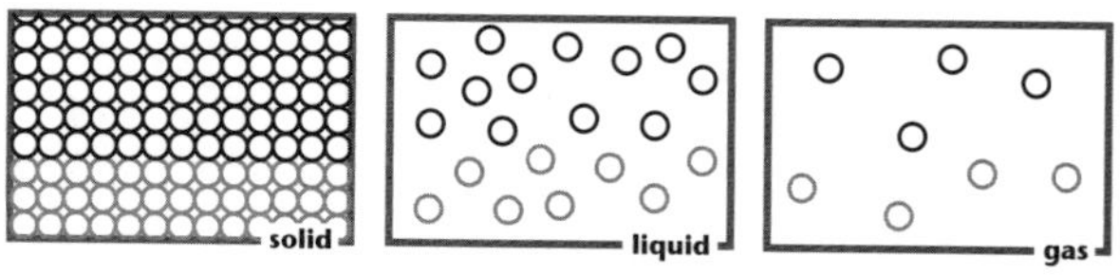

ISBN: 978-1-897457-80-1

B. 1. volume 2. more
3. less 4. mass
5. same 6. ratio

C. A: $\frac{850-50}{400} = 2$ (g/mL)

B: $\frac{850-50}{500} = 1.6$ (g/mL)

C: $\frac{1250-50}{800} = 1.5$ (g/mL)

C ; B ; A

D. 1a. water in its solid state
b. water in its liquid state
Particles in liquid water are more closely packed than particles in the solid state of water.
2. They float because water in the solid ice form is less dense than water in the liquid form.

3 Buoyancy

A. 1. fluid 2. weight
3. displaces 4. =
5. 200 g 6. 400 g

B. 1. fluids 2. force
3. gravity 4. greater
5. density 6. strength
7. difference
8.

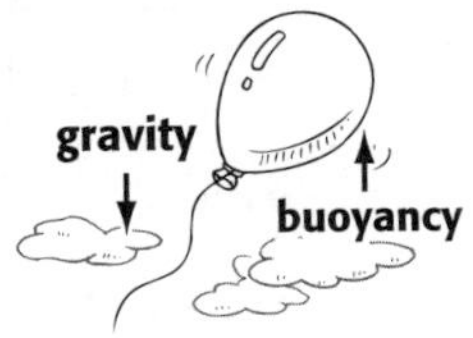

< ; floats

9.

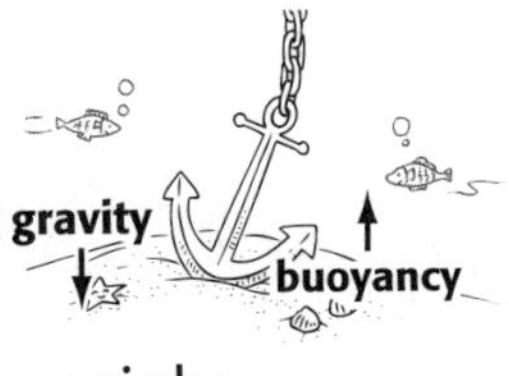

> ; sinks

C. 1.

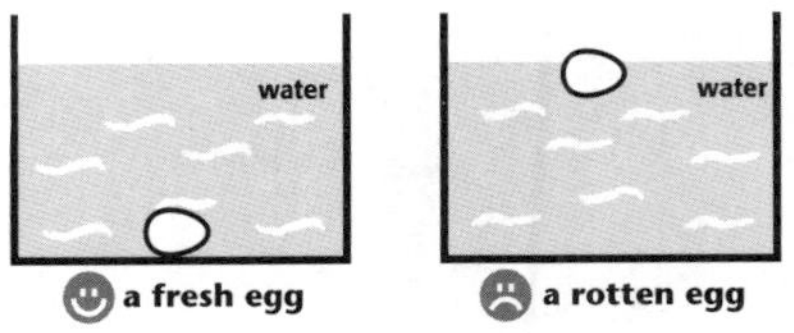

2. As an egg ages, air from outside enters the air pocket of the egg. It becomes less dense than water, so it floats.

3.

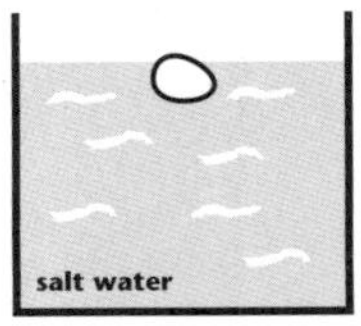

A rotten egg floats on fresh water. Since salt water is denser than fresh water, a rotten egg floats on salt water as well.

Experiment

(Individual experiment outcomes)

4 Compressible Fluids

A. 1. Liquid

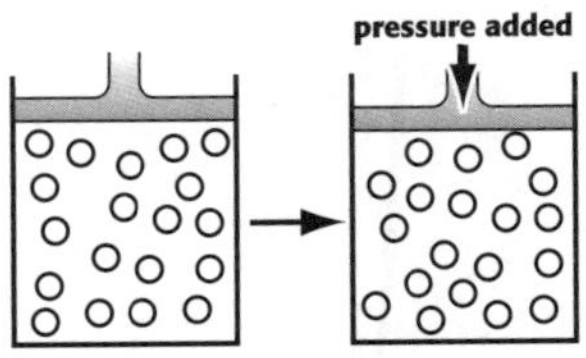

a small ; distance

2. Gas

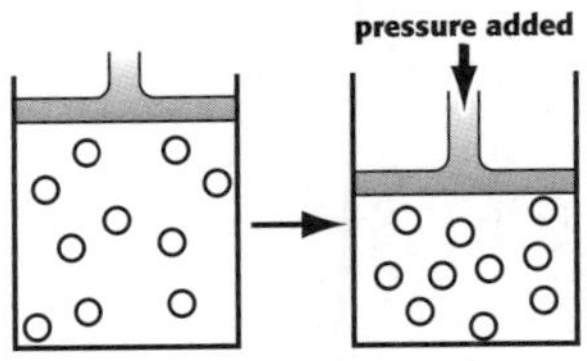

smaller ; decrease

B. 1. hudro — water
pneuma — wind (moving air)

2. fluids ; multiply ; location

3.

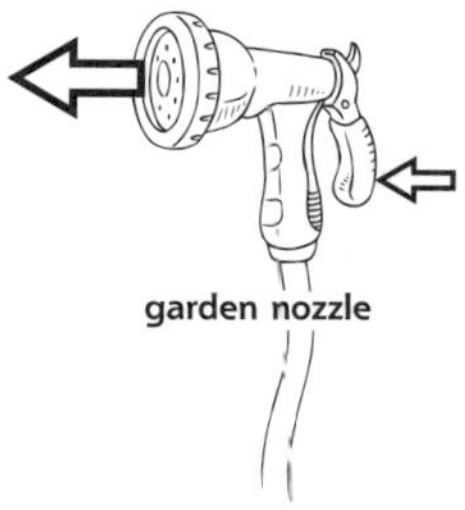

4.

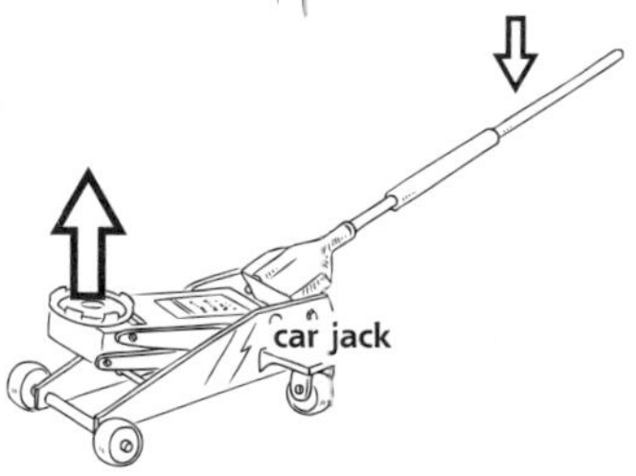

5.

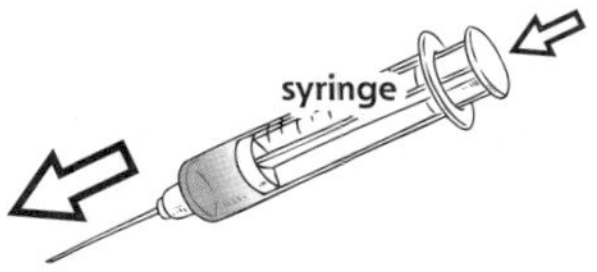

C. 1. A gas has higher compressibility because its particles are farther apart than those of a liquid, so there is more room for compression.
2. Solids are incompressible because their particles are closely packed.
3. A pneumatic system makes use of the compressibility of a gas to magnify an input force so that the output force at another part of the system is much greater.
4. A, C, B

5 Fluids and Pressure

A. 1. pressure 2. confined
3. directions 4. undiminished
5. A 6. B

B. 1. A: force
B: transmitted ; movement
C: pressure ; initial
D: greater
E: load
2. (Suggested answer)
To lift a heavier load, the diameter of the cylinder with the small piston should be reduced.

C. 1. less ; decreased ; pressure
2. rises ; faster ; expands ; more
3. A: The contents in the container are compressed, their volume decreased, and so they exert more pressure.
B: With increased heat, the particles of the contents move faster and expand. An increase in volume exerts more pressure, and so the container may explode.

6 Fluids and Society

A. 1. shape
2. density ; buoyancy
3. flow
4. compressibility

B. C ; A ; D ; B

C. (Suggested negative impacts)
1. D ; E ; affects water quality when spills happen
2. A ; F ; causes noise pollution
3. C ; B ; is often unavailable to everyone

D. 1a. flow restrictor
b. cut-off valve
c. air
2. They can help reduce water consumption.
3. It allows the user to halt the flow of water easily while soaping up.

Experiment

Result:
Circle: is ; is ; increases ; sinks

Review

A. 1. F 2. T 3. F
4. F 5. F 6. T

ISBN: 978-1-897457-80-1

B.

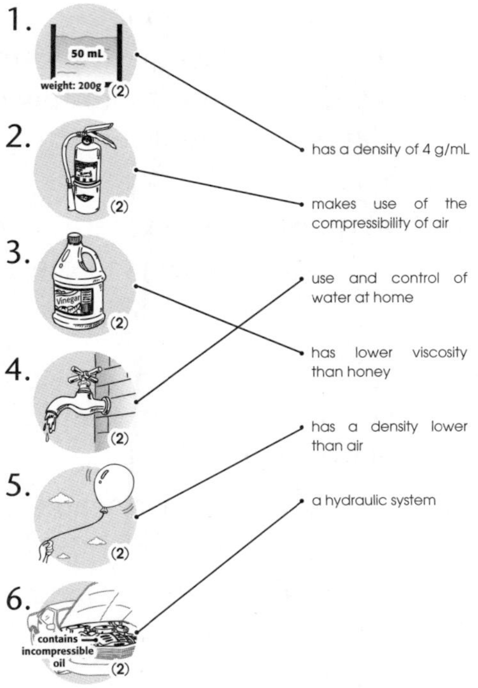

C. 1. rises ; Helium has a lower density than air, so the helium balloon rises in the air.

2. floats ; The ball filled with air is less dense than the water, so the force of buoyancy is greater than the force of gravity and the ball floats.

3. warm ; The viscosity of a fluid decreases with an increase in temperature, so the warm honey is less viscous and the candy sinks to the bottom first.

D. 1. A: $\frac{0.396}{0.2} = 1.98$ (kg/m^3)

B: $\frac{0.16}{0.2} = 0.8$ (kg/m^3)

C: $\frac{0.24}{0.2} = 1.2$ (kg/m^3)

2. A

3. The gas in each container is compressed and its volume decreased.

4. B ; A ; C

Gas A has the greatest density and so the least compressibility, while gas B has the lowest density and so the greatest compressibility.

E. 1a.

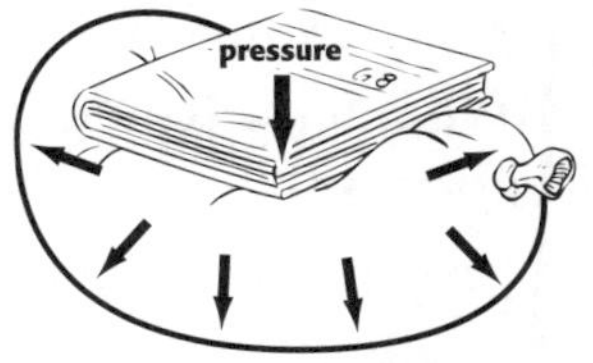

b. Pressure exerted anywhere on a confined fluid is transferred equally in all directions and is undiminished to every point of the fluid.

2a. hydraulic b. small

c. A d. great

e. B

f. When a force is applied to the handle of the car jack, the pressure is transferred through the incompressible oil to the load side. The output force is many times greater than the input force and can lift a heavy car.

Section 4

1 Water on Earth

A. 1. solid 2. liquid
3. gas 4. temperature
5. low 6. ice
7. steam 8. evaporation
9. water vapour 10. altitude
11. height

B. 1. water 2. recycled
3. states 4. evaporation
5. transpiration 6. condensation
7. precipitation 8. surface runoff
9. infiltration 10. groundwater
11a. condensation
b. transpiration
c. surface runoff
d. precipitation e. evaporation
f. infiltration g. groundwater

ISBN: 978-1-897457-80-1

12. Groundwater is fresh water. It comes from rain that gets into the ground through infiltration.
13. Water from precipitation falls directly or finds its way to water bodies through rivers and streams, while some infiltrates into the ground and becomes groundwater. Evaporation occurs in water bodies and transpiration takes place in living things, through which water changes to water vapour and then condenses to form clouds. With increased weight, water droplets fall back to the Earth as precipitation.
14. 1
15. (Suggested examples)
    whale ; water lily ; salmon

2 The Watershed

A. water ; downhill ; network ; surface ; rivers ; high ; ridges ; divides

B. 1. lake 2. water divide
   3. river 4. precipitation
   5. stream 6. groundwater

C. 1. aquatic ecosystems
   2. recreational activity
   3. climate/weather condition in the watershed
   4. land animals and plants ; human population

D. 1. naturally ; household cleaning products, pesticides, and fertilizers
   right amount:
   supports a healthy aquatic ecosystem
   excessive amount:
   causes excessive algae growth, which leads to depletion of dissolved oxygen
   2. One of the main objectives:
   to improve water quality by reducing the loading of phosphorus to the lake
   Major sources of phosphorus:
   effluent from sewage treatment plants, septic systems, stormwater runoff, and airborne dust
   Action taken:
   limiting phosphorus discharges from sewage treatment plants to the lake

3 The Water Table

A. 1. groundwater 2. Permeable
   3. space 4. impermeable
   5. saturated 6. water

B. 1a. water table b. surface water
   c. unsaturated zone
   d. saturated zone
   e. impermeable rock
   2. Rises due to:
   heavy rainfall ; N
   lake seepage ; N
   melted snow and glaciers ; N
   removal of deep-rooted trees ; H
   Falls due to:
   bottled water industry ; H
   persistent drought ; N
   inefficient showers and toilets ; H
   groundwater mining ; H
   structural change in soil due to construction ; H

C. 1. An aquifer is an underground storage of water.
   2. Water from aquifers was cleaner and safer for drinking than surface water because as water seeped through the soil to aquifers, many pollutants were filtered out.
   3. Agricultural chemicals, landfills, leaking oil tanks, and accidental spills cause the pollution of aquifers.
   4. (Individual answer)

ISBN: 978-1-897457-80-1

Experiment

(Individual experiment outcome)

4 Glaciers and Polar Ice Caps

A. size
Glaciers: downhill ; equator
Polar Ice Caps: polar

B. 1. temperature ; increases
2. precipitation ; decreases

C. 1. Warmer 2. flooding
3. disappear 4. Rivers
5. lakes 6. fresh water
7. hydroelectric

D. 1. The Earth underwent long periods of low temperatures when ice caps might have reached far past the Arctic and Antarctic circles.
2. glaciation: the process of the growth and establishment of glaciers
moraines: accumulations of silt to boulder-sized rock deposited by glaciers
3. A: 3 ; B: 1 ; C: 2

5 Water Systems and Climate

A. 1a. slower b. longer
c. extreme d. Winnipeg
e. mild f. Prince Rupert
2a. water b. topography
c. winds d. latitude

B. 1.

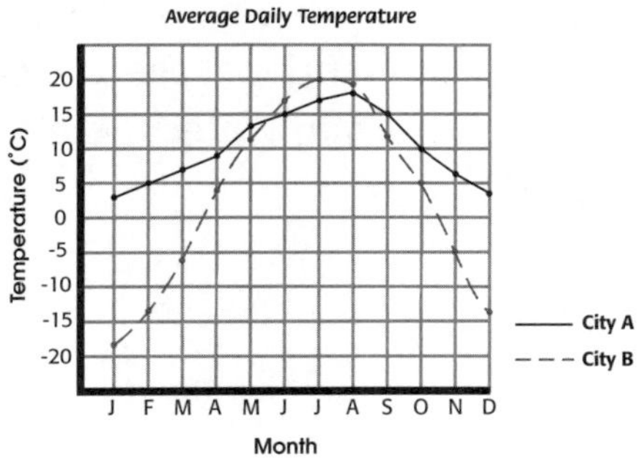

2. 15°C ; 38°C

3. City A: marine ; with mild temperatures
City B: continental ; with extreme temperatures
4. City A, which has a marine climate, would be Vancouver, BC because Vancouver lies on the coast of the Pacific Ocean and so has a marine climate.

C. 1.

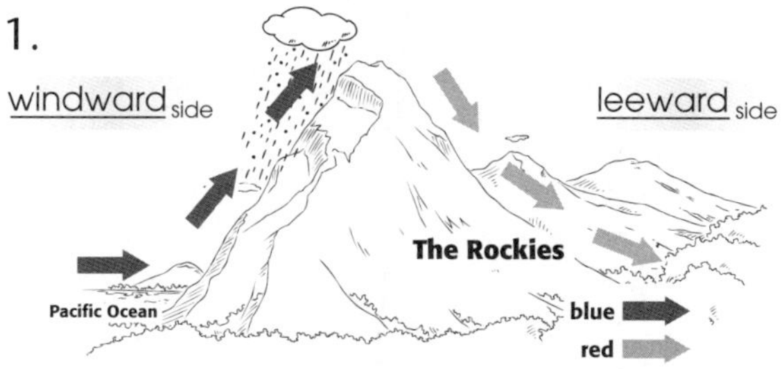

2. It is a westerly wind that descends the leeward side of the Rockies and brings warm and dry weather to places east of the Rockies.
3. The moist wind from the Pacific Ocean is forced to rise and rain on the western side of the Rockies, and it becomes dry and warm when it goes down the eastern side.

6 Society and Water Systems

A. 1. desalinate 2. pressure
3. reservoir 4. discharged
5. fluoridate 6. distribute
7. treat

B. 1. rural 2. wells
3. cities 4. distributing
remove ; tank ; bottom ; filter ; fluoride ; pipes ; sewage ; natural

C. A: The oil spill pollutes the water and leads to a decrease in water supply.
B: The release of chemicals into the water pollutes the water and leads to a decrease in water supply.
C: The dam can store water for local population and regulate water supply.

ISBN: 978-1-897457-80-1

D: Water regulations aim to conserve water in order to ensure adequate water supply for people's basic needs.

Experiment

(Individual experiment outcome)

Review

A. 1. T 2. F 3. F
4. F 5. F 6. T

B. 1. 2. 3. 4. 5. 6.

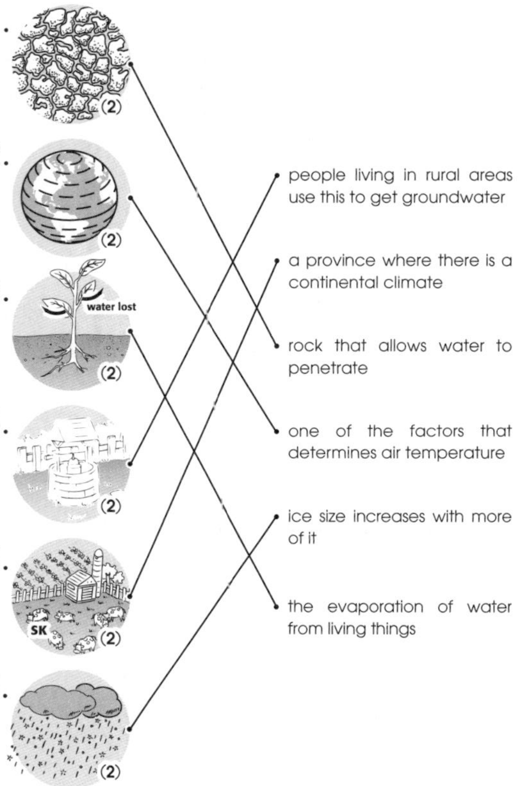

C. 1a. lake b. water divide
c. river d. precipitation
e. stream f. groundwater

2. watershed:
a geographical area within which all water from precipitation and melted ice and snow drains downhill into the same body of water
water divide:
a line that follows the highest geographical parts and separate watersheds
3. Groundwater can be found in the saturated zone, where all the space between rock and soil particles are filled with water.
4. They are industrial activity, agricultural activity, forestry activity, and recreational activity.

D. 1a. surface water
b. unsaturated zone
c. water table
d. saturated zone
e. impermeable rock
2.

The water level in the well is determined by the water table.
3. cause: warm temperature
effect: (Suggested answer) flooding
4. (Suggested factors)
The water table rises. Heavy rainfall and lake seepage are other factors that cause the water table to rise.

E. 1. A ; D ; E ; F
2. 2 ; 4 ; 5 ; 3 ; 1
3. 2 ; 3 ; 1 ; 4

ISBN: 978-1-897457-80-1

TRIVIA Questions

ISBN: 978-1-897457-80-1

ISBN: 978-1-897457-80-1

True or False

When you are sleeping, your brain is taking a rest too.

What percentage of the Earth's oxygen does the Amazon Rainforest produce?

A. about 5%

B. about 20%

C. about 70%

In which body of water can you stay afloat most easily?

A. the ocean

B. a pool

C. a lake

True or False

Hot springs are too hot for any organisms to live in them.

ISBN: 978-1-897457-80-1

Answer:

B. about 20%

Answer:

false

When you are sleeping, the brain processes memories.

Answer:

false

Some species of micro-organisms are commonly found in hot springs. They can survive in temperatures even above 100°C.

Answer:

A. the ocean

Due to the salt content in the ocean, its water has a higher density than the water in pools and lakes.

ISBN: 978-1-897457-80-1

About how much water will a faucet that drips once every minute waste in a year?

A. 13 litres

B. 130 litres

C. 1300 litres

True or False

Extracting energy from biomass is a recently developed practice.

True or False

Phytoplankton produce half of the oxygen we breathe.

What is the world record of the fastest temperature change?

A. 7°C in 2 minutes

B. 17°C in 2 minutes

C. 27°C in 2 minutes

ISBN: 978-1-897457-80-1

Answer:

false

People in prehistoric times already burned wood, a kind of biomass, for light and heat.

Answer:

B. 130 litres

Every 4000 drips make 1 litre, so about 130 litres of water will be wasted in this case.

Answer:

C. 27°C in 2 minutes

On January 22, 1943 in South Dakota, the U.S.A., a Chinook wind brought a sudden rise in temperature from -20°C at 7:30 a.m. to 7°C at 7:32 a.m.

Answer:

true

Phytoplankton are small plant-like organisms that live in the ocean. Like plants, they absorb carbon dioxide and produce oxygen.

ISBN: 978-1-897457-80-1

What is the shape of a raindrop?

A. roughly spherical
B. the shape of a teardrop
C. both A and B

Where can we find most bacteria in our body?

A. digestive system
B. nervous system
C. circulatory system

True or False

Volcanic eruptions can trigger lightning.

True or False

The colour and shape of the nails can tell the health problems one might have.

ISBN: 978-1-897457-80-1

Answer:

A. digestive system

Most of these bacteria are beneficial to us. They help digest food, absorb nutrients, and break down waste.

Answer:

C. both A and B

Raindrops are roughly spherical when they form in the atmosphere due to the surface tension of water. Then gravity pulls them to the shape of teardrops when they fall.

Answer:

true

The state of your nails can help doctors spot health problems including respiratory, circulatory, and skin problems.

Answer:

true

In the last two centuries, more than 150 volcanic eruptions were accompanied by spectacular lightning.

ISBN: 978-1-897457-80-1

True or False

The Earth is the only planet in the solar system where lightning takes place.

How acidic is acid rain?

A. as acidic as stomach acid
B. as acidic as lime juice
C. as acidic as tomato juice

What causes bad breath?

A. dying cells on the tongue
B. bacteria in the mouth
C. saliva

Can spiders spin webs in space?

ISBN: 978-1-897457-80-1

Answer:

C. as acidic as tomato juice

Answer:

false

Lightning also occurs on some other planets, like Jupiter and Neptune.

Answer:

Yes, they can.

Spiders were sent to space to test their web spinning skills, and the result was that they could do so, though the webs were not quite the same as those on Earth.

Answer:

B. bacteria in the mouth

Odour-producing bacteria accumulate on the food left in the mouth and between the teeth.

ISBN: 978-1-897457-80-1

True or False

A sunflower seed is not a seed but a fruit.

If you could drive 100 km/h in a straight line from the Earth's surface to the centre, how long would it take?

A. about 10 hours

B. about 64 hours

C. about 6 days

Why were the outer concrete surfaces of the two towers of Toronto City Hall designed to be ribbed?

A. to give a more distinctive look

B. to counteract the effect of erosion

C. to prevent the damage due to the expansion of the surfaces

True or False

Rock particles in clay are so small that they do not contain any minerals.

ISBN: 978-1-897457-80-1

Answer:

B. about 64 hours

The average distance from the Earth's surface to the centre is about 6400 km.

Answer:

true

Sunflower seeds are a type of dry fruit. They are not seeds at all.

Answer:

false

Rock is made up of one or more minerals, no matter how big or small it is.

Answer:

C. to prevent the damage due to the expansion of the surfaces

Since the towers are curved outwards, if the exterior surfaces were not ribbed, the materials could be easily ripped and damaged due to expansion.

ISBN: 978-1-897457-80-1

True or False

The bigger a star is, the longer its lifespan.

How old was the oldest seed to grow into a plant?

A. 25 years old

B. 500 years old

C. 2000 years old

What was the wingspan of the largest prehistoric dragonfly?

A. 5 cm | B. 20 cm
C. 75 cm | D. 200 cm

At what temperature is water the densest?

A. -4°C

B. 4°C

C. 40°C

Answer:

C. 2000 years old

A 2000-year-old date palm seed was found in Israel and planted in 2005. It grew into a healthy plant and is still living.

Answer:

B. 4°C

Water is less dense at temperatures colder or warmer than 4°C.

Answer:

false

Very massive stars can exist for thousands of years while small stars can exist for billions of years.

Answer:

C. 75 cm

Prehistoric insects were much larger than they are today.

ISBN: 978-1-897457-80-1

True or False

Mount Everest is the highest mountain not only on Earth but also in the solar system.

What is the most abundant metal on Earth?

A. aluminum

B. gold

C. silver

The water pressure at the Challenger Deep, the deepest part of the ocean, is like having...

A. 2 trees piled on top of you.

B. 50 jumbo jets piled on top of you.

C. Jupiter on top of you.

When a dolphin sleeps, which side of its brain stays awake?

A. the right side

B. the left side

C. the two sides take turns

ISBN: 978-1-897457-80-1

Answer:

A. aluminum

Aluminum makes up 80% of the Earth's crust.

Answer:

false

The highest known mountain in the solar system is a volcano named Olympus Mons on Mars. It is 27 km high, about 18 km higher than Mount Everest.

Answer:

C. the two sides take turns

Being half awake allows dolphins to continue breathing while they rest.

Answer:

B. 50 jumbo jets piled on top of you

ISBN: 978-1-897457-80-1

Where will you not find any penguins?

A. the Arctic
B. South Africa
C. the equator
D. all of the above

True or False

The descent in 1960 was the first and only manned descent to the Challenger Deep.

The Statue of Liberty is a monument that France gave the United States as a gift in 1886. What did the monument also function as?

A. a stadium
B. a radio tower
C. a watchtower
D. a lighthouse

True or False

Some jellyfish can live forever.

ISBN: 978-1-897457-80-1

Answer:

true

Only 2 unmanned descents but no other manned descents have been made since then.

Answer:

A. the Arctic

Answer:

true

The turritopsis nutricula is a type of jellyfish that can convert its cells to become young again. Theoretically it can live forever, but it tends to get eaten at some point in time.

Answer:

D. a lighthouse

It was the first lighthouse that was powered by electricity in the United States. It stayed in service until 1902.

ISBN: 978-1-897457-80-1

How far can you stretch a spider silk without breaking it?

A. 40% of its length
B. 100% of its length
C. 250% of its length
D. Spider silk is not stretchable.

How hot is lava?

A. about 100°C
B. about 500°C
C. about 1000°C

The world's largest dome structure is Cowboys Stadium in Texas, the U.S.A. The diameter of this structure is the total length of...

A. 2 to 3 soccer fields.
B. 5 to 6 soccer fields.
C. 9 to 10 soccer fields.

True or False

There are trees that are taller than a 15-storey building.

ISBN: 978-1-897457-80-1

Answer:

C. about 1000°C

Answer:

A. 40% of its length

That means you can stretch a 10-cm-long spider silk to 14 cm.

Answer:

true

Trees are the largest kind of plant.

Answer:

A. 2 to 3 soccer fields.

The structure has a diameter of 273 m.

ISBN: 978-1-897457-80-1

How many official constellations are there?

A. 10
B. 12
C. 50
D. 88

The Armadillo Lizard has skin covered with thick, protective scales. What distinctive defensive posture does it have?

A. It grabs its tail in its mouth and curls into a ring.
B. It inflates its body like a puffer fish does.
C. It shoots its scales to scare off predators.

True or False

It took a highly viscous liquid several years to form a drop and fall through a funnel.

Mercury is closer to the sun than Venus, but why is the latter hotter?

A. Mercury has water to cool itself down.
B. Mercury reflects light and Venus absorbs it.
C. Venus has a much thicker atmosphere to trap heat.

ISBN: 978-1-897457-80-1

Answer:

A. It grabs its tail in its mouth and curls into a ring.

This position allows it to expose only its armoured back and protect its soft underbelly.

Answer:

C. Venus has a much thicker atmosphere to trap heat.

Answer:

D. 88

Though there are 12 zodiac constellations, there are actually 88 official constellations.

Answer:

true

In the pitch drop experiment, a highly viscous liquid that appears solid in a funnel started flowing in 1930, with its eighth drop fell in 2000.

ISBN: 978-1-897457-80-1

True or False

All animals' tongues are pink.

Sripuram is a temple in India. What is this temple famous for?

A. It is the world's largest temple.
B. It is the only temple in India.
C. The entire temple is made of gold.

What is the eroding rate of Mount Rushmore?

A. 2.5 cm in 1 year
B. 2.5 cm in 10 years
C. 2.5 cm in 10 000 years

True or False

Earth is the only planet that has an atmosphere.

ISBN: 978-1-897457-80-1

Answer:

C. The entire temple is made of gold.

This temple covers 5100 m^2 and its construction was completed in 2007.

Answer:

false

Some animals, like polar bears, have blue tongues.

Answer:

false

All planets have atmospheres, though some have thicker ones and others have thinner ones.

Answer:

C. 2.5 cm in 10 000 years

Despite its exposure to natural occurrences, the rock of Mount Rushmore is composed of smooth, fine-grained granite which is very durable.

ISBN: 978-1-897457-80-1

Which substance boils at room temperature?

A. mercury B. water

C. oxygen D. aluminum

True or False

Canada has the longest covered bridge.

True or False

The Earth spins very slowly. That is why we cannot feel it spinning.

Bamboo is the fastest-growing woody plant. How fast does it grow?

A about 3 cm/day

B. about 30 cm/day

C. about 3 m/day

Answer:

true

This bridge, called Hartland Bridge, is 391 m long. It crosses the Saint John River at Hartland, New Brunswick.

Answer:

B. about 30 cm/day

Since it grows so fast, people can watch this plant grow.

Answer:

C. oxygen

Oxygen is in its gas state at room temperature, which means a room temperature is high enough for oxygen to boil. To be exact, oxygen boils at -182.95°C.

Answer:

false

At the equator, the Earth spins at about 1720 km/h and rotates around the sun at 107 800 km/h.

ISBN: 978-1-897457-80-1